PEN

TRA

Charles Nicholl is a historian, biographer and travel writer. His books include *The Reckoning* (winner of the James Tait Black prize for biography and the Crime Writers' Association 'Gold Dagger' award for non-fiction), *Somebody Else: Arthur Rimbaud in Africa* (winner of the Hawthornden Prize) and the acclaimed biography, *Leonardo da Vinci: The Flights of the Mind*, which has been published in seventeen languages. His *The Lodger: Shakespeare on Silver Street*, was nominated as 'Book of the Year' twelve times in 2007. He is a Fellow of the Royal Society of Literature and has lectured in Britain, Italy and the United States.

The Chemical Theatre

A Cup of News: The Life of Thomas Nashe

The Fruit Palace

Borderlines

The Reckoning: The Murder of Christopher Marlowe

The Creature in the Map

Somebody Else: Arthur Rimbaud in Africa

Journeys (anthology)

Leonardo da Vinci: The Flights of the Mind

Shakespeare and his Contemporaries
(National Portrait Gallery)

The Lodger: Shakespeare on Silver Street

Traces Remain

Essays and Explorations

CHARLES NICHOLL

PENGUIN BOOKS

PENGUIN BOOKS

Published by the Penguin Group
Penguin Books Ltd, 80 Strand, London WC2R ORL, England
Penguin Group (USA) Inc., 375 Hudson Street, New York, New York 10014, USA
Penguin Group (Canada), 90 Eglinton Avenue East, Suite 700, Toronto, Ontario,
Canada M4P 2Y3 (a division of Pearson Penguin Canada Inc.)
Penguin Ireland, 25 St Stephen's Green, Dublin 2, Ireland (a division of Penguin Books Ltd)
Penguin Group (Australia), 707 Collins Street, Melbourne, Victoria 3008, Australia
(a division of Pearson Australia Group Pty Ltd)
Penguin Books India Pvt Ltd, 11 Community Centre, Panchsheel Park, New Delhi – 110 017, India
Penguin Group (NZ), 67 Apollo Drive, Rosedale, Auckland 0632, New Zealand
(a division of Pearson New Zealand Ltd)
Penguin Books (South Africa) (Pty) Ltd, Block D, Rosebank Office Park,
181 Jan Smuts Avenue, Parktown North, Gauteng 2193, South Africa

Penguin Books Ltd, Registered Offices: 80 Strand, London WC2R ORL, England

www.penguin.com

First published by Allen Lane 2011
Published in Penguin Books 2012
002

Copyright © Charles Nicholl, 2011

The moral right of the author has been asserted

Details of original publication of the essays are given in the notes

Typeset by Jouve (UK), Milton Keynes
Printed in Great Britain by Clays Ltd, St Ives plc

A CIP catalogue record for this book is available from the British Library

ISBN: 978-0-1-402-9682-2

www.greenpenguin.co.uk

MIX
Paper from
responsible sources
FSC
www.fsc.org   FSC™ C018179

Penguin Books is committed to a sustainable
future for our business, our readers and our planet.
This book is made from Forest Stewardship
Council™ certified paper.

For Arthur

Contents

List of Illustrations

Preface

Traces [*plural*] – 'Vestiges or marks remaining and indicating the former presence, existence or action of something'

– *OED*

In this book I have gathered together twenty-five essays and articles written over nearly as many years. Their area of interest is mostly historical, biographical and literary – people, places, books, journeys, puzzles. Quite a few belong in the puzzle category, among them three mysterious disappearances, two unmarked graves, two murder cases, one missing Shakespeare play and one enigmatic portrait discovered in a Herefordshire attic.

The title of the collection, *Traces Remain*, is not intended to suggest some unifying theme, but to sum up a particular approach or emphasis. The traces I am thinking of are those 'vestiges or marks' of past lives which are otherwise called historical evidence. I mean the real stuff: the bits and pieces of primary evidence; the raw data, the eyewitness report, the casual detail. I am not sure whether it is a virtue or a failing, but I have always found the details of history more interesting, or anyway more evocative, than the larger perspectives of History. They are trivial and particular and often refreshingly anomalous, especially when they have to do with some distant historical figure or cultural hero whose *curriculum vitae* we thought we were familiar with. That young man who is spotted at Mrs Benchkin's house in Canterbury on an autumn day in 1585, and who reads out her will so 'plainely and distinktly' to the assembled company in the parlour – can it really be the firebrand poet and blasphemer Christopher Marlowe? The documentation (a statement by his brother-in-law, John Moore, who was also present) tells us unquestionably that it is, and reminds us that even firebrand poets spend a lot of their lives doing ordinary, non-combustible things. It is not a major revelation, and is mentioned in these pages only in passing, but it has that quality which always grips me – the sudden presence, the glimpse behind the curtain, the episode measured in minutes and preserved across the centuries. Elsewhere in the book you will find similar brief vignettes, some faintly comic and some more poignant: William Hazlitt eavesdropping outside his landlady's kitchen door; Leonardo da Vinci eating a meal of eels and apricots; Beatrice Cenci crying out in the night 'I will not be burned'; Colonel Fawcett playing his ukulele for some Xingù Indians a few days before vanishing in the Mato Grosso jungle.

That traces remain is the guiding principle of archaeologists and crime-scene investigators, and though I do not have their particular expertises, I share with them a belief that the evidence of the past, whether distant or recent, is something to be examined at close quarters, to be sifted, combed through, picked over. Most of the pieces here, particularly the longer ones, are guided by a general principle of *poking around*, whether physically *in situ*, in what archaeologists would call 'the field', or in libraries and archives. Poking around may not quite count as an expertise, but if purposeful enough it can usually turn up something of interest. Sometimes it involves re-examining a known piece of evidence, and trying to ask new questions about it; and sometimes it is just hopefully prospecting. You never know where the evidence will turn up – that tantalizing document beneath the paw of a medieval hunting-dog, for instance, as seen in the detail from Vittore Carpaccio's wonderful *Due dame veneziane* reproduced on the cover. It looks unlikely, however, that the dog will let you see what's in it.

Out in the field the traces are largely associative – a building, a gravestone, a curve in the street, a disregarded corner; and with them a faint sense or scent of someone who was here long ago. These are more the French sort of *traces*, whose primary meaning is tracks or footsteps, though given one's late arrival on the scene they are only metaphorical footsteps. More often it is the document down in the dusty unglamorous archive which is actually a tangible trace of the past. One reads it as a text, with varying degrees of difficulty, but one also attends to it as a physical relic, the product of a unique conjunction of particularities: a certain person at a certain place and time; their very gesture, and in some cases their very mood and disposition, recorded in those 'vestiges or marks' on the paper. Often when writing something which hinges in one way or another on manuscript evidence, I feel a kind of wonder at the tenacity and toughness of old documents. Houses are demolished, inscriptions merge back into stone, the old mulberry tree is felled, but against all the odds that fragile-seeming, almost weightless object – a bit of paper – remains.

★

With a couple of exceptions these pieces were first published in British magazines and newspapers. They began as articles but now that they have moved in between hard covers they prefer to be known as essays. A number of them – the longer ones that were essays all along – first appeared in the *London Review of Books*, and I acknowledge a debt of gratitude to Karl Miller, Mary-Kay Wilmers and Jeremy Harding (editors past, present and associate) for their welcoming of proposals which other editors might have deemed obscure or eccentric. I am grateful to them, and to the editors of *Granta*, *The Times Literary*

Supplement, the *Sunday Times*, the *Daily Telegraph*, the *Independent*, the *Mail on Sunday* and the *London Magazine*, for permission to republish what first appeared in their pages.

Though none of these pieces goes back that far, I wish also to remember those whose encouragement meant so much to me at the beginning, on what was still literally Fleet Street – John Anstey and David Holloway of the *Telegraph*, Tom Hopkinson and James Cameron. And, yet further back, Robin Dickinson and Jo Bain who first awoke me to Shakespeare; and my late mother, Josephine, whose enthusiasm for history kindled mine, and whose later work as a graphologist opened up that physical, time-capsule sense of the manuscript which I have spoken of. I am, as ever, grateful for the loving companionship of my wife, Sally, and of our children, William, Georgia, Sasha and Kit, and grandchildren, Arthur and Matilda.

As for the book itself, my thanks to Stuart Proffitt, David Godwin, Donna Poppy, Richard Duguid, Shan Vahidy, Tom Meagher and Denise Perry. Some more specific debts are acknowledged in the notes at the back of the book.

I have made a few minor changes and corrections in the texts, but have not in general tried to update them. They belong to their time – to specific occasions and commissions and, in the case of review-essays, publications. I state boldly in an opening paragraph that John Aubrey was buried '300 years ago today', a statement that was only true on 7 June 1997, when the article in question was first published. It would be simple to excise it, but then the piece would somehow lose its point, which is celebratory. Each piece is dated on its opening page, and I am sure the reader can handle the arithmetic. Where there is significant new material to report I do so in the notes.

The essays are lightly grouped, though fairly miscellaneous within the grouping. The first ten belong to sixteenth- and seventeenth-century England, particularly to the Shakespearean period – the decades either side of the turn – which is a period I never leave for long. There follow some pieces with an Italian Renaissance theme, and then the rest are on nineteenth- and twentieth-century subjects, including a trio of Latin American adventures. The latest date, in terms of subject-matter, is 1981, which is thirty years ago as I write, and thus certainly history. Nearer than that I do not venture – as Robert Louis Stevenson once remarked, 'The obscurest epoch is today.'

Charles Nicholl
Corte Briganti, September 2011

The Field of Bones

Thomas Coryate's Last Journey
[1999]

The old fortress town of Mandu stands high on a rocky plateau above the plains of Madhya Pradesh in central India. After a tortuous ascent from Dhar, the road squeezes between two stone bastions and enters through the Dihli Darwaza, or Delhi Gate, where remains of inset blue enamel can be seen on the dilapidated sandstone archways. Up this road and through this gate, on a day in early September 1617, came the eccentric English author and traveller Thomas Coryate. He was a smallish, bearded man with a long, rather lugubrious face. 'The shape of his head', according to one description, was 'like a sugar-loaf inverted, with the little end before.' He wore simple native clothes, and was thin to the point of emaciation. He had travelled down from the city of Agra, 400 miles to the north, and it is a fairly safe bet he had done so on foot.

Coryate is not much heard of nowadays, but in his time he was famous. He had, and still has, a paradoxical reputation. On the one hand he was a kind of comedian, a learned buffoon, a butt for courtly wits and poets like John Donne and Ben Jonson, who both knew him well. On the other hand he was the immensely tough and courageous traveller, whose journeys through Europe and Asia were all the more remarkable for being made almost entirely by foot. This is the boast entailed in his favourite description of himself as a 'legstretcher'; he also styled himself a 'propatetique', in other words 'a walker forward on feete' (as opposed to a 'peripatetic', who merely walks around). Both these reputations, the comic and the adventurer, were diligently cultivated by Coryate himself – he was a great self-publicist – and both are expressed in his best-known book, *Coryats Crudities*, published in 1611.

In the *Crudities* he gives an exhaustive account of his travels in Europe, but his long peregrinations in the East are more sparsely documented. His last extant writing is a letter from Agra to his mother, dated 31 October 1616. By the time he reaches Mandu the following year, he is travelling – textually at least – in silence.

Having completed whatever formalities were required by the Mughal guard at the gate, he made his way to a disused mosque close to the southern escarpment of the plateau. Here he found other Englishmen, about half a dozen of them, with assorted servants and stragglers. Though you would not think it to look at them, this bedraggled little band constituted the first official English embassy to India. The flag of St George fluttered above their bivouac. The ambassador was Sir Thomas Roe, a tough, intelligent, rather prickly man who seems a kind of blueprint for future administrators of British India. He had been in Mandu six months, grappling with exhaustion and acute dysentery, and dancing attendance on the Mughal emperor Jahangir, the 'World Grasper', whose whimsical progresses he was forced to follow. Roe knew Coryate quite well. They had first met back in England, in the courtly ambit of Henry, Prince of Wales, and Coryate had been loosely attached to the embassy since Roe's arrival in India two years previously. The ambassador had an ambivalent attitude to this eccentric but deeply experienced traveller.

Also in the English party was the embassy chaplain, a young man called Edward Terry. He met Coryate for the first time here in Mandu. The two men were billeted together; a friendship formed between them. Years later Terry published a memoir of his Indian travels, and one is grateful that he did, for this obscure volume – *A Voyage to East-India* (1655) – contains almost the only information we have about Coryate's last months.

Coryate was then about forty, but his years in India had taken their toll. Already the omens were bad, as a recollection of Terry's shows:

> Upon a time, he being at Mandoa with us, and there standing in a room against a stone pillar, where the Embassadour was, and myself present with them, upon a sudden he fell into such a swoon that we had very much ado to recover him out of it. But at last come to himself, he told us that some sad thoughts had immediately before presented themselves to his fancy, which (as he conceived) put him into that distemper; like Fannius in Martial, *Ne moriare mori*: to prevent death by dying.

These intimations of mortality proved accurate, for it was from Mandu that Coryate set out on his last journey, which ended in his death, at the Indian port-city of Surat, in December 1617.

★

Thomas Coryate or Coriat was a Somerset man, born in about 1577 in the village of Odcombe, where his father was rector. He habitually attached the adjective 'Odcombian' (or 'Odcombiensis') to himself and his productions, both out of genuine local pride and because the name accorded so well with his own celebrated oddity: 'Tom of Odcombe, that odd jovial author', Jonson calls him. After schooling at Winchester he went up to Oxford, where he 'attained to admirable fluency in the Greek tongue', but left without taking a degree. His skill in languages was frequently noted: among his last writings was a speech delivered in Persian.

What we know of the Elizabethan Coryate is unremarkable: an obscure country parson's son. As a piece of 'self-fashioning', a term very appropriate to him, Coryate is an essentially Jacobean product. Sometime after the accession of King James in 1603, he gained entry to the court of the precocious young Prince of Wales. According to Bishop Fuller, 'Prince Henry allowed him a pension and kept him for his servant. Sweetmeats and Cory-ate made up the last course on all court entertainments.' His position was probably not as formal as this implies – there is no record of him in the extant check-rolls of the prince's household – but it seems he had found some kind of niche in Henry's circle as a jester or entertainer. We have no first-hand record of a Coryate entertainment, but plenty of clues to the nature of it. Fuller says: 'he was the courtiers' anvil to try their wits upon, and sometimes this anvil returned the hammers as hard knocks as it received . . . Few would be found to call him fool, might none do it save such who had as much learning as himself.' Learning was probably the chief feature of Coryate's act: the Classical tags and jocular neologisms found in his pub-lished texts. His speciality was the comic oration. In a letter to Sir Edward Philips (the Somerset landowner who probably introduced him to Prince Henry) he refers to his 'linsey-wolsey orations' and 'extravagant discourses'. Elsewhere he speaks of a certain 'harangue' he delivered to the prince. He was also fond of that tiresome literary game called 'Macaronicks' – doggerel verses full of foreign words and mock-Latinisms – and this was probably part of his patter too. The overall feel is of Coryate as a combative, bombastic, garrulous figure, the scatterbrain among the smoothies of the Jacobean court.

Coryate is part of a subgroup of Elizabethan and Jacobean entertainers who were not wholly actors or writers or orators or clowns, but a little of each, and who achieved a brief popularity as 'characters' playing a kind of burlesque version of themselves. These are men like the braggadocio Peter Shakerly; the railer Charles Chester, who was the model for Carlo Buffone in Jonson's *Every Man Out of His Humour*; Humfrey King, the poetic tobacconist; the barber-surgeons Tom Tooley and Richard Lichfield; the tavern joker John Stone. These loquacious odd-balls found a small economic niche as ad hoc entertainers; they are haunters of St Paul's Churchyard and the Inns of Court, of revels and *convivia*. One might call them early prototypes of the stand-up comedian.

In 1608, in his early thirties, Coryate set out on the European journey which made his name. (The death of his father the previous year perhaps made this financially possible.) There is an element of the publicity stunt about it. The comic actor Will Kemp had morris-danced from London to Norwich in 1599 and had published a book about it, *Kemps Nine Daies Wonder*; Cory-ate walking through Europe was perhaps something similar. This is not to deny the genuine hunger for travel that impelled it. 'There hath itched a very burning desire in me', he wrote, 'to survey and contemplate some of the chiefest parts of this goodly fabric of the world.'

By his own estimate, Coryate covered 1,975 miles in a little over five months, and visited forty-five cities. He then settled back in his study at Odcombe, and painstakingly relived the journey on paper. The book took him three years and in the first edition runs to 654 pages. Its full title is itself a small masterpiece:

> Coryats Crudities, Hastily gobled up in five Moneths travells in France, Savoy, Italy, Rhetia commonly called the Grisons coun-try, Helvetia alias Switzerland, some parts of High Germany and the Netherlands; newly digested in the hungry aire of Odcombe in the county of Somerset, & now dispersed to the nourishment of the travelling members of the Kingdome.

'Crudities' is to be taken in the French sense, *crudités* – pieces of raw food, or in this case raw experience, 'hastily gobbled up' on the journey and now 'digested' back home and 'dispersed' to his readers. The metaphor inescapably suggests the travel book as a kind of postprandial fart.

The title page is adorned with engravings depicting note-worthy comic events during the journey: his seasickness on the crossing to Calais, the time he slept in straw and was pissed on by a horse, his altercation with certain Jews in Venice from whom he fled in fear of being forcibly circumcised, and so on. In pride of place is the portrait of Coryate engraved by William Hole; around its cartouche lounge a trio of bosomy ladies representing France, Germany and Italy, one of whom (Germany) is shown vomiting over his head. Another illustration by Hole, inserted in the text, shows Coryate bowing in greeting to a famous Venetian courtesan, Margarita Emiliana. This catches a note of misplaced gravitas which is comic and slightly poignant: the diminutive *cavaliere* ('Il Signior Tomaso Odcombiano') with his solemn, elongated face and his Jimmy Hill beard. His eyes are lowered, for the point of it all is his pilgrim-like abstinence from her proffered charms. 'As for thine eyes,' runs the text nearby, 'shut them and turn them aside from these venerous Venetian objects; for they are the double windows that convey them to thy heart.'

Various luminaries contributed verses to the *Crudities*, among them Donne, Jonson, Hugh Holland, John Davies of Hereford and Inigo Jones. The vein is one of mock-commendation, but the sheer bulk of the endorsements gives to the publication the buzz of a literary event. In the autumn of 1611 Coryate was guest of honour at a gathering at the Mitre Tavern in Fleet Street. This 'Convivium Philosophicum' is celebrated in a dog-Latin poem which was read out on the occasion. Most of it is a comic eulogy of Coryate himself, but many who contributed verses to the *Crudities* are also addressed, and were perhaps present (Donne among them, addressed as 'Factus'). It seems likely this event was a sort of launch party for the *Crudities*.

Following the success of the book, Coryate hastily knocked

up a sequel, or second course, which he called *Coryats Crambe, or his Colwort twise sodden*. There is also a pamphlet entitled *The Odcombian Banquet*, but this is really just a reprint of the commendatory verses in the *Crudities*. Its publisher was Thomas Thorpe, better known as the publisher of the first edition of Shakespeare's *Sonnets*. It is probably an opportunist edition – a book 'printed in hugger-mugger', as Coryate put it – though it is not impossible he had a hand in it.

The *Crudities* is a triumph of self-advertisement. In a year not short of literary achievements – Shakespeare's *Tempest* and Jonson's *Alchemist* were on stage, Donne was writing the 'Holy Sonnets', the King James Bible was published – this big bubble of a book gets noticed. But it has also more solid virtues. After the extended badinage of the prefatory matter, the actual travelogue is delivered in a direct, unfussy style. Jonson hits the right note when he calls Coryate a 'bold carpenter of words'. Much of the text is practical, indeed statistical (journey times, populations, dimensions of notable buildings, etc.). It was, in short, a very useful book as well as a caper; travellers carried it with them as a *vade mecum*, or guidebook. Coryate himself would meet the adventurer Sir Robert Shirley in the hinterlands of Persia, and be chuffed when he drew forth from his luggage 'both my bookes neatly kept'.

This kernel of sensibleness in the *Crudities* makes one think again about Coryate the jester, the 'linsey-wolsey' orator. One sees it more clearly as a contrived performance, a *métier*, a job. Behind the comedian's bluster there is this more conventional, punctilious, inquisitive man. He might just enjoy being a bit boring, as a change – or a relief – from being funny.

*

In the autumn of 1612 Coryate left England, for what would prove to be the last time, en route for the East. Sometime before his departure he bequeathed his old travelling shoes to the parish church at Odcombe. They were still to be seen hanging there in the eighteenth century. Having meandered around Asia Minor and the Holy Land for some time, he set out from Jerusalem for lesser-known territories in April 1614. At Aleppo he waited for a caravan to accompany; here he wrote up some notes on his journey, a few of which survive, and sent some letters which are lost. He set out in September, *en caravane*, and within a few days crossed the Euphrates into Mesopotamia. Here he visited Ur (Orfah), 'a very delicate and pleasant city'. It was the birthplace of the biblical Abraham, but the diligent inquirer could find 'no part of the ruins of the house where that faithful servant of God was born'. Four days out of Ur he waded across the Tigris River, finding it 'so shallow that it reached no higher than the calf of my leg'. From here he travelled through Armenia and Persia to 'Spahan' (Isfahan), where he waited once more 'for an opportunity of caravans to travel withal'. The caravan he eventually joined had 2,000 camels, 1,500 horses, 1,800 mules and 6,000 people.

Four months out of Isfahan, Coryate crossed 'the famous river Indus which is as broad again as our Thames at London', and not long after arrived at Lahore, which he found to be 'one of the largest cities in the whole universe, for it containeth at least xvi miles in compass, and exceedeth Constantinople itself in greatness'. Having rested here, he set off for Agra, the capital of the Mughal Empire. He thought it a 'goodly city' (though he could not see its chief attraction of today, the Taj Mahal, which was only built in the 1620s by Jahangir's son, Shah Jahan). From Agra he turned west to Ajmer, where the Mughal court then was. He arrived around the middle of July 1615, and was hospitably received by the small group of English merchants resident in the city. Here, at the English 'factory', he set up his staff and settled in to rest – and to write – after this incredibly tough journey.

From Jerusalem to Ajmer, he estimated, was a distance of 2,700 miles, and he had 'traced all this tedious way afoot'. It had taken him 'fifteen months and odd days', though nearly six months of this was spent waiting for caravans in Aleppo and Isfahan. He was thus actually on the road for about nine months, covering an average of seventy miles a week in extremely harsh conditions. He is particularly emphatic on the economies of his travel. 'Betwixt Aleppo and the Mughal's court', he spent just £3, 'yet fared reasonably well every day'. Of that £3, moreover, he was 'cozened of no less than ten shillings by certain lewd Christians of the Armenian nation'. His actual expenditure for the journey works out at just over a shilling a week.

In November 1615 he dispatched to England four long newsletters, from which the above itinerary is drawn. One of them is addressed to the 'Fraternitie of Sireniacal Gentlemen that meet the first Fridaie of every month at the signe of the Mere-maid in Bread streete in London' – a reference to the celebrated Mermaid 'club', whose membership has been hopefully expanded to include Shakespeare. These newsletters were collected and printed in a short pamphlet entitled *Thomas Coriate, Traveller for the English Wits: Greeting from the Court of the great Mogul* (1616). The title page has a woodcut of Coryate riding an elephant (see Plate 1). His last letter to his mother (31 October 1616) also found its way into print. It appeared posthumously in 1618, as *Mr Thomas Coriat to his Friends*, with some rather slighting introductory verses by the boatman John Taylor, known as the 'Water Poet'. These writings are only a fraction of what he had produced en route. 'His notes are already too great for portage,' Sir Thomas Roe wrote, 'some left at Aleppo, some at Hispan [Isfahan], enough to make any stationer an alderman who shall but serve the printer with paper.' In 1619 the ledgers of the English factory in Isfahan mention that one George Strachan has 'certayne bookes' which he has either brought 'out of England, or got since by the death of some that could not carrye them to Heaven'. Might these be Coryate's lost notebooks? Might they still be there, mouldering in some chest or cupboard in Isfahan?

Coryate stayed at the Ajmer factory for over a year, an honoured guest (or inveterate sponger), 'not spending one little piece of money'. His hosts included the East India Company's agent at the Mughal court, William Edwards, and the company chaplain, Peter Rogers, who carried his newsletters back to England. On 22 December 1615 Coryate was in the reception committee assembled outside Ajmer to welcome the arriving ambassador, Sir Thomas Roe. He insisted on greeting the exhausted Roe – who was in his own words 'scarce a crow's dinner' – with a long oration. Roe describes him in his journal as 'the famous unwearied walker, Tho. Coryatt, who on foote had passed most of Europe and Asya and was now in India, beeing but the beginning of his travells'. That nonchalant flourish at the end sounds like a Coryate catchphrase echoed verbatim. In a letter from India to the Earl of Pembroke, Roe speaks warmly of Coryate, 'whom the fates have sent hither to ease me', but it was not long before tensions arose between them. The cause was Coryate's addressing an oration, in his newly acquired Persian, to the Mughal emperor Jahangir. He did this without Roe's permission, knowing the latter would have 'barricadoed all my proceeding therein'. Roe was indeed angry when he found out. It was, he said, 'to the dishonour of our nation that one of our country should present himself in that beggarly and poor fashion to the King, out of an insinuating humour to crave money from him'. Coryate says he answered the ambassador in 'stout and resolute' terms, and so constrained him 'to cease nibbling at me'.

The text of Coryate's oration to Jahangir is given, in both Persian and English, in his letter to his mother. It begins: 'Lord Protector of the World, all hail to you. I am a poore traveller

and world-seer, which am come hither from a farre country'. In
the original Persian, Coryate uses the word *fakir* to describe
himself. A similar idea is found in Edward Terry's account of
this episode, which concludes: 'The Mogul gave him one hundred rupees, looking upon him as a derveese or votary or
pilgrim, for so he called him.' One glimpses here, fossilized in
these texts, an emergent new identity. In the context of the
Jacobean court he could only be a buffoon; in India he is
the wandering fakir or dervish. It is a small shift, a new spin on
the old Coryate, but one feels it mattered to him. It is an achieving of dignity.

In early 1617 he was wandering again – to Hardwar, to celebrate the Hindu new year, and to Kangra, where he visited the
temples of Mata Devi and 'Jallamakee' (Jawala Mukki). Terry's
description of these sites in his Indian memoir is entirely based
on Coryate's information: they were 'seen and strictly observed
by Mr Coryat'. He was back in Agra by early July. On 20 July,
from Mandu, Roe wrote to the English factors at Agra; he
had heard of Coryate's return, and asked to know what his
plans were – 'for England or stay; or if I take any new course,
whither he will go with me'. The interesting subtext of this
note is that Roe seems to need, or anyway value, Coryate's
presence in his retinue.

On the strength of this letter, Coryate decided to head down
to Mandu, where he arrived, as we have seen, around the
beginning of September 1617.

★

Mandu today is a ghost city, a reverie of deserted palaces, pavil-
ions, mosques, tombs, and great stonework water-tanks the size
of small lakes. An old Sanskrit inscription shows there was a
hill-fort on the site at least as early as the sixth century, but the
city's heyday was in the fourteenth and fifteenth centuries, when

it was entirely rebuilt by the Muslim sultans then ruling the region. The style is Afghan: sumptuous in scale, austere in mood and – judging by the current state of preservation – remarkably strong in construction. Then the city's fortunes changed once more. In 1561 the last Sultan of Mandu, Baz Bahadur, was defeated by Mughal forces, and by the time Coryate and Roe were here Mandu had become a distant and increasingly neglected outpost of the Mughal Empire. Today there is just a small village, straggling round a crossroads, surrounded by the empty hulks of the old city brooding quietly in the sun.

It seems a suitable place to search for ghosts, but that of Coryate – 'who while he lived was like a perpetual motion' – is hard to pin down. Where exactly was the mosque which housed him and the British Embassy in Mandu? Some sketchy information is given in Roe's journal (or rather in the precis of it published by Samuel Purchas in 1625; Roe's original journal for this period is lost). He describes the site as a mosque and tomb enclosed within a spacious 'well-walled courtyard'. He says that it was on the southern side of the settlement, near a precipice leading down to the River Narbada; and that it was some two miles from the palace which housed Jahangir and his court.

There are two mosques in Mandu which broadly fit these specifications, though neither does so completely. They are the Mali Mughid Mosque, and a smaller, unnamed mosque to the west of Rupumati's Pavilion. Neither is two miles from the royal enclave: the small mosque is the further of the two, but it is no more than a mile. Mali Mughid has the 'well-walled court-yard' and a large tomb next to it, and though it does not overlook the Narbada, it does stand near a precipice overlooking a tributary, the Nala. In the heat of the day the colonnades of Mali Mughid are a refuge. I contemplate the rows of honey-coloured columns – earlier Hindu work incorporated into the fifteenth-century mosque – and wonder if one of them is the 'stone pillar' against which Coryate was leaning when he passed out in the presence of Roe and Terry. One cannot know. One is left with physical sensation as the only bridge back to Coryate in Mandu – the flinty pathways beneath his feet, the elephantine trunks of the baobab trees, the moonlight on the water-tanks, the chatter of beautiful Bhil tribeswomen, the strident chirruping of the giant fruit-bats that rise up over the Kapoor Tank on wings of polished black leather.

In Mandu, Coryate was quartered with Edward Terry. Thereafter, says Terry, 'he was either my chamber-fellow or tent-mate, which gave me a full acquaintance of him.' Terry was in his mid twenties, a mild-mannered, devout young Oxford graduate. Roe thought him 'sober, honest and civil', and found him a source of strength in these testing circumstances. He had originally signed up as ship's chaplain aboard an East India Company merchantman, the *Charles*, but on his arrival in India in 1616 had been co-opted into Roe's embassy, whose previous chaplain had died.

Terry gives an acute sketch of Coryate's charms and flaws, as they seemed to him on those long days together in Mandu:

> He was a man with a very coveting eye, that could never be satisfied with seeing (as Salomon speaks, *Eccles*. ii 8), though he had seen very much; and I am persuaded that he took as much content in seeing as many others in the enjoying of great and rare things. He was a man that had got the mastery of many hard languages . . . If he had obtained wisdom to husband and manage them, as he had skill to speak them, he had deserved more fame in his generation. But his knowledge and high attainments in several languages made him not a little ignorant of himself, he being so covetous, so ambitious of praise that he would hear and endure more of it than he could in any measure deserve; being like a ship that hath too much sail and too little ballast.

These catch something of the man – the infectious curiosity, the buttonholing manner, the sensitivities no longer so well concealed behind the big words and florid gestures. There is in all who knew him a note of dismissiveness, a shake of the head: he does not quite add up to what he might have been. He has the multilingual words but not the wisdom to go with them: he is a mere verbal showman. One thinks of Hamlet's 'antic disposition', that craziness which may be a front or may be real, and not even he is quite sure which. This is the fascination of Coryate's silence. Without the words, without the elaborated Odcombian persona, what exactly is left?

Even here at Mandu, however, he is not entirely silent. There remain a few scattered notes from his hand, which were preserved after his death by Roe and were later published in Purchas's *Pilgrimes*. One of these, at least, was demonstrably written at Mandu. It concerns the dire water shortage which was caused by Jahangir's sudden descent on the town, and which is frequently complained of by Roe. It reads:

> Remember the charitie of two great men that, in the time of this great drought, were at the charge of sending ten camels with twenty persons every day to a river called Narbode [i.e. Narbada] for water, and did distribute the water to the poor; which was so dear that they sold a little skin for eight pise.

The text of this last fragment is the bleak struggle for survival.

On 24 October 1617 Jahangir's imperial circus pulled out of Mandu, its destination uncertain. Roe was obliged to follow, noting gloomily that he was 'very weak, and not like to recover upon daily travell in the fields with cold raw muddie water'. The embassy decamped on 29 October, with Coryate in the company, and soon caught up with the emperor's cavalcade in the plains around Dhar.

It was here that occur two episodes, recorded by Terry, which show the continued gnawing ambiguity of Coryate's status. On 2 November an East India Company adventurer named Richard Steele returned from England, bearing some long-awaited pearls which Roe had promised the emperor. Steele told Coryate that King James himself had 'enquired after' him, but then added, with what sounds like deliberate malice, that when he told the king he had met Coryate in India, the king replied: 'Is that fool yet living?' When Coryate heard this, Terry says, 'it seemed to trouble him very much, because the King spake no more nor no better of him; saying that kings would speak of poor men what they pleased.' The second slight came in the form of a note of recommendation penned for him by Roe, addressed to the British consul at Aleppo, in which Roe wrote: 'When you shall hand these letters, I desire you to receive the bearer of them, Mr Thomas Coryate, with courtesy, for you shall find him a very honest poor wretch.' Coryate was furious. He told Terry: 'For my Lord to write nothing of me by way of commendation but "Honest poor wretch" is rather to trouble me than please me with his favour.' He took his complaint to Roe, who rewrote the offending sentence. Terry says these episodes show how 'tender' Coryate was in the face of disparagement. They suggest also a stasis or stagnancy which mocks the 'perpetual motion' of the traveller. After all the miles he has covered he is still – to the English, at least – where he was before: the king's fool, my lord's wretch.

Soon after this Coryate left the embassy encampment, travelling alone. 'My Lord [Roe] willed him to stay longer with us,' writes Terry, 'but he thankfully refused that offer, and turned his face presently after towards Surat, which was then about three hundred miles distant from us.' The river-port of Surat, close to the Gujurati coast north of Bombay, was the chief point of entry and departure for English shipping. Possibly he was thinking of sailing back to England, though that note of recommendation to the Aleppo consulate suggests his more customary mode of travel. Either way it seems he was heading home. The day of his departure is probably established by a bill of exchange, which records that he deposited thirty-five rupees with the ambassador and was authorized to draw the same amount from the English factors in Surat. The date of this bill is 13 November 1617. Two extant letters from Roe to the Surat factors, dated 11 and 12 November, were probably also in Coryate's meagre luggage when he set out.

The itinerary of his last lonely trudge can only be surmised. A plausible route would be to strike south-west from Dhar, via the village of Bagh, to rejoin the same Narbada River which flows past Mandu. Here he could take passage down into the coastal lowlands of Gujurat, to the small but ancient river-port of Baruch (now often called by its Anglicized form, Broach) and from there by the caravan-road to Surat.

All we actually know of the journey is that he made it to his destination, that he was suffering badly from dysentery when he arrived, and that he died a few days later. Terry gives the circumstances as follows:

He lived to come safely thither, but there being over-kindly used by some of the English, who gave him sack which they had brought from England; he calling for it as soon as he first heard of it, and crying: 'Sack, sack, is there such a thing as sack? I pray give me some sack'; and drinking of it (though, I conceive, moderately, for he was a very temperate man), it increased his flux which he had then upon him. And this caused him within a few days, after his very tedious and troublesome travels (for he went most on foot) at this place to come to his journey's end; for here he overtook Death in the month of December 1617. *Sic exit Coryatus*, and so must all after him, for if one should go to the extremest part of the world East, another West, another North and another South, they must all meet at last together in the Field of Bones, wherein our Traveller hath now taken up his lodging.

★

An early seventeenth-century traveller enthused about Surat's 'fair, square' stone houses, its 'goodly gardens with pomegranates, pomecitrons, lemons, melons, figs', and its tall handsome people 'clothed in long white calico or silk robes', but nowadays – according to my *Lonely Planet* guidebook – the city 'is of little interest to travellers, except those with a fascination for urban decay, mayhem, noise and pollution'. An industrial city of nearly two million people, Surat is known for silk production and diamond-cutting, and for an outbreak of pneumonic plague which killed a hundred people in 1994. The first ominous tower-blocks in smudged concrete merge up out of the littoral. A few images detach themselves – a cow with blue-painted horns, a truck nicknamed 'Lucky Bharat', a woman in a flowing lilac sari picking her way across a rubbish tip – and then the cacophony of the city engulfs you in a fog of auto-rickshaw smoke.

The site of the former English factory where Coryate died is almost completely obliterated. It stands on the southern bank of the Tapi River, half a mile upriver from the old Mughal fortress and the great sweep of the Tapti Bridge. Some fragments of the old building can be seen by peering through the concertina-gates into the courtyard of the Irish Presbyterian Mission School for Girls. It was here that I at last met an Indian who had actually heard of Thomas Coryate. 'But he is the English fakir,' he exclaims, and turns to the straggle of onlookers to explain my purpose. He is a tall, bespectacled man in his forties named Jolly Wellington Christie – a missionary christening, needless to add. He lives near by, in a little terrace of mission houses whose address, Mughalsarai, harks back to Mughal days. He is the scholar of the area. In his house, piled horizontally on the kitchen table, stacked in cabin-sized bedrooms, are hundreds of books, all covered in brown paper with their Hindi titles inscribed in schoolmasterly ink.

Beside the school is the Irish Presbyterian Church, and there he shows me a grave. It holds the remains of the Reverend Alexander Fyvie, who died here in 1840, aged forty-six. He was sent to Surat by the London Missionary Society; he built the church himself; he fell out of that window there, and died. The curious thing is that his grave points south. 'It seems', says Jolly solemnly, 'to have been moved.'

This brought me to the question of Coryate's last resting-place, and the conflicting accounts concerning its location. In November 1627, ten years after Coryate's death, an Englishman named Thomas Herbert arrived in Surat in the retinue of Sir Dodmore Cotton, English ambassador to Persia. Shortly afterwards he attended the funeral of a Persian nobleman named Nagd Ali Beg, who had died on the voyage out. Beg was 'entombed' in Surat, Herbert noted in his journal, 'not a stone's throw from Tom Coryate's grave, known by two small stones that speak his name'. This modest grave was still visible nearly fifty years later, when the travel-writer John Fryer visited Surat. He says he saw the grave of Nagd Ali Beg just outside the Broach Gate (now called the Kataragama Gate), 'not far from whence, on a small hill on the left hand of the road, lies Thomas Coriat, our English fakier (as they name him), together with an Armenian Christian, known by their graves lying east and west'. This would place Coryate's grave close to the later English cemetery, which is still there; but not quite in it, as the cemetery lies to the right of the Broach Road. There is no record of burials there before the mid 1640s.

According to his friend Edward Terry, however, Coryate was not buried at Surat at all, but 'at the East India shore of Swally, on the banks thereof, amongst many more English that lie there interred'. Swally is Suvali, the small sea-port twelve miles west of Surat. Terry's evidence has weight because of his personal interest in Coryate, and because he seems to have seen the grave on his journey home in 1619. He describes it as 'a little monument, like one of those are usually made in our churchyards'. If there was an English graveyard at Suvali, it has long since disappeared under silt, and has left no documentary traces other than this.

Local tradition has favoured Terry's version. A mile north of Suvali, outside a hamlet called Rajgiri, stands a solitary, domed edifice, perhaps twenty foot tall. Exactly when this came to be known as 'Tom Coryate's Tomb' is unclear: the name first appears, as a coastal landmark, on a British Admiralty sea-chart of 1837. It is worth the pilgrimage, out through the cloying suburbs of Surat, along a narrow road loomed over by vast factories and refineries, finally to touch the sea at Swally Point. The tomb, if such it is – 'a monument in Mahommedan style', as an old handbook describes it – stands on a gentle rise sparsely scattered with palm trees. It looks out over the broad reaches of the Gulf of Cambay and is soothed by sea breezes. It would be a peaceful corner of the 'field of bones' to lodge in, though whether it is Coryate's corner is uncertain.

Almost everything about Coryate's last journey is uncertain. Its precise route cannot be traced, its circumstances cannot be recovered. He disappears from view in the plains below Mandu; he turns up later on the riverfront at Surat. One glimpses him out of dusty bus windows: a ragged man walking alone down a road.

2

A 'Naughty House'

Mr Mountjoy at the Magistrates' Court
[2010]

Among the cases before the magistrates at the Middlesex Sessions of 1 December 1613 was one which involved three French
'goldworkers' resident in the parish of St Giles without Cripplegate, and a woman from Whitechapel called Frances Williams.
The charge was fornication. Though not in itself unusual, the
charge had an extra twist, repeated with minor variations in
most of the entries relating to it: 'they were all 4 seene in bed
together at one tyme.' The documentation is scanty, and we have
no Jacobean tabloids to furnish us with further juicy details –
'Immigrants in Group Sex Romp!' – but one fact which makes
the case worth pursuing is the involvement of Shakespeare's
former landlord Christopher Mountjoy. There is an obvious
link: like the three goldworkers, Mountjoy was French. Also
like them, he lived in the Cripplegate area (though his house was
within the London City walls, on respectable Silver Street,
whereas the alleged fornicators lived out in the rougher extra-
mural suburb of St Giles). These are community connections.
But what else – what more specifically – has drawn him into this
prosecution, and into the rather murky story that lies behind it?

This new material about Mountjoy does not impinge directly
on Shakespeare, who had not lived at his house for some years,
and who is anyway not answerable for the behaviour of his landlord. But it does throw further light on the character and
circumstances of a man who was part of Shakespeare's London

life, and who had a precisely identifiable, and in some measure domestically intimate, relationship with him. They first met, according to Shakespeare's own recollection, in about 1602. Mountjoy was a tiremaker – a maker of the decorative headgear for ladies known as 'tires' or 'attires' – and the first contact between them may have been in the ambit of theatrical costuming. By 1604, certainly, Shakespeare was lodging with the Mountjoys (Christopher and his French wife, Marie), and in that year he assisted in the engagement, or 'troth-plighting', of their daughter Mary to one of their apprentices, Stephen Belott. Some years later Belott sued Mountjoy for an unpaid dowry of £60, and Shakespeare was among those called to give evidence at the Court of Requests in Westminster. He did so on 11 May 1612, though – somewhat conveniently for Mountjoy – he could not remember what sum of money had been promised for the dowry. This was his last recorded dealing with Mr Mountjoy, a year and a half before this rather different kind of court case at the Middlesex Sessions.

I explored the story of the Mountjoy family in my book *The Lodger: Shakespeare on Silver Street* (2007), but missed this later morsel of evidence. I should not have missed it – indeed I had already seen a signpost to it, in the old ledgers of the French Church in Soho Square, which mention that Mountjoy had been '*tiré au Magistrat*', though without saying where or when. For this new reference I am grateful to the sharp eyes of Andrew Wilson, who spotted Mountjoy's name by chance (or by alphabetical serendipity: he was researching a family ancestor called Merryweather) and kindly alerted me to it. The reference leads us to this case of multiple fornication, as outlined in two sets of Middlesex court documents now held at the London Metropolitan Archives. They are the Sessions Roll of November 1613, which lists the 'recognizances' of those standing bail for the accused; and the Sessions Register, which briefly records, *in situ*, the proceedings of their day in court. Mountjoy makes an appearance in both.

★

On 20 November 1613 'Christoferus Mountioy de Silverstreet london Marchant Taylor' pledges himself as a surety for the three accused Frenchmen. They are named as Jacobus Mullett, Abrahamus Trippie and Jacobus Depre. (The two Jacobi would, of course, be Jacques in French and James in English. Mullett is elsewhere written as Millett, and Trippie as Tippey.) Mountjoy puts up £20 – half of the required bail – to guarantee their appearance at the forthcoming Sessions of the Peace, where they are 'bound to answere their incontinencye wth one ffra: Williams: they were all 3 in bed together with her at one tyme.' The other half of the bail is posted by one Richard Meade, also of St Giles parish, whose occupation is given as 'gardiner'. A few days later the procedure is repeated, and two other men stand surety for the fourth defendant, 'ffrancisca Williams de whitechappell, spinster'. The designation 'spinster' is misleading, for it appears from later entries that she was married. Her husband, possibly estranged, was James Williams of Whitechapel, described as a 'yeoman', which means he owned some kind of property. Frances's marital status does not at all preclude the possibility she was a prostitute, or at least one of the legion of semi-professionals in that trade – a 'light-tayled huswyfe', as the pamphleteers liked to put it, the spelling halfway between 'housewife' and its eroded variant, 'hussy'. Finally, on 29 November, we meet the accuser, Adam Bowin. He is a man in the textile business – a 'tuft taffatamaker' – from the parish of St Botolph's, Bishopsgate. He puts up his own security to appear in court to give evidence against the Frenchmen (which will also be evidence against Frances Williams, though she is not actually mentioned). He is 'bound to Justifie an informacion he hath given against the said parties for incontinency: 3 men with one woman in a bed'.

And so the scene is set for the brief courtroom drama of 1 December 1613. This takes place in the newly erected Sessions House in Clerkenwell, known as Hicks Hall because it was built by the rich mercer and financier Sir Baptist Hicks, who was himself one of the Justices of the Peace on the Middlesex circuit. Sessions had previously been held in the less salubrious surrounds of the nearby Castle tavern. Hicks Hall, which opened in 1612, was an imposing three-storey house standing at the bottom end of St John's Street, not far from Smithfield Market. When it was built the street had to be rerouted around it, which did not please the residents, and one of the first to appear at the new court was a local apothecary's wife, Grace Watson, charged with 'giving reviling speeches against Sir Baptist Hicks touching the building of the Sessions House'. A later writer describes it as 'a shapeless brick lump containing a great warehouse in the centre for the court, and houses for the officers all round and joined on to it'. In the eighteenth century the area below the oval-shaped courtroom was used for dissecting the cadavers of criminals: it may be the locale shown in the famously gruesome anatomy scene in Hogarth's *Four Stages of Cruelty*.

Nothing survives today of Hicks Hall. One sees only the bellying out of the street where it once stood, and the disused Victorian warehouse ('Geo. Farmiloe & Sons, Lead & Glass Merchants') which more or less marks the spot. But what does survive is the written record, and within it the tumultuous throng of petty offenders who passed through here, accused rightly or wrongly of picking pockets, filching cloaks, making affrays, calling constables knaves, committing lewd acts, enticing other men's apprentices, keeping disorderly tippling-houses, and a hundred and one other minor infractions – a rich sociological soil-sample of life out in the suburbs of London, an area which in parts would have had the attributes we associate with 'suburban', but which was mostly considered a 'noysome' sprawl full of poverty, crime and vice.

On that day in 1613, the case of the fornicating Frenchmen was only one of about 150 cases which the magistrates heard. There was the miller charged with 'putting in musty corn instead of sweet' and selling 'heavy sacks for light, 2 lb in every sack'. There was the cardsharp up for 'cozening Giles Hall at decoy', and another trickster for 'cheating a Derbyshire gentleman with counters instead of silver', and a burglar, Thomas Mason ('alias Humming Tom'), who had broken into the house of Sir Walter Cope. There was the woman from Finsbury accused of 'cozening Elizabeth Barnes of certain money for a little powder in a paper' – she had promised that Elizabeth 'should have her purpose of musicion by carryenge the powder about her', apparently meaning it would attract some musician she fancied, but clearly it hadn't. And among these mischief-makers (and a few more serious cases which the magistrates sent straight up to the Gaol Delivery Sessions at Newgate) there were the carnal sinners of one sort and another. I count a dozen cases, including that of the three Frenchmen, in this category. Among them are Susan Browne, 'taken in bed with a Scotsman in a common bawdy house'; Anthony Horne, tailor, 'locked up in a shed in Chiswell Street with Margery Blague in the night, and apprehended by the constable'; Henry Manne, gentleman, 'complained to be a very disordered fellow, and keeping company with Alice Sherwood, a common whore'; Joan Wilson, 'charged with incontinency and keeping company with Richard Ganny in uncivil manner, upon the complaint of the said Ganny's wife'; Susan Ellington, 'for keeping very evil rule and light huswifery in her house'; and – lest these quaintly phrased veneries obscure a harsher reality – Mary Pilkinton, spinster, the inmate of a brothel on Whitecross Street, who was charged with 'burying a bastard child in a yard in the same'.

Most of these people, we may assume, were there to answer the charges against them, in that milling, echoing, warehouse-like courtroom in Clerkenwell, where a log fire smokes in the ornate fireplace inscribed with phrases of gratitude to Sir Baptist. And amid them we find Christopher Mountjoy, waiting for the case of the three Frenchmen to be called. He is already somewhat disgruntled, because one of the three musketeers, Abraham Trippie, has failed to show up, thus breaking the conditions of his bail, and putting in jeopardy the not inconsiderable sum of £20 which Mountjoy has pledged as surety. As we know from the earlier case of the unpaid dowry, he was not someone who spent money gladly. 'He would rather rott in prison,' he had said in the hearing of a neighbour, than give his daughter and son-in-law 'any thinge more'; other witnesses in that case recall similarly crabbed and blustery comments.

In 1613 Mountjoy was a man probably in his late fifties. He was a widower, a householder, a tax-payer and a 'denizen', or naturalized citizen, who had lived in London for over thirty years; he was a supplier of headgear *à la mode* to an upmarket clientele which had at one time included King James's fashion-mad consort Queen Anne; and he was – not least – a familiar acquaintance of Shakespeare. A rather respectable figure, it may seem from this summary, an immigrant success story, though there is also some evidence to suggest another, less respectable side to him. Just a few months earlier he had been 'censured' before the Spiritual Court of the French Church for living in sin with his maidservant, by whom he had fathered '2 bastardes'. His lifestyle is described as 'debauched' and 'disordered' ('*déreglé*'). That, at least, was the view of the Calvinist elders of the French Church, and perhaps he already has an inkling that the Middlesex Justices are about to take a similar line.

So far his only involvement in the case has been in this perfectly neutral role of providing surety for his fellow Frenchmen. But as the hearing unfolds at Hicks Hall we find him more deeply implicated in the affair. It is revealed that the 'fornicacion' in question took place in a property owned or leased by him (though it is not the house on Silver Street where he lived). We learn this from the committal proceedings, which record the offence and the summary judgment of the magistrates upon it:

> James Millett and James Depree committed to putt in good sureties for their good behaviour for committing fornicacion with one ffrancis williams they two with one Abraham Tippey all at one tyme att severall tymes for a fortnight together in the house of one Christopher Mountioye a Tiremaker in St Giles without Cripplegate in most beastlyke manner. The said Christopher Mountioye likewyse committed to putt in very good sureties p.b.g. [*pro bono gestu*, for his good behaviour] and to bringe forthe Abraham Tippey for whom he is bayle.

The same judgment follows for Frances Williams, who is also 'committed *p. bono gestu*'.

It is clear the magistrates consider Mountjoy culpable. Like the other offenders he is bound over for good behaviour: he has himself become one of the offenders. Quite what the charge is against him is not stated, though the obvious inference is that, at the least, he knew about the 'beastlyke' behaviour going on in that house in St Giles. We also note, from the phrasing of the committal, that this congress *à quatre* was not just a one-off Saturday-night orgy, but something that had happened 'at several times' over the space of a fortnight. This too might bear on Mountjoy's culpability as an accessory. He could reasonably have disclaimed knowledge of a single lewd act, taking place in a house which he owned but did not live in. A continuous arrangement of lewdness sounds more suspicious.

The sentence he receives, along with the other guilty parties, is lenient enough, and fairly standard for this sort of case. It is a reprimand more than a punishment, though it involves him in the business of 'putting in' sureties – money which will be forfeited if he is in trouble again within a specified period, usually one year. A later entry names his sureties: they are a local vintner, Benjamin Flint, and a Cheapside goldsmith, Laurence Strowbridge. We hear Mountjoy's social world in this – wine and gold – though Strowbridge may just be a moneylender, offering to pay the surety as a loan with interest, rather than a personal contact.

★

Further hints as to the nature of Mountjoy's offence are to be found in the 'act book' of the French Church. As noted earlier, this mentions that he had been brought before a magistrates' court; the date of the entry, 27 February 1614, makes it pretty certain that it refers to his appearance in Clerkenwell three months previously. The statement is brief: Mountjoy has been '*tiré au Magistrat pour ses paillardises & adultères*'. These words suggest he had been charged with something more than just being an accessory. In Randle Cotgrave's French–English dictionary, published in 1611, *paillardise* is defined as 'lecherie, whoredom, venerie, obscenitie, uncleanness', in fact 'any filthie or beastlie humour', while the related verb *paillarder* is glossed as 'to haunt bawdie howses' and 'to bitch-hunt it'. (These words derive from *paille*, 'straw', via an association of cheap straw mattresses, or *palliasses*, with prostitution.) The other word used is '*adultères*'. Mountjoy was at this time unmarried (Marie Mountjoy had died in 1606, and his subsequent marriage to Isobel d'Est was not until 1615), so the primary sense of 'adultery' is not strictly applicable. However, in early usage the meaning was 'extended to unchastity generally' – the *OED* cites an example from the

1590 Geneva Bible, a book much prized by the Calvinists of the French Church.

The gist of the synopsis seems clear enough. The Church elders are saying that Mountjoy had been charged with some kind of illicit sexual activity. As they had themselves recently 'censured' him for sleeping with his maid, they no doubt thought the charge was just. Indeed, I wonder if these two accusations against Mountjoy in 1613 – the censure of the Spiritual Court in May; the charges at the Middlesex Sessions in December – might actually be the same accusation made twice. The maid is not named in the French Church document: she is simply called his '*servante*'. It has been assumed she was herself French, but we know of two earlier maids in the Mountjoy household – Margaret Brown and Joan Langford – and both were English. Could Mountjoy's servant and concubine in 1613 be Frances Williams? This is speculation, of course, though it would explain why Mountjoy ends up being charged along with the three Frenchmen. As the evidence of their fornication with Frances is presented to the magistrates, it emerges that Mountjoy has himself been fornicating with her over a period of years (long enough, anyway, to have produced those '*2 bastardes*' attributed to them). I have suggested that Frances was a prostitute: she may more precisely be a servant housed and employed by Mountjoy and pimped out by him when occasion serves.

It would be useful at this point to learn something more about the accuser, Adam Bowin, whose initial complaint – 'an information he hath given against the said parties' – brought them all to court, and whose evidence led to their conviction. What do we know of him? He is described in the Sessions documents as a resident of Bishopsgate, and his occupation is given as 'tuft taffetamaker'. This immediately suggests that he too was French or Flemish, the production of taffeta ('a light thin silk

stuff with considerable lustre') being a speciality of the immigrant silk-weavers. 'Tuft' (or tufted) taffeta, which Bowin
produced, was woven with raised patterns, to produce a velvety
pile of a different colour to the ground. Huguenot and Walloon
craftsmen were the first to manufacture this costly fabric in England. Our accuser is very likely the Adam Bowin whose daughter
Suzanne was married at the French Church in 1621; the marriage register tells us she had been born in London, so Bowin
was certainly in England by the early years of the seventeenth
century. He may have been there a good deal longer. In the
1593 Return of Strangers – a detailed census of immigrants in
London – there are nineteen 'taffety-makers' listed: there is no
Adam Bowin among them, but there is an Adam Boren, and
given the fluid spelling of foreign names in these documents,
they sound like the same man. If so, he was a French-speaking
Walloon from 'Torney', or Tournai, in what is now southern
Belgium, and he had a wife called Marie from the same city.
Tournai was a centre for taffeta-weaving: twelve of the 'taffety-
makers' listed in the census came from there. In 1593 he was a
householder, with four children, all English-born: the eldest
was a girl of ten. Tournai had been occupied by Spanish forces
under the Duke of Parma in 1581; many refugees came to England at that time, and Boren or Bowin was probably among
them.

It seems Adam Bowin was a successful Huguenot craftsman
in the fashion business, who had been living and prospering in
London since the early 1580s – someone, in short, very like
Christopher Mountjoy. They must certainly have known one
another. How much they liked one another can perhaps be
gauged from events at the magistrates' court, where Bowin's
'information' about the three Frenchmen leads to embarrassing
disclosures about Mountjoy himself. Bowin was a member of
the French Church. He would have already known about

Mountjoy's promiscuous lifestyle, censured by the elders in May, when he lodged his complaint about the goldworkers around November. Without wishing to turn this into a conspiracy theory, I suspect that the real target of the complaint was Mountjoy (or Mountjoy and his strumpet, Frances), and I wonder if there isn't someone else in the background: another Frenchman living in St Giles, and one who certainly had a motive to cause Mountjoy trouble – Stephen Belott, his son-in-law, and his bitter antagonist in the still unresolved case of the missing dowry. When it is said that the foursome were 'seene' *in flagrante*, one assumes it was Bowin who saw them. Did he somehow stumble upon them, with a cry of affronted piety? Or was there a word in his ear, discreetly directing him to the house of Mountjoy, where he could conveniently catch them in the act?

I have searched in vain for further information on the troublesome trio of goldworkers. Jacques Depree (nowadays generally spelt Du Pré) has a name too common to be helpful. At least two of them appear in the registers of the French Church in the 1620s, but nothing connects them with the offender of 1613. Jacques Mullett may be the silk-weaver's servant James Mulett, who appears in a list of 'strangers' living in Bishopsgate, but that was back in 1583, thirty years earlier. And Abraham Trippie is perhaps related to René Tripier, a native of Le Mans, who was living in the parish of St Stephen's on Coleman Street in the late 1590s (and who was therefore a neighbour of the mercer Henry Wood, a business associate of the Mountjoys and a rather overheated admirer of Mountjoy's sparky wife, Marie). This Tripier was married at the French Church in January 1601, but Abraham cannot be a son of this marriage – the presence of a twelve-year-old in that overfreighted bed is not impossible, but the description of him as a goldworker would be very unlikely. The

three Frenchmen remain bodiless, apart from the very corporeal
record of them in 1613.

★

The last entry concerning Mountjoy in the Sessions Register is
merely administrative – it records the payment into the
Exchequer of the £40 surety for his good behaviour – but it
adds to our store of information by giving a more precise address
for the scene of the crime: 'his house in whitecrostreete'. Whitecross Street was a long narrow road leading northwards from
the City walls up to Old Street. We can further specify that the
house stood on the upper stretch of the street, north of its inter-
section with Chiswell Street, because that was the only part of
the street which was in Middlesex, and which therefore came
under the jurisdiction of the Middlesex magistrates. The southern part of St Giles parish, though outside the City walls, was
administratively part of the City; walking north you crossed the
county boundary into the badlands of Middlesex.

One notes the intensely local flavour of the case. Mountjoy's
surety Benjamin Flint lives on Whitecross Street (or perhaps,
since he is a 'vintner', runs a tavern there). So does one of Frances
Williams's sureties, Robert Bowker (who is described in one
entry as a carpenter and in another as a glover), while her other
surety, a scrivener called West, lives a block away on Golding
Lane. The gardener Richard Meade, co-surety for the three
Frenchmen, is not far away either, being of the Middlesex part
of St Giles. The name is a common one, but he may be related
to John Meade of Golding Lane, a porter, who features at the
Sessions in 1614 (bound over to keep the peace) and twice in 1615
(standing bail for a prostitute, and prosecuting a local barber for
'cozening' him).

This northern stretch of Whitecross Street is all that remains today – the rest, bombed out by the Luftwaffe in 1940, now lies under the giant Barbican estate. Halfway up this pleasant, quiet-ish, intermittently scruffy street you come to a turning on the left into Fortune Street, and many who walked up here in 1613 would have been heading for precisely this spot, for the street marks the site of the Fortune Theatre, which stood between Whitecross Street and Golding Lane. A squarish wooden struc-ture which is said to have accommodated a thousand spectators, it was built in 1600 by the impresario Philip Henslowe, worried about falling revenues at his Southwark playhouse, the Rose, due to competition from Shakespeare's company at the newly opened Globe. Henslowe's partner in the Fortune venture was his son-in-law, the actor Edward Alleyn, who capitalized on it by buying some lettable properties on Whitecross Street. There were actors living on the street – Roger Barfield of Queen Anne's company, who rented one of those tenements owned by Alleyn; and William Stratford of Prince Henry's troupe, who lived 'at the upper end' of the street, and was buried at St Giles in 1625. Former colleagues of Shakespeare such as William Sly and Nicholas Tooley are also found in the St Giles registers, as is his younger brother Edmund, also a player, who buried an infant son there, 'base-born', in 1607: he was perhaps acting at the Fortune in that year.

Where there were playhouses and players there was infallibly that ad hoc outgrowth of leisure and pleasure which so worried the authorities – taverns, dicing-houses, bowling-alleys and, above all, brothels. One such tavern might be Benjamin Flint's, and one such brothel the Whitecross Street establishment run by Helen Clare, 'a harbourer of lewd persons', whose girls included Mary Pilkinton, charged at the sessions of December 1613 with burying her baby in the backyard of the house. Another name to mention here is that of George Wilkins, hack author and brothel-keeper: another St Giles character until he shifted operations to Clerkenwell in about 1610. Wilkins frequently appeared before the Middlesex magistrates, sometimes on charges of gross violence against the prostitutes who worked for him. He has documented dealings with Mountjoy and Stephen Belott, and indeed – perhaps through this connection – with Shakespeare, with whom he collaborated on the writing of *Pericles* in 1607/8. An unpleasant character (though also an underrated writer), Wilkins belongs to the overall tone of this story, but seems to have no specific link with it.

Mountjoy's house on Whitecross Street is not mentioned in the lawsuit about the dowry, heard at the Court of Requests the previous year. At the hearing on 19 June 1612 (which Shakespeare did not attend), witnesses were asked about Mountjoy's financial state, including the specific question 'What leases of houses or tenements hath he, and where do the said houses or tenements lie?' Two of the respondents – Mountjoy's brother Noel and a near-neighbour Christopher Weaver – gave clear answers, agreeing in most details. We learn that Mountjoy 'hath but the lease of two houses'. One is the property on Silver Street 'wherein he dwelleth', which is 'divided into two tenements', one for himself and one rented out. The other is a property in 'Brainforde' (now Brentford), which he sublets. From these 'he gaineth an overplus of rent more than he payeth', and this profit is estimated by both deponents as about £18 per annum. They are witnesses generally favourable to Mountjoy, and they would favour his cause by downplaying his disposable income, but it is unlikely they are both lying about how many houses he had. A more plausible deduction is that Mountjoy acquired the Whitecross Street property sometime after June 1612.

The most significant part of Mountjoy's property portfolio in 1612 is the house in Brentford. Though now a neat and orderly West London suburb, Jacobean Brentford had a lurid reputation. It was a 'place of resort' for Londoners, with numerous brothels, and is frequently mentioned in plays and pamphlets as a place for a dirty night or weekend. 'Let's to mine host Dogbolt's at Brainford,' says an adulterous gallant in Dekker and Webster's *Westward Ho!* (c. 1606). 'There you are out of eyes, out of ears: private rooms, sweet linen, winking attendance, and what cheer you will.' There are similar references in Ben Jonson's *The Alchemist* (1610), and in the theatrical smash of 1611, Dekker and Middleton's *The Roaring Girl*, where the beau Laxton makes a 'lecherous voyage' to Brentford with Moll Cutpurse.

I have wondered whether Mountjoy's house in Brentford was just such a place of amorous assignation – a pleasure-den or bawdy-house, if not quite a full-scale brothel – and I gave reasons in *The Lodger* for thinking it might be. The new evidence from the Middlesex Sessions rather vividly corroborates this idea. To his house in disreputable Brentford can now be added this other house, in the equally disreputable purlieus of the Fortune playhouse. And to the speculation that he had a sideline in the sex-trade can now be added this eyewitness report, which takes us right inside one of the rooms in his house, and shows us three men in bed with a 'light-tailed' lady whose services they may well be paying him for.

'If it be not a bawd's house,' says Constable Elbow, it is certainly a 'naughty house'. He is talking of Mistress Overdone's brothel, a place so dodgy that even the irreproachable Mrs Elbow might be 'accused in fornication, adultery and all uncleanliness there'. The phrasing is apt for this case at the Sessions, with its teasing glimpse into Mountjoy's real-life 'naughty house' in Whitecross Street; and apt also because Shakespeare's *Measure for Measure*, in which Elbow appears, can be dated to about 1604, and was therefore probably written in his lodgings at Mountjoy's other house in Silver Street. Shakespeare has no connection with this case nearly a decade later, except that it shows us more of the louche and not entirely likeable Frenchman he had once lived with, and more of the dark and dirty side of Jacobean London which he drew on when writing the brothel scenes in *Measure for Measure* and *Pericles*. This tawdry episode brings us briefly into that quotidian world of people and streets and rooms which lies, for the most part unreachably, just the other side of those texts.

3
Noticing Everything

A Celebration of John Aubrey
[1997]

That tireless scribbler John Aubrey died suddenly, aged seventy-one, sometime during the first week of June 1697. His funeral was held at St Mary Magdalen Church in Oxford 300 years ago today. The parish register records: 'John Aubery a stranger was buryed Jun 7th.'

The term 'stranger' means merely that he was not of the parish – he lived all his life in the Wiltshire hamlet of Easton Piers, near Malmesbury – but it carries a certain resonance of the man. Aubrey never quite belonged: he was an observer more than a participant. In academic circles he was a marginal, quirky figure, and he remains so in the eyes of posterity. He spent a lifetime recording 'curiosities' of all sorts, and is now considered something of a curiosity himself. The range of his interests defies classification – biographer, topographer, antiquary, mathematician, folklorist, archaeologist: the list could go on. He is sometimes described as a 'miscellanist', a term redolent of a bygone age of genial scholarly browsing. This is partly right, but does not catch Aubrey's out-and-about quality – he was 'never off horseback' – nor his reportorial relish for gossip and raciness. Contemporaries described him variously as a 'learned honest gentleman', a 'professed virtuoso, always replete with new discoveries' and a 'shiftless person, roving and maggoty-headed'.

There is a memorial plaque on the west wall of St Mary Magdalen, put there in the 1980s, but his true monument lies a few hundred yards away at the Bodleian Library. It is a monument of paper – fifty assorted leatherbound volumes of his manuscripts and letters, packed with his small, rapid, slightly obsessive handwriting. Leafing through these cluttered pages, abuzz with addenda and marginalia, with doodles and diagrams, you seem almost to be looking into his mind.

★

Aubrey is best known for his marvellous collection of biographical sketches, *Brief Lives*, of which he said: 'These remaines are *tamquam tabulata naufragi* ['like the fragments of a shipwreck'] that after the Revolution of so many years and governments have escaped the teeth of time.' This catches the nature of their perennial appeal. Jotted down over decades, unpublished until 1813 – and then only in very bowdlerized form – the *Lives* are a gold mine for the historian. They are full of rackety details and contemporary gossip, of irresistible if usually unverifiable anecdotes – Sir Walter Ralegh 'getting up one of the Maids of Honour up against a tree'; Ben Jonson drinking canary wine in an old 'coachman's coat, with slits under the armpits', and so on.

Equally piquant are the many minor, forgotten figures who appear in its pages: Dr Willis, who had 'dark brindle hair like a red pig' and 'stammered much'; Sir Jonas Moore, who 'cured his sciatica by boiling his buttock'. Here is the entire brief life of Dr Richard Stokes:

> Scholar to Mr William Oughtred for Mathematiques (Algebra).
> Made himself mad with it, but became sober again, but I feare
> like a crackt glasse. Became Roman Catholique. Married unhappily at Liège, dog and catt, etc. Became a sott. Dyed in Newgate,
> prisoner for debt, April 1681.

Aubrey is the master of biographical compression (something today's 800-page merchants could learn from) and the cryptic

but suggestive aside. Apropos the Countess of Kent, 'I remember in 1646 or 1647 they did talk also of my Lady's she-
blackamoor.' He had a nose for salacious stories about the great
and good. Mistress Overall, wife of the Dean of St Paul's, was
discovered *in flagrante*, lying 'upon Sir John Selby's bed as flat as
any flounder'. The Countess of Pembroke – Sir Philip Sidney's
sister – had a 'videtto', or peep-hole, made for her at Wilton
House so she could watch the stallions 'leape the mares' and
then 'act the like sport herself with her stallions'. (In the manuscript this passage is scored out, apparently by Aubrey himself,
though not enough to make it illegible.)

The *Lives* are an accretion of notes rather than a finished
work. They were 'set down tumultuarily', he said, 'as if tumbled out of a sack'. Oliver Lawson Dick, whose excellent edition
appeared in 1949 (and who sadly died in his mid forties in 1964),
reckoned the total number of lives as 426. But some are merely
copied from other sources, and some take brevity too far –
Aubrey's life of John Holywood consists of a single sentence:
'Dr Pell is positive that his name was Holybushe.' Lawson Dick
stitched together 136 lives out of this Aubreian 'gallimaufry' of
fact and anecdote.

The lack of method seems now a positive quality. The *Lives*
have a rawness and intimacy. He compared the biographer to
a 'conjuror' who 'makes them walk and appear that have layen
in their graves many hundreds of years'. One catches too a sense
of Aubrey himself, the inquisitor at large. Scattered through
the manuscripts is the word *Quaere*, or simply *Q* – a memo
to himself to ask someone something. '*Quaere* Dr Pell, what is
the use of those inverted logarithmes?', '*Quaere* whether there
are mussel-shells in the Thames', and so on. He was the great
inquirer, the pursuivant of fugitive details. His interviewees
sometimes found him tiresome. Dr John Newton 'told me he
was borne in Bedfordshire, but would not tell me where'. And

'the Earl of Carnarvon does not remember Mr Brown; I ask't his
Lordship lately if any of his servants do; he assures me NO.'

The chaos of the Civil War made Aubrey acutely aware of
the precariousness of historical remembrance. He woke up in a
cold sweat thinking of all those interesting old parchments now
being used to wrap herrings and stop mustard-pots. He rescued
a rich stratum of oral history about the Elizabethans, of whom
our personal knowledge is scant. He quizzed a dying generation
of eyewitnesses and childhood reminiscencers. (He was to the
Elizabethans, chronologically, as we are to the Edwardians.) In
London, in the old theatrical quarter of Shoreditch, he found a
son of Shakespeare's colleague Christopher Beeston; another
old-stager called Lacey supplied him with memories of Ben
Jonson. He tapped into the Ralegh family via Sir Walter's great-
nephews, who were at school with him.

*

Aubrey's own life is less well known, outwardly uneventful but
rich in charm and curiosity. He records its small dramas –
mortgages, lawsuits, bungled courtships, hawking trips – with
the nonchalant irony that marks the *Lives*: 'This yeare [1666] all
my businesses and affaires ran kim-kam.'

The son of a minor Wiltshire squire, he was a sickly, studious
child, prone to agues and colics, 'mild of spirit' and 'mightily
susceptible of fascination'. His 'phansie', or imagination, was
'like pure chrystal water which the least wind does disorder and
unsmoothe'. He grew up in a secluded farmhouse, looking out
over the 'thin blew lanskape' of Wiltshire, walking river banks
riotous with 'calver-keys, hare-parsley, wild vetch, maiden's
honesty, polypodium, foxgloves, wild vine, bayle, and many
vulnerary plants now by me forgot'.

He studied at Trinity College, Oxford, but the outbreak
of war in 1642 forced him home. He was torn between

gregariousness and seclusion. He never married, though there were doomed alliances, most notably with Joan Sumner, to whom 'I made my first addresse, in an ill-howre' in 1665. Little is known of the relationship. That she told him of a recipe used by thieves to stop dogs barking – a mixture of boar's fat and cumin seeds – is pungent if not quite romantic. It ended in law-suits, 'opprobrious speeches', and the embarrassment of an arrest on Chancery Lane.

An expressive portrait by William Faithorne (see Plate 2) shows him in 1666, at the age of forty. He has big eyes, a thin moustache and long curly hair like a Dobson cavalier. It is a very likeable face, but has an unexpected air of uncertainty or even bitterness.

The following year Aubrey met the irascible Oxford don and gossip Anthony Wood. They spent 3s. 8d. drinking 'at Mother Web's'. Wood writes: 'Mr Aubrey was then in a sparkish garb, came to town with his man and two horses, spent high, and flung out A. W. at all reckonings.' It was the caustic Wood who described Aubrey as 'maggoty-headed'. He complained that Aubrey fed him 'fooleries and misinformations', but this is sour considering how much of Aubrey's research he used, with-out acknowledgement, for his own biographical collections, *Athenae Oxonienses* (1691–2).

Aubrey's most measurable achievement was as a founder member of the Royal Society. He was a great experimenter. A hundred years before the first manned balloon flight he wrote: 'Fill or force in smoke into a bladder, and try if the bladder will not be carried up in the ayre; if it is so, several bladders may draw a man up into the ayre a certain height.' He was also a pioneering archaeologist, who first drew attention to the ancient stone-ring at Avebury. He wrote brilliantly about places as well as people. (Having grown up in Surrey, I have a soft spot for his neglected *Perambulation of Surrey*, last published in 1719.)

His only work to be published in his lifetime was simply called *Miscellanies* (1696). A grab-bag of superstitions and occultisms, it is largely unreadable – may even be, as the learned cleric Dr Stratford described it, 'a mad book' – but the title is apt for his maverick eclecticism. Aubrey's genius lies precisely in his dilettantism, in his capturing of the diverse and ephemeral, the common currency, the lightweight truths of an age: 'cookery, chemistry, cards'. His manuscripts contain a world, lovingly observed and preserved amid the upheavals of war. The historian G. M. Young sums him up eloquently: 'Across this shifting landscape he flits, noticing everything.'

His last dateable note was written on 1 June 1697, a few days before his death. It is a memo to the bookseller Awnsham Churchill, directing his attention to 'a very pretty remarque concerning apparitions' in the *Athenian Mercury*. He hopes it can be inserted into the next edition of his *Miscellanies*. He gives the exact volume, number and date. The precision is with him to the end, and the enthusiasm, and the poignant overtone of pointlessness.

He once described himself as 'surprised with age', and he was probably surprised with death as well; at any rate, he died intestate. It was perhaps a recurrence of the 'apoplexy', or stroke, which he had suffered three years earlier. An air of surprise attends his whole life: everything is so curious, so puzzling, so worthy of 'remarque', and down it goes into the notebook whose pages one opens up today, as if uncorking an old dusty phial marked 'Tonick' and finding the contents still fresh and full of zest.

4
Death of an Alchemist
Edward Kelley in Bohemia
[2001]

The winter night falls early in the small Czech town of Soběslav, and with it comes a cold, creeping fog laced with coal-smoke that leaves a bitter coating in the mouth. The town square is deserted, the tall-spired church a hulk. There is a cramped little beer-cellar full of gaming machines, but it is decidedly not the old 'inn' which stood on the square in the days when Soběslav was a staging-post between Prague and the southern stronghold of Český Krumlov, seat of the powerful Rožmberk family. It was at this inn, on the evening of 3 May 1591, that the English alchemist, clairvoyant and con-man Edward Kelley was arrested by officers of Emperor Rudolf II.

At the time of his arrest Kelley was an internationally famous figure, but thereafter the story grows confused – he disappears from view into the dungeons of Bohemia. News of his death reached England in late 1595, and for a long time this provided the death-date in such biographies of him as existed (there is still no full biography). But the report was false. He is discernible in Bohemian documents for a couple of years after this: the date of his death is more probably November or December 1597, at the age of forty-two. I have always had a sneaking fascination for Kelley, and hoped that a visit to the Czech Republic might shed some light on the foggy circumstances of his last years.

*

The best-known part of Kelley's story concerns his long part-nership with the magus John Dee. It begins with his arrival at

Dr Dee's house, in the Thameside village of Mortlake, near London, in early March 1582. Dee, then in his mid fifties, was the queen's chief consultant on all matters occult. He was renowned as a mathematician, physician, astrologer, geographer and, in the popular parlance, 'conjuror'. His visitor was, at this point, an altogether more shadowy figure. We know that he was twenty-six years old, and came from Worcester; that he had served apprentice to an apothecary; that he had been in trouble with the law. And we know that he was using an alias, for he first appears in Dee's diary not as Edward Kelley but as Edward 'Talbot'.

The purpose of his visit that morning was, in Dee's words, 'to see or shew some thing in spiritual practice' – in other words, to display his gifts as a 'skryer', or spirit-medium. Dee was cautious, and had reason to be. He was quick to make clear that he had no dealings 'in that vulgarly accounted magick'. He was, however, 'desirous to have help' in his philosophical studies, 'through the company and information of the blessed angels of God'. Having made this important distinction between the conjuring of evil spirits and the invocation of *angeli boni*, Dee brought out his 'shew stone', or crystal ball (possibly the small globe of greyish smoky quartz which is now in the British Museum, though he had others). The *soi-disant* Talbot 'then settled himself to the Action . . . and within one quarter of an hour (or less) he had sight of one in the stone'. The angel identified itself as Uriel. It spoke 'plainly', in a mixture of Latin and English, 'to the hearing of E. T.'. The séance proceeded smoothly – perhaps suspiciously so – and the successful skryer was engaged, informally at first, and later at a generous salary of £50 per annum.

Kelley remained Dee's link to the angels for a further seven years, first at Mortlake, and then, from 1583, during their long and controversial travels in Central Europe. Their names are for ever linked, invariably with Dee as the reverend but credulous old magus, and Kelley as his unscrupulous deceiver and exploiter. He is variously described as a 'grand Imposter', an 'egregious scoundrel' and a 'terrible zombie-like figure'. This last comment – the phrase is Edith Sitwell's – glances at a ghoulish feature of the Kelley image: it is said that he had no ears, having had them cut off in the pillory in his youth. The Dee–Kelley partnership has inspired plays and novels, from Ben Jonson's *The Alchemist* to Peter Ackroyd's *The House of Dr Dee*. Its apotheosis, in this picaresque sense, is the notorious occasion at Trebon Castle in southern Bohemia, when the spirits revealed to Kelley their wish that he and Dee should 'hold their wives in common'. In the embroidered versions Jane Dee tends to be blonde and beautiful. This is not attested in any document I know of, but it is a fact that she was nearly thirty years younger than Dee, and had been one of the queen's ladies-in-waiting. Dee consented to this 'doctrine of cross-matching' reluctantly, and Jane even more so. 'She fell a-weeping and trembling for a quarter of an hour,' but at length she resigned herself to it, saying: 'I trust, though I give myself thus to be used, that God will turn me into a stone before He would suffer me, in my obedience, to receive any shame or inconvenience.' The shenanigans that followed are cryptically recorded in Dee's diary. Nine months later Jane bore a son. He was christened Theodorus Trebonianus, meaning 'the gift of God at Trebon'.

Kelley the spirit-medium (or cunning ventriloquist) has gone down in the folklore, but in Europe he became more celebrated in another branch of the occultist repertoire: alchemy. Dee believed Kelley to be an alchemical grand master – a climactic moment is recorded in May 1588: 'E. K. did open the great secret to me, God be thanked.' Another devotee was the poet and diplomat Sir Edward Dyer, who 'laboured much in chymistry' under Kelley's tutelage, and was present at one of his transmutations in Prague. 'I am an eyewitness thereof,' Dyer affirmed, 'and if I had not seen it I should not have believed it. I saw Master Kelley put of the base metal into the crucible, and after it was set a little upon the fire, and a very small quantity of the medicine put in, and stirred with a stick of wood, it came forth in great proportion perfect gold, to the touch, to the hammer, to the test.'

Alchemy was the passion of the age, and nowhere more so than at the court of Emperor Rudolf II in Prague. When Dee returned to England in 1589, Kelley stayed. His bruited alchemical skills brought him fame and fortune, and even a Bohemian knighthood: he is henceforth Sir Edward Kelley of the noble 'house of Imamyi in the county of Conneghaku'. (I always took this heraldry to be a concoction of Kelley's – indeed, 'Imamyi' sounds like one of the spirits he professed to converse with – but in the old Irish genealogy *An Leabhar Muimhneach*, or 'Book of Munster', the Kelley are said to be descended from the Maine, whose Gaelic form, Uí Mhaine, is also written 'Imany'. The Maine held territory in Galway and Roscommon: these are in the province of Connaught, which in the Bohemian documents comes out as 'Conneghaku'. Kelley's self-styled lineage is thus grandiose but not incorrect.)

In a letter to Lord Burghley of July 1590 Kelley describes his lofty situation in Bohemia. He is 'siezed in lands of inheritance yielding £1,500 yearly, incorporated into the kingdom in the second order, of some expectation and use more than vulgar'. He has even been invited to join Rudolf's Privy Council, but is 'not yet sworn, for the love I bear unto my sacred Queen & Country'. Rudolf, it should be remembered, was Habsburg and a Catholic, and was nominally – though not personally – an enemy of Elizabeth. Kelley was in regular correspondence with Burghley, the queen's chief adviser, who earnestly entreated him to return home, 'to honour Her Majesty . . . with the fruits of such great knowledge as God hath given him'. Or, if he could not personally return, perhaps he might send her a small sample of his gold-making powder, 'in some secret box' – just enough 'as might be to her a sum reasonable to defer her charges for this summer for her navy'.

★

This is the climax of Kelley's fortunes; the sudden fall – the inn at Soběslav – is just around the corner. But even here, in this better-lit part of his life, I find it hard to grasp his personality and motivations. Behind the folkloric stereotypes – the hypnotic Svengali, the sham magician, the trickster – the face is unclear. What was he like?

The only known portrait, by the Dutch engraver Franz Cleyn, dates from the mid seventeenth century and is probably guesswork (see Plate 3). It shows a gaunt, long-faced, bearded man, wearing a fur-trimmed cloak and a four-cornered hat like a cleric's biretta. The only contemporary hints I can find seem rather at odds with this, for an Englishman who visited him in Bohemia in 1593 describes him as 'fat and merry'; another source calls him a 'weighty' man. Certainly Kelley was no ascetic. His fondness for wine is often mentioned. A drunken incident in Prague gives us a vividly nasty glimpse of him: 'In this company of drinking was Alexander [a Polish servant] unto whom E. K. (when the drink on a sudden had overcome him) said he would cut off his head, and with his walking-staff did touch him fair and softly on the neck, sitting before him.' The following morning there was a further altercation: 'E. K. took up a stone and threw after him, as after a dog, and so came into the house again in a most furious rage.' Kelley's violent temper and mood changes are often noted by Dee.

The walking-stick with which Kelley stroked Alexander's neck may itself be significant. In a letter from Prague in April

1586, the Papal Nuncio refers to '*Giovanni Dee e il zoppo suo compagno*'. *Zoppo* means 'lame'. It is possible that Kelley was disabled in some way (and disability is traditionally associated with the psychic powers he claimed). There is a reference, during one of the séances, to his difficulty in kneeling.

And then there is the question of his ears, or lack of them. This is sometimes said to be a late tradition, dating from the eighteenth century, but it is not. It first appears in print in John Weever's *Ancient Funerall Monuments* of 1631: 'Kelley (otherwise called Talbot) that famous English alchymist of our times . . . lost both his ears at Lancaster.' Another, independent testimony is found in the manuscripts of a Czech alchemist, Šimon Tadeáš Budek, who speaks of Kelley's 'missing ears'. It turns out these reports are only partly correct, however, for the earliest comment on the matter is in a letter from Prague dated 20 July 1593, in which an Englishman named Parkins reports being questioned about Kelley by one of Rudolf's councillors. Among the inquiries was: 'if I could give any account of the diminishing of one of his ears, or of his good or evil behaviour in England'. Parkins knew Kelley, and the councillor who was questioning him probably did too, so this phrasing is backed up by eyewitness. It seems that Kelley had had just one ear cropped in the pillory. The alchemist Budek also describes him as having 'long hair' – as he has in the Cleyn engraving – which may in part be to conceal this disfigurement, and the criminal record it betokened. 'Crop-ears' are 'privileged to wear long locks by ancient charter', says a humorous pamphlet of the day. Concealment of the clipped ear may also be the reason why 'Mr Talbot' declined to take off his hat before praying to the angels, as complained of by Dee in a diary entry of May 1582.

The limping, fleshy, boozy, long-haired and aggressive character who emerges from contemporary reports is rather different from the daemonic deluder of legend, though scarcely more admirable or likeable. Yet in a way this aura of unpleasantness makes his success even harder to understand. What was it about him that – despite all this – held so many in his spell?

In his dealings with Dee, the sheer scale of his deception is staggering. Dee left reams of manuscripts recording the messages of angels and spirits, all of them dictated to him by Kelley: the 'spirituall diaries', as they are called. The first printed edition, *A True & Faithful Relation of what passed for many yeers between Dr John Dee and some spirits*, edited by Méric Casaubon and published in 1659, is a stout folio running to several hundred pages. In the conventional view, these messages and visions came from Kelley himself – he made them up – in which case we are dealing not just with a story of sustained deception, but with an extraordinary feat of imagination. The utterances of Uriel and Madimi, of El and Il and King Carmara and scores of others, are not voicings from the spirit-world, but improvised dramatic monologues performed by Kelley. Most of it is high-sounding esoteric flannel, but often the words have a strange rolling beauty: 'I will hold up his house with pillars of hyacinth, and his chambers shall be full of modesty and comfort; I will bring the east wind over him as a lady of comfort, and she shall sit upon his castles in triumph.' Here is an edited transcript of Kelley in full flight, in front of the 'shew stone', at their lodgings in Prague near the Bethlehem Chapel:

> E. K.: I see a garland of white rose-buds about the border of the stone: they be well-opened. But while I consider these buds better, they seem rather to be white lilies. They are 72 in number, seeming with their heads, *alternatim*, one to bend or hang toward me and another to you. A voice cometh shouting out from the lilies, saying Holy, Holy, Holy, and all the lilies are become on fire. The noise is marvellous great which I hear

coming through the stone: as it were of a thousand water-mills going together.

A voice: *Male & in summo: & mensuratum est.*

Another voice: The seal is broken.

Another: Pour out the sixth viol that the earth may know herself.

E. K.: Now I see beyond like a furnace-mouth, as big as 4 or 5 gates of a city. It seemeth to be a quarter of a mile off. Out of the furnace-mouth seemeth a marvellous smoke or smother to come. Bye it seemeth to be a great lake of pitch, and it playeth or simpereth as water doth when it beginneth to seethe.

Often the visions are lurid and apocalyptic – 'Here appeareth . . . a man in the fire, with flaxen hair hanging down upon him, and is naked unto his paps, and seemeth to have spots of blood upon him.' But sometimes there is a touch of surreal humour – 'E. K. saw three little creatures walk up and down in the sunshine'; they were 'very small, not a handful long, like shadows or smokes, and the path wherein they walked seemed yellow'; they pipingly identify themselves as Da, Za and Vaa. We are not far here from the fairy-world of *A Midsummer Night's Dream*; elsewhere we seem to have strayed into an early draft of *Doctor Faustus*. Sometimes the sessions are accompanied by optical tricks – objects are miraculously discovered; books lie conveniently open – and sometimes by strenuous physical effects on Kelley. 'He thought verily that his bowels did burn' . . . 'His body had a fiery heat, even from his breast down unto all his parts, his privities and thighs' . . . 'He started, and said he felt a thing creeping within his head, and in that pang became all in a sweat, and he remained much misliking the moving and creeping of the thing in his head.'

These are brief extracts from a rolling seven-year performance.

Reading them *in extenso* (which one can now do conveniently in the new edition of Dee's diaries by Edward Fenton) it is sometimes hard to believe that they are just inventions. The performance is so good. Is it possible, after all, that Kelley himself believed in it? That he *did* hear voices and see things when he knelt in front of the 'shew stone'? The instabilities of his personality could support this idea – in other words, the 'spirituall diaries' are a casebook of schizophrenic imaginings – but the many instances where the spirits say and show things thoroughly convenient to Kelley tend to argue against it: the 'cross-matching' episode is only the most notorious of these. We must take him as a showman, a con-artist, a brilliant actor, though one whose very brilliance may suggest an ambiguous closeness to the part he is playing.

It is, in fact, as another kind of actor that Kelley makes his first appearance in Dee's life – as a spy. This is quite clear from Dee's diary, though it features surprisingly little in the Kelley mythos. The suspicion that 'Mr Talbot' was some sort of spy or provocateur was in Dee's mind from the beginning: he had long experience of the parlousness of his occult studies, and of unscrupulous people who tried to make capital out of this. Over the next few months his suspicions were amply confirmed. On 29 May 1582: 'I understood of Ed. Talbot his wicked nature and his abominable lies &c.' On 16 July 1582: 'I have confirmed that Talbot is a cozener' (a cheat). Perhaps it is at this point that Talbot's real name is revealed: in the next reference to him he is, for the first time, 'E. Kelly'. A fragmentary entry on 1 August 1583 seems also to be about Kelley – 'a Worcestershire man, a wicked spy, came to my house: whom I used as an honest man and found nothing being as I used.' Further cracks appear when Dee finds Kelley has been snooping through his diary, and even brazenly altering it. Thus in the original manuscript, the entry reading 'I have confirmed that Talbot is a cozener' is scored through, and beside it Kelley has written: 'a horrible and slanderous lie'.

None of this quite explains what Kelley was up to as a 'wicked spy'. One answer is given by Dee in an undated marginalium, in which he comments on Kelley's first arrival at Mortlake – 'his coming was to entreat me if I had had any dealing with wicked spirits, as he confessed oftentimes after: and that he was set on, &c.' This has to be treated with caution – it is Kelley's own account of it, as 'confessed' to Dee – but it is plausible enough. His intention was to provoke Dee into forbidden magical practices, to incriminate him as a 'conjuror'. By whom he was 'set on' does not appear: one could round up the usual suspects. Dee was the figurehead of a growing fascination with the occult in late Elizabethan England, and he had many enemies, both doctrinal and political, who considered his influence subversive.

These jottings and erasures are physical traces of the first edgy stages of their relationship. Dee knows that 'Talbot' is a cheat and a spy, yet is also so clearly in his thrall, both because he believes him to be genuinely gifted as a medium, and because there is some magnetic power Kelley holds over people. He makes poor Dr Dee positively palpitate: 'my heart did throb oftentimes this day, and thought that E. K. did intend to absent himself from me.' He has an unsettling effect on Jane Dee as well: 'Jane in a marvellous rage all that night and next morning till 8 of the clock, melancholic terribly for the cozening.' This was in early May 1582; that 'the cozening' refers to the deceptions of Kelley is confirmed by his attempt to deface the entry. A couple of years later, in Poland, Kelley transmitted the following ominous vision concerning Jane:

He [the spirit Nalvage] showeth an house, and six or seven on the top of it with torches. They are like shadows; when they sit they are like apes. They set a fire on it and it burneth mightily. Now your wife runneth out, and seemeth to leap over the gallery rail, and lie as dead. And now come you out of door, and the children stand in the way toward the church, and you come by the yern door, and kneel, and knock your hand on the earth. They take up your wife; her head waggleth this way and that way. The stone house quivereth and quaketh, and all the roof of the house falleth. Your wife is dead; the right side of her face, her teeth and all, is battered. She is bare-legged. She hath a white petticoat on.

There is a scarcely veiled erotic charge in this: a motif of sexual violence – the waggling head, the battered face, the rucked-up petticoat – which adds another grim twist to the later 'cross-matching' episode in Trebon, and to the 'weeping and trembling' of Jane when she submitted to it.

This leads into another Kelley puzzle: his marriage. The first mention of this is on 29 April 1582, when he tells Dee the spirits have 'commanded' him to marry, adding darkly: 'which thing to do I have no natural inclination'. The date of the wedding is not recorded, but it was before the end of April 1583, when Dee first refers to Kelley's wife. She was Joan Cooper or Cowper, of Chipping Norton in Oxfordshire; her age was nineteen. Things did not start well. In early July, Kelley rants: 'I cannot abide my wife, I love her not, nay I abhor her.' Dee describes him as 'marvellously out of quiet against his wife' and says certain friends of hers have made 'bitter reports against him behind his back'. Again, on 18 August 1583 – 'Great tempest of wind at midnight; E. K.'s very great anger against his wife.' That Kelley was an ill-tempered and possibly violent husband need not surprise us, but the situation is more complicated. It has recently been discovered that Joan Cooper was already a widow when she married Kelley, and had two children. Her earlier marriage to John Weston, 'clerk', had taken place at Chipping Norton in the summer of 1579, and she had buried him in the same church on 6 May 1582. Kelley's first mention of marriage, as recorded by Dee, was made just a week before Weston's funeral. His reluctance may suggest that he was under some kind of pressure to marry the young widow; that he was, in his own word, 'commanded' to do it.

Whatever the circumstances, Joan's future, and that of her two children, lay with Kelley in Bohemia. Her daughter, Elizabeth Jane Weston, became quite well known there as a Latin poet and scholar, and died in Prague in 1612. That she was the stepdaughter of Edward Kelley was unknown before the discovery of Joan's previous marriage. This is confirmed beyond doubt by a poem of Elizabeth's, *In obitum dominae Ioannae*, published in Prague in 1606. This rare work is an elegy on her mother ('Lady Joanna'), who died that year, and who is identified in the preface as the 'widow of the magnificent and noble Sir Edward Kelley of Imany, Golden Knight of His Holy Imperial Majesty's Council'. In the poem Elizabeth speaks of her childhood: how her father died when she was still a baby, but 'the fates pitied her' and provided her with a stepfather, 'for which I was happy'. Of him she says, *'ceu pater alter amavit'* – 'he loved me as another father.' Here is another, hitherto unsuspected piece of the Kelley jigsaw: the family man. We can allow him some credit, after centuries of bad press, as the protector and perhaps even educator of his scholarly stepdaughter. His stepson, John Francis Weston, seems to have been academic as well: he was enrolled at the University of Ingolstadt, but died there in 1600, aged about twenty.

*

We glimpse a little of the reality behind the *grand guignol* of the Kelley legend, but the circumstances of his last years remain shadowy. We do not know the exact reason for his fall from the emperor's favour. The usual telling of the story is that Rudolf had ceased to believe in him – Kelley's promises, particularly with

regard to heaps of transmuted gold pouring into the treasury, had
proved empty. This may be true, though there were other
speculations voiced at the time, for instance that he was an English spy feeding intelligence back to Lord Burghley, which may
also be true. There is also vague mention of a duel he had
fought: a troublesome figure, he had doubtless made enemies.
The documents do not tell us why it happened, perhaps because
no one really knew, but they can tell us how it happened. The
royal edict, indicting Kelley as a criminal and a fugitive, is dated at
Prague Castle, 'this Thursday, St Sigismund's day, 1591'. The date
referred to is 2 May 1591 (actually the Thursday before that saint's
day, which falls on 6 May). The man ordered to bring him in
was Rudolf's 'quartermaster', Gregor Böul. The wheels of court
payment ground slowly, and years later Böul had still not been
reimbursed for his efforts – which is fortunate for our purposes,
because his complaint to this effect, delivered on 22 March 1597,
gives a detailed account of the operation. This can now be added
to certain English intelligence reports from Prague, to provide for
the first time a full account of Kelley's arrest and imprisonment.

Around midday on Tuesday, 30 April, a deputation of officials and soldiers descended on Kelley's house in the Na
Slovanech district of Prague. They had 'commandment to bring
him up bound, the cause concealed'. They came 'in great number', carrying chains and fetters and 'irons of torture'. But Kelley
was not there. He had slipped away the previous night, 'so
secretly as his own family was kept from it'. The soldiers con-
tented themselves with ransacking the house – they 'broke open
his doors, thrust their halberds through his beds' – and arresting
the servants; 'chief extremity' was used on his younger brother
and confidant, Thomas Kelley. The house was put under guard,
and Kelley's laboratory sealed up. All the 'elixirs' in it were
impounded; also certain 'boards', perhaps wall-panels, painted
with arcane hieroglyphs.

Learning of Kelley's escape, Emperor Rudolf 'cursed in the Dutch manner', and issued the promulgation of 2 May referred to above. Armed with this edict, Quartermaster Böul left Prague with a posse of officers and soldiers: twenty-five people travelling in four wagons. They headed south, towards the fiefdom of Count Rožmberk, Kelley's powerful patron. By midday on 3 May, they had reached Tábor, a beautiful little town founded by the famous Czech Protestant Jan Žižka: you can still see the maze of underground passages beneath the town, where the Protestant rebels hid. In the afternoon Böul pressed on, with a small guard, to Soběslav, ten miles south of Tábor, and here, in that no longer extant inn on the square, they found Kelley. Böul does not describe the actual arrest, but that able English intelligencer Thomas Webbe, dispatched to Prague a few weeks later, gleaned the following:

> He [Kelley] went six Dutch miles towards the Lord Rosenberg, to a certain town under his jurisdiction, where he being weary, and without suspect, he reposed himself after dinner on a bed, and slept. In which time, the Emperor's guards entered, took him, entreated him very ill, cut his doublet open with a knife, searching him, and told him they were by the Emperor's commandment to carry him back again dead or alive, which they cared not. And so prisonered he was carried back again.

A curt report is also found in the Rožmberk annals, written by the count's secretary, Václav Březan: 'Eduardus Kelleus, the cheating alchemist, escaped from Prague, was pursued by His Majesty's soldiers, and arrested at Soběslav.'

The following morning, Böul brought his prisoner back to Tábor, where the rest of the search party was, and thence to Sedlčany. Here a courier met them with express orders from the emperor: Kelley was not to be brought up to Prague, but taken directly to Křivoklát Castle. So the party turned their wagons west, and crossed the Vltava River. They journeyed for two days, via Dobříš and Beroun, along a route that can be traced quite easily today, through beech woods and apple orchards and old broken hedges rampant with snowberries, and at around midday on Monday, 6 May 1591, Kelley was handed over to the safekeeping of the castellan of Křivoklát, Jan Jindrich Prolehofer von Purkersdorf.

Křivoklát Castle, known also as Pürglitz, stands sternly on a precipitous wooded bluff which is made almost an island by the curving course of a small river, the Rakovnický, below it (see Plate 4). Kelley was held in the Huderka Tower, a squat, squarish building in the northern corner of the castle's outer courtyard. It has the look of a large oven, or perhaps even an alchemist's 'athanor', or furnace. The door of the tower is massive, studded with a lattice of iron; the lintel is carved, like others in the courtyard, in the form of drapery, as if a stone curtain had been rolled up above the door. A series of newsletters from Prague, written by an agent of the Fugger banking house, provide some glimpses of Kelley's circumstances. 'He was not even allowed a bread knife: everything was taken away' (8 May). 'The English alchemist, who was recently taken to Pürglitz as a prisoner, appeared to be in the depths of despair these latter days, and refused to partake of food, so it was feared he might die' (15 May). He was imprisoned 'with no air but that which comes through a hole, through which he can reach for his food bit by bit' (2 July). An English report confirms that Kelley was 'closely kept, without any manner of access to him'. An undated petition from his wife to the Imperial Chamber complains of Kelley's conditions: he has to 'eat pieces of rotten cow-meat'. She herself has 'not enough money to get her bowl mended'.

Joan Kelley was under great pressure. At the time of Kelley's apprehension she had been placed under house-arrest, probably at Nova Liben, near the gold-mining town of Jilové, south of

Prague; this estate was part of a huge grant of lands from Count Rožmberk. Then came news of the heavy fine meted out to Kelley: 15,000 thalers, some of it apparently a 'debt' to the royal Exchequer, to defray the costs of his arrest and imprisonment (though we know from Gregor Böul's later submission that his own expenses amounted to only 160 thalers). In the autumn of 1591 Kelley's estates at Nova Liben were impounded. Early the following year we hear of two officials installed there, 'in charge of the house and its lands, and of other lands at Jilové'. The death of Count Rožmberk in 1592 lost Kelley his last ally.

He remained at Křivoklát for more than two years. A jovial Moravian woodcarver I met there knew about him, and told me, while selling me a cherrywood butter dish I didn't really want, how Kelley tried to escape one night, and the rope snapped, and he fell, breaking his leg so badly that he was brought back to Prague to have it amputated. We stared down from the battlements at the patch of rock and scrub where this fall might have landed. I have heard and read this elsewhere, but there is no evidence at all that it happened at Křivoklát. It is probably a refraction of what happened later, and fatally, at another castle; alternatively, it is part of a Bohemian folklore arising from the fact that Kelley was disabled. There are various contemporary reports of Kelley's release, and none mentions anything about an escape or injury. In July 1593 Christopher Parkins reports from Prague that Kelley has been promised 'his enlargement presently', but still 'remains in hold' at Křivoklát. According to Dee's diary he was released on 4 October, but the best source puts the date a couple of days later – 'As concerning Sir Edward Kelley, his delivery has been the 16th day of October, new style' (i.e. 6 October in England, which was still on the pre-Gregorian system). The writer of this, Abraham Faulkon, had actually seen Kelley, back home at Nova Liben, in rude health: 'his Honour . . . received me very courteously, and [I] must sit at table both dinner and supper, what guests soever his Honour had . . . His Honour did fish a pond, and gave me good store of fish home with me.' Kelley's fondness for fishing is elsewhere mentioned by Dee.

The record of the following years is mainly one of crippling debt. Still liable for the 15,000 thaler fine, Kelley is to be found scrounging credit at high interest – 1,100 thalers from a Prague brewer; 3,380 thalers from a Silesian named Balthazar Wagen. He is forced to sell his houses in Prague to his sister-in-law Ludmila or Lydda, the Bohemian wife of Thomas Kelley. One recalls a comment of Dee's, that above all things Kelley 'feared want and beggary'. To begin with he was banned from the court. Other alchemists were now in favour with Rudolf, among them the flamboyant Italian Giovanni Scotta and the Pole Michael Sendivogius, author of the influential *Novum lumen chemicum* (1604). Both these men were known of in England: in Ben Jonson's *Volpone* (1606) the fictitious mountebank 'Scoto of Mantua' was suggested by Scotta (though he was actually from Parma), and the same author's masque *Mercury Vindicated from the Alchymists* (1615) was based on a work by Sendivogius. But it seems Kelley clawed his way back into favour, for in August 1595 he was in touch with Dee, with something of the old lofty manner – Dee describes his letters as written on the emperor's behalf, 'inviting me to his service again'. He also wrote to Sir Edward Dyer, recalling their alchemical studies: 'Yea, honourable Sir, you know very well what delight we took together.' Other than these, nothing is known of his activities in 1595. There seems no particular reason for Dee's mistaken belief that Kelley was 'slaine' in November that year. It was a rumour or false report which became an unfactual fact.

In late 1596, at Nova Liben, Kelley was arrested again. The precise cause or pretext is again unknown: it may be the prosaic one of debt. His lands were confiscated and sold. Joan and the children were permitted to keep a house and brewery in Jilové, but these too were forced from her. She received a token sum of 900 kopa for them. She and her daughter Elizabeth, now fifteen, fought long in the Bohemian courts for restoration of these appropriated estates. Among those who helped them was a young Prague lawyer, John Leo, who became Elizabeth's husband.

Kelley was transported to the far north of Bohemia, to Hněvín Castle overlooking the town of Most (or, in German, Brüx). The chief archival record of his imprisonment is, once again, an unpaid bill. Expenses were claimed by the castellan, Balthazar Stecher, for Kelley's firewood and food, a servant and a guard of four soldiers; the outstanding sum was 334 kopa. The period covered in this accounting is just less than a year, from 7 November 1596 to 1 November 1597. It is possible these dates record the day of Kelley's incarceration at Most and the day of his death. Hněvín Castle no longer exists: after the horrors of the Thirty Years War, the citizens of Most decided that the presence of a castle only increased the likelihood of military attack, and in 1651 Emperor Ferdinand II gave permission for it to be demolished. What stands on Castle Hill today is a loose replica, built in the early twentieth century and now serving as a restaurant and conference centre, but the tall, circular tower, which is built of glazed bricks from the kilns of Branany, is demonstrably set on a pre-existing base, and thus approximates to Kelley's last abode. The rooftops of Most, over which he looked, have vanished also. The old town was demolished in the 1960s, to open up the rich seams of lignite beneath it; the site is now a huge open-cast mine. With it went the graveyard of the old Church of the Assumption – possibly Kelley's burial-place – though the church itself was moved, on a specially constructed railway, and now stands forlorn among some old factory buildings on the edge of the coal-workings. If you were superstitious, you might say that the whole town has been cursed by the alchemist's ghost, but today the only Briton whose name you're likely to hear among the tarnished tower-blocks of the new town is that of the racing driver David Coulthard, who is the official patron of the city's race-circuit down near Highway 15.

Sequestered in his lugubrious quarters at Most, Kelley spent some of his time writing. His alchemical treatise *De lapide philosophorum*, published at Hamburg in 1676, was written here. It opens with an indignant letter, in Latin, addressed to Emperor Rudolf: 'Though I have now twice suffered chains and imprisonment in Bohemia, an indignity which has been offered to me nowhere else in the world, yet my mind remaining unbound, has all the time exercised itself in the study of that philosophy which is despised only by the wicked and foolish.' Despite the 'calamity' of his imprisonment, he says, he is 'utterly incapable of remaining idle'. He concludes:

> Nothing is more ancient, excellent or desirable than truth, and whoever neglects it must pass his whole life in the shade. Nevertheless it always was and always will be the way of mankind to release Barabas and crucify Christ: this I have (for my good, no doubt) experienced in my own case. It is my hope, however, that my life and character will so become known to posterity that I may be counted among those who have suffered much for the sake of truth.

This is audacious to the point of poignancy – Kelley the sufferer for truth; the sacrificed Christ-figure. Another, very different kind of writing is a manuscript copy, in German, of the Bohemian 'land constitution', now in the National Museum Library in Prague. A colophon on the last page states that the copy was compiled by 'Herrn Edwardo Kelleo von Imanii' together with another man named Ritter; this note, perhaps signalling the completion of the task, is dated 22 May 1597, at 'Brüxer Schloss' (i.e. Most Castle). Some of the text is indeed in Kelley's hand – the fluent, rather well-formed script that can be seen in his letters to Burghley in the British Library: surprisingly normal, except for a thick, disruptive backstroke in the *A* and *d*, which slices up through the rightward flow of the script. This copy of the land constitution makes an oddly secretarial conclusion to a lurid career. Perhaps he was preparing some legal battle for his estates; perhaps it was just something to do, in the terrible boredom of prison life. Even as he writes, an image of his captivity stares up at him – the paper has a watermark showing two castellated towers and a gateway, and below it the letter *H*, no doubt for Hněvín Castle.

There is only one account of Kelley's death which has any claim to authenticity. It comes from the manuscript by the Czech alchemist Šimon Tadeáš Budek, which I quoted earlier on the subject of Kelley's ears; it was written in about 1604. Budek described himself as Rudolf's 'prospector' for 'treasures, metals, precious stones, and all hidden secrets of nature'. It is possible he had met Kelley; that he describes him as having a wooden leg sounds like an exaggeration (one would surely have heard it mentioned) but may be a loose phrasing for the lameness mentioned by others. Budek's account, which has not been given in English before, runs as follows:

Edward Keleus was sitting there in the castle of Most, with his wooden leg, and his missing ears, and his long hair; and he was kept apart from his wife and daughter. Then at Christmas-time in 1597 he climbed down from his prison; his brother was waiting with a cart down below. But he fell into the moat, and broke his other leg in three places. He was taken back to the castle for his injuries to be tended. He was going to be transported down to the emperor [i.e. to Prague]. He asked that his wife and daughter be permitted to visit him, and this was allowed. He spoke English to his wife, and German and Latin to his daughter. He asked to be given some water, and then he drank the water, and died.

This is, at the least, a contemporary Bohemian view of what happened. Certain later accounts, which cannot be based directly on Budek, confirm the scenario. John Weever, though wrongly placing the scene in Prague, says: 'he fell down from the battlements, broke his legs and bruised his body, of which hurts a while after he departed this world.' And Dr Dee's son Arthur, who as a boy had known Kelley and had on occasions 'scryed' alongside him, said much the same many years later, adding the flourish that Kelley had given 'opium in drink to the keepers'. But I prefer Budek's version. At least one of its details can be supported – the presence of Kelley's wife and stepdaughter in Most is confirmed by a letter of Elizabeth's written there in 1597. The rest is circumstantial, but one seems at the last to see a real man, with no more tricks up his sleeve, drinking a cup of water.

5

Mugshots and Miniatures

English Portraiture in the Sixteenth Century
[1995]

'If we will have anything well painted, carved or embroidered,' grumbled Sir Thomas Elyot in 1531, 'we abandon our own countrymen and resort unto strangers.' His complaint is borne out by *Dynasties*, the Tate Gallery's fascinating exhibition of painting in Tudor and Jacobean England. The home-grown talent is here – Nicholas Hilliard, George Gower, Inigo Jones, William Larkin, Sir Nathaniel Bacon and others – but the exhibition is dominated, statistically at least, by foreign artists, mainly Dutch and Flemish. Some of these 'strangers' were visitors, like Holbein and Van Dyck, but many settled here and became naturalized Englishmen, or 'denizens'. They brought an invigorating new range of techniques that transformed English art.

Most of the paintings and drawings on show here are portraits, but the exhibition is not the dour gallery of Tudor mugshots that this might suggest. They come in a variety of styles, and in all shapes and sizes, from the fastidious miniatures of Hilliard and Isaac Oliver, painted on two-inch snippets of vellum glued on to bits of playing-card, to the tall, lush, overbearing canvases of Stuart court artists.

There is also a variety of ideas as to what a portrait is, and what it should say about its subject. We see here, as Karen Hearn says in her catalogue, 'an ebb and flow in the desire for naturalistic representation'. Among the earliest works are exquisite Holbein sketches from the 1530s, where every hair on a young woman's eyebrows seems alive, but for much of the Tudor period

the capturing of physical and personal detail seems almost inci-
dental. The portrait is seen more as a mode of display, a finely
tuned statement of the sitter's status and allegiance, a creating of
his or her 'image' in the public relations sense of the word we use
today. These are pictures to be read as much as viewed, their
messages signalled in costume details, Latin mottos and heraldic
devices, and in a range of symbolic props in which everything
from a gemstone to a goldfinch has an emblematic meaning.

The chief 'dynasties' portrayed here are the Tudors and Stu-
arts, but there is a powerful presence of those other great English
families – aristocrats, *arrivistes*, merchants, politicians – whose
flair, energy and greed were as decisive in the history of the
period as the policies of the monarchs themselves.

One of the most arresting pictures is the Cobham family portrait (see Plate 5). Painted in 1567 by an unnamed artist in the
service of the Countess of Warwick, it shows William Brooke,
tenth Baron Cobham, at the age of about forty, together with
his wife and sister, his six young children and their assorted pets.
It is mealtime, specifically dessert: a scene of domestic together-
ness, but painted with that deliberate waxy stiffness, that sense
of ceremonial hush, which takes one away from the everyday
and into the realm of the painting's messages and meanings. The
message is precisely dynastic. The Latin inscription compares
Lord Cobham to Old Testament patriarchs like Jacob and Job.
'God grant that the line of Cobham beget many offspring such
as Joseph.' The prayer is already answered by the clutch of doll-
like children below; indeed the whole composition has the
diagrammatic look of a family tree.

On the table there are fruit: apples, pears, grapes, walnuts – a
tribute to the prolific orchards of Cobham Hall, and a restate-
ment of the picture's message of fruitfulness and dynastic harvest.
Another symbolic prop is the diamond pendant Lady Cobham
wears, in the shape of an ocean-going ship. This suggests another

kind of harvest: the riches of maritime trade filling the Cobham coffers. The parrot and the monkey – imported New World pets – are part of the same idea. The ship also signifies happiness, alluding to a Roman emblem showing a ship named *Felicitas*.

The Cobham portrait seems almost a kind of talisman, an invoking of familial health, wealth and stability in an age of slippery fortunes. In fact, there are historical ironies to the picture. The title was inherited by Henry, seen here as a two-year-old with a puppy on his lap. Implicated in a conspiracy against King James in 1603, he was attainted for treason and stripped of his peerage, thus bringing to an abrupt end the dynastic aspirations expressed in this painting. We catch the Cobhams in a moment of eminence which proves somewhat temporary. Portraits of the Catholic Howards have a similar resonance, particularly the canvas of the Earl of Surrey, the nobleman-poet, bursting with confidence and Italianate elegance. It was painted in 1546, when he was twenty-nine; a year later he was beheaded on a trumped-up charge of treason.

*

The Brookes and the Howards were powerful but expendable satellites around the central dynasty of the monarchy. Royal portraits form the heart of the exhibition. The earliest (*c.* 1500) is the poignant little portrait of Prince Arthur, Henry VIII's elder brother, who died at the age of fifteen. This was rediscovered in 1993, at Castle Forbes in Ireland, and is seen here for the first time. How it came to be owned by the earls of Granard is unclear. It exactly fits the description and measurements of a portrait listed in the collection of Charles I, showing Arthur 'in a black capp and goulden habbitt houlding in his right hand a white gillifloore'. The gillyflower, a kind of carnation, was associated with betrothals, and the painting may have been done for Catherine of Aragon, whom Arthur married in 1501.

An entire room is devoted to images of Queen Elizabeth. She

was the most cultish of all the Tudors, and fully exploited the
propagandist element of portraiture. Most of the surviving pictures of her are known by some symbolic device or allusion.
Here we have the 'Armada Portrait', and the rather ghostly
'Sieve Portrait'. The most striking is the 'Phoenix Portrait'
(*c.* 1576), attributed to Hilliard, though it is not the symbolic
paraphernalia that catches the eye – the phoenix jewel and the
Tudor rose – but the brilliant detail of Hilliard's workmanship.
The gold embroidery of the dress is represented by paint, prin-
cipally lead-tin yellow, rather than by the actual gold leaf used a
generation earlier (for example, in the 1544 portrait of Mary
Tudor). This kind of technical advance contributed to the growing autonomy of the artist, enabling him to represent precious
materials without having to afford them.

The portraits of Elizabeth do not invite personal or biographical interpretations, but the study of King James, by the
Dutchman Adrian Vanson, certainly does. Painted in 1595, it
shows a very human James at the age of twenty-nine (though
some of its unusual intimacy is a result of a later cutting-down
of the picture). The face is sallow, the gaze weary, the mouth
thin and ironic. One thinks of the personal traumas of his childhood: the murders, the night flights, the execution of his
mother. He seems slightly slumped. His tall sugarloaf hat is
tipped back, giving him the air of a melancholy young *boule-
vardier* resting between bouts of absinthe.

Right beside this is a portrait of the wily Sir Robert Cecil,
painted by Johan De Critz in about 1602, on the eve of James's
succession to the English throne, which Cecil as secretary of
state had done so much to engineer. Here is a man in control of
his own destiny – far more so, one feels, than the droopy young
king next door. On his table are folded dispatches, a seal-bag, a
bell to summon his amanuenses and clerks. This is the new man,
the bureaucrat, the political string-puller. The motto on the

portrait, '*Sero sed serio*' ('Late but in earnest'), is usually associated with tardy repentance, but here suggests the politic skills of patience and decisiveness; it shows him of the same mind and method as his father, Lord Burghley, whose motto '*Prudens qui patiens*' associates prudence with patience.

In the portraits of Cobham and Cecil, and in the lesser-known merchants and gentry staring huffily out, one gets a sombre, mafioso sense of Elizabethan power-mongering. But there is plenty of the more flamboyant side, the peacockery and swagger, as in Hilliard's famous miniature of George Clifford, third Earl of Cumberland, in an extravagant costume of azure and gold embroidered with astrological and alchemical devices. He is dressed up for the Accession Day Tilt, a mock-chivalric festival in which aspiring courtiers jousted for the queen's favours.

Cumberland – an inveterate gambler and a courageous sea-captain – epitomizes the panache of the era. Even more eye-catching is Richard Sackville, third Earl of Dorset, painted by William Larkin in 'cloth of silver embroidered all over in slips of satin, black and gold'. He is the perfect dandy, from his doily-like ruff down to his pom-pommed pantofles. This probably shows him at the wedding of Princess Elizabeth and the Elector Palatine, on 14 February 1613, at which it was said he 'dazzled the eyes of all who saw'.

Among all the monarchs and magnates are a few pictures of the artists themselves. Easily missed is the wry self-portrait by George Gower (1579). It is the only large-size self-portrait in existence by a sixteenth-century British artist. He holds a palette and a paintbrush. An inscription celebrates his work 'by pencil's trade' and the rewards it has brought him: 'What parents bore by just renown, my skill maintains.' And so a new professional group edges up the increasingly crowded and competitive social ladder. Essentially of artisan class – servers of apprenticeship, members of guilds, guarders of trade secrets – they have acquired an indispensable role as the image-makers of Tudor high society.

6

Canterbury Tale

Christopher Marlowe's Boyhood
[1988]

The late William Urry knew more than anyone about Christopher Marlowe's early life in Canterbury. His 'forthcoming book' on the subject was mentioned by one of Marlowe's biographers as long ago as 1965. Here at last it is, seven years after his death, edited from drafts by his former colleague Andrew Butcher.* The text runs to less than a hundred pages, but there are ample appendices and source notes, and anyway these hundred pages of dense documentary detail are worth a thousand of theorizing.

Our historical knowledge of Elizabethan writers like Marlowe ultimately rests on this kind of deep archival work. Toiling through mouldy reams of municipal Latin, poring over act books and close-rolls, pleas and recognizances, baptisms and burials, borough-mote surveys and consistorial court proceedings, scholars like Urry provide a constant supply of rich contextual trivia, and just occasionally, down some documentary back-way, they stumble upon the great and famous, and retrieve some precious nugget of raw information about them. The classic instance in Marlowe's case was the unearthing by Leslie Hotson, in 1925, of the coroner's inquest on Marlowe's violent death. While Urry has made no comparable discovery – perhaps no one will – he has lit up many small corners of Marlowe's life, particularly of his childhood.

* William Urry, *Christopher Marlowe and Canterbury* (Faber, 1988).

Christopher Marlowe – or Marley, in the more common contemporary spelling, and the one he used in his only extant signature – was born in St George's parish in Canterbury in February 1564. He was the son of John Marlowe, shoemaker, and Katherine *née* Arthur, a Dover woman. They had nine children, though only five survived childhood. Christopher was the eldest son and, after the death of his sister Mary in 1568, the eldest child in the family. His father was 'rowdy, quarrelsome, awkward, improvident, busy, self-assertive and too clever by half', in Urry's estimate. He appears often in local records, sometimes in positions of minor responsibility – warden of the Shoemakers' Company, sidesman at the parish church, constable at Westgate – but more often when being sued for debt, nonpayment of rent or breach of the peace. He was fined for giving his apprentice Lactantius Preston a bloody nose in 1576, and was himself assaulted by another apprentice a few years later. It is hard to avoid seeing Marlowe's touchy aggressive temper – intellectual and physical – prefigured in his father. His sister Anne seems to have been a handful as well. Like him she was known as a 'swearer' and 'blasphemer of the name of God', and in 1626, well into her fifties, she set about an unfortunate neighbour, one Prowde, with a staff and a dagger.

Marlowe's origins were provincial and artisan: an earlier generation in Canterbury were tanners; his sisters married a tailor, a shoemaker and a glover. This tough, industrious class nurtured much of the budding literary talent of the time, and the Elizabethan leather industry provided a livelihood not only for Marlowe's family, but also for that of Robert Greene and William Shakespeare, sons respectively of a Norwich saddler and a Stratford glover. Even here in Canterbury there were other young writers growing up: John Lyly, son of Peter Lyly, clerk to the consistorial court; and Stephen Gosson, a joiner's son. We have here a miniature blueprint for late Elizabethan theatrical

tastes: Marlowe the tragedian, whose high-octane poetry packed
them in at the public theatres; Lyly the author of dapper courtly
comedies for the boy-actors of St Paul's; and Gosson the contro-
versialist, whose *Schoole of Abuse* (1579) was a polemic against the
theatre, and provided a prototype for the Puritan attitudes that
were to dog Marlowe's brief career.

In terms of Marlowe biography, Dr Urry's canvas is less par-
tial than might appear. Marlowe was getting on for seventeen
when he left Canterbury for Cambridge University in late 1580.
He died at the age of twenty-nine, so this study covers a good
half of his life – often the more obscure half in a distant historical figure. Urry recovers the young Marlowe's immediate
human and social surroundings: extended family, neighbours,
apprentices, schoolfellows. He reels off the names of the Mar-
lowes' neighbours as if he were doffing his cap to them in the
street: Alderman Rose the woollen-draper; Harmon Verson the
immigrant glazier; Laurence Applegate the tailor, who spoke
'bawdy words' about Mistress Hurt; Goodman Shaw the basket-
maker, into whose house John Marlowe stormed one evening in
1579 and said, 'Michael Shaw thou art a thief, and so I will prove
thee to be'; and Gregory Roose the capper, husband to the local
midwife, Goodwife Roose, who probably brought Christopher
Marlowe into the world.

*

Though compact – population about 3,500 – Elizabethan Canterbury was a cosmopolitan city. Its ecclesiastical eminence
drew visitors from all over Europe, and its position on the
through-road from Dover to London brought a broader cross-
section of travellers, soldiers, sailors and sturdy vagabonds. Like
other cities, it hosted Protestant war-refugees from France and
the Low Countries. A wave of French Huguenots arrived after
the St Bartholomew's Day Massacre in 1572, an event Marlowe

later worked over in his lurid political drama *The Massacre at Paris*.

Religion, not surprisingly, loomed large in Canterbury. The only book in the family home – at least by the time of John Marlowe's death in 1605 – was the Bible. In St George's parish, lying between the cathedral and the city's eastern gate, Marlowe grew up literally in the shadow of the Church. He witnessed its finest pomps and perhaps also its grisly punishments. He would become one of its most reckless critics, scoffing at the 'bugbeares and hobgoblins' of superstition, and dangerously arguing that religion was just a political tool 'to keep men in awe'. Here, too, Urry gives a local, human face to religious controversy. At King's School, which Marlowe entered on a £4-a-year scholarship in 1578, his fellow pupils included Samuel Kennett, who became a Catholic exile and missionary, and died a Benedictine monk in 1612, and Henry Jacob, who later founded one of the first Congregationalist Churches in England. Near by lived a young Puritan called Robert Cushman, a grocer's assistant. Many years later he returned from exile in Holland and was the prime mover in the hiring of the ship *Mayflower*.

Marlowe's first headmaster at King's was a Cambridge man, John Gresshop, and an interesting document published here is the catalogue of Gresshop's library, drawn up on his death in 1580. It contained over 350 volumes – nothing like the Mortlake library of Dr John Dee (4,000 volumes) or the thousand-plus books collected by Lords Burghley and Lumley, but it shows the kind of reading available to a bright young scholar. There are the plays of Plautus and Terence, the poems of Juvenal and Ovid, a strong Italian presence including Boccaccio, Petrarch, Valla and Ficino. There is More's *Utopia*, Munster's *Cosmographia* and the works of Chaucer.

One senses the emancipation, the new mental world opening up for the cobbler's son – but with it come dangers. Among the

theological tracts on Gresshop's shelves was a work by John
Proctour, *The Fall of the Late Arrian*, a broadside against Arian or
Unitarian views which questioned the divinity of Christ. This
was already an old book, published in 1549, but it contained large
chunks of the heresy it was written to confute. Scroll forward to
11 May 1593, and the arrest of the playwright Thomas Kyd in
London. Among his papers was found a four-page digest of
Arian views, copied verbatim from Proctour's book. Questioned
about these 'vile hereticall conceipts', as the interrogators called
them, Kyd said the manuscript belonged to Marlowe: it had got
'shuffled' with his papers when the two writers were sharing
a chamber in 1591. A week later Marlowe was himself summoned before the Privy Council for questioning. That 'hereticall'
manuscript was doubtless on the agenda, along with other supposed evidence of his blasphemy and atheism. Words he once
might have read with impunity in his headmaster's library had
acquired a new dangerousness in the sedition-hunting atmosphere of 1593. Whether the manuscript really was his – and
whether all this has a connection with his violent death in a
Deptford lodging-house on 30 May – is another matter.

*

After his departure for Cambridge, just two further visits to
Canterbury remain on record. On a Sunday morning in November 1585 he was at the house of Katherine Benchkin on Stour
Street, together with his father, his brother-in-law John Moore
and his uncle Thomas Arthur. There, in the parlour, Mistress
Benchkin asked him to read out her new will, which he did
'plainely and distinktly', and shortly afterwards signed it as a
witness. The will was discovered by another Canterbury bur-
rower, Frank Tyler, in 1939. It gives us the only known example
of Marlowe's signature; the orthography has similarities with
the 'Collier Leaf' – a manuscript fragment of *The Massacre at*

Paris, now in the Folger Library – but probably not enough to prove that the 'leaf' is in his hand.

Marlowe's last recorded spell in Canterbury was in September 1592. Typically, it was a fight that makes it memorable. On Friday, 15 September, close to the corner of Mercery Lane, Marlowe attacked William Corkine, tailor, with a staff and a dagger. John Marlowe, ironically, was acting as local constable at that time: possibly he had to arrest his son, certainly he paid the twelve-pence surety required to keep Christopher out of jail. Corkine sued for assault, but by the time it came to court they had patched up their differences, and the case was dismissed. Twenty years later, a William Corkine published a lute accompaniment to Marlowe's famous lyric 'Come Live With Me'. This was probably the Canterbury tailor's son.

The scuffle with Corkine brings to a close a troubled year, which had begun with Marlowe's arrest in the Netherlands for 'coining', or counterfeiting money – a very serious charge, which could lead to the gallows. That he escaped punishment may suggest that this Dutch episode (which was only discovered in 1974) is another piece in the jigsaw of Marlowe's secret political activities. Deported back to England under escort in late January 1592, Marlowe was certainly free by May, when he was bound over to keep the peace after abusing a pair of constables in Shoreditch.

Marlowe had only one brother, Thomas. He was four when Marlowe left for Cambridge, sixteen at the time of the Corkine fracas. To him Marlowe must have been half a stranger, someone who returned home from time to time, trailing notoriety from London. Thomas may have died young too – there is no mention of him in his mother's will of 1605 – but he may just be the Thomas Marloe who travelled to America in the ship *Jonathan*, and who was living in 1624 at a settlement near Jamestown, Virginia, breathing the freer air of America that would so much have suited brother Kit.

Marlowe was an extraordinary man, yet his life, like everyone else's, constantly intersected with ordinariness. This book tells us about him because it tells us what it was like for him to grow up in that time, in that street, in that income bracket. In his perceptive introduction Andrew Butcher suggests that this kind of close-focus contextual study is now really the frontline in Elizabethan literary history. It recovers the contingencies – the 'formative tensions', as he puts it – of a writer's life. It finds him not in quill-wielding solitude, but precisely at his points of contact, his mingling with certain very particular sectors and groupings of Elizabethan life, shaping them and being shaped by them. Some may find Dr Urry's book too dense with detail. But the details are a kind of intimacy, and this portrait of the budding poet often seems more human, more actual, than the constructs of more conventional biography.

7

'An Explorer'

Ben Jonson and the Uses of Comedy
[1991]

Ben Jonson is remembered as a master of English comedy, but you would hardly think so from his portraits. There are two contemporary images – an oil painting by Abraham van Blyenberch, done before 1620 and showing him in his mid forties; and an engraving by Robert Vaughan from a few years later. The engraving is particularly dour (see Plate 6): the face is jowly, bearded, heavily lived in. In both portraits it is the eyes that speak out: harassed and wary in the Blyenberch, shadowed and morose in the Vaughan. Comedy, they seem to say, is no laughing matter. It was one of Jonson's sayings that 'he would not flatter, though he saw death,' and his look seems to challenge the artists not to flatter him either. You can see the glisten on his skin from too much sweet Canary wine ('his beloved liquor', according to Aubrey), and a suggestion of the warts and blemishes which more malicious caricaturists like Thomas Dekker dwell on: 'a face full of pockey-holes and pimples . . . a most ungodly face, like a rotten russet apple when 'tis bruised'. And you can guess at what was by then his vast bulk. In his youth he was tall and rangy, a 'hollow-cheekt scrag', but by middle age he was pushing twenty stone. In his poem 'My Picture Left in Scotland' (1619) he mocks his unwieldy frame –

> So much waist as she cannot embrace
> My mountaine belly and my rockye face

– yet seems also to celebrate its craggy solidity. This sense of stature comes through in the portraits. Here, in every sense, is a big man.

Jonson's literary career was a triumph of volume and stamina. It spanned three reigns and four decades, from the first flexing of comic power in *The Isle of Dogs* (1597) to the last melancholy fragments of *The Sad Shepherd* (*c.* 1636). During that time he wrote eighteen plays, thirty-seven masques and court entertainments, two volumes of poetry and a volume of epigrams. This list does not include the lost plays from his days as one of Henslowe's hacks at the Rose, nor the mass of work unpublished at his death: over a hundred miscellaneous verses, a translation of Horace's *Ars Poetica*, an English grammar, and the compendium of jottings, musings and mini-essays later collected under the title of *Timber* (or 'Discoveries Made Upon Men and Matter').

In an age when most writers burned out young, Jonson kept on going. Right at the end, embattled by debt and alcoholism, half paralysed by a stroke, he was still at work. Among his last pieces was probably the *English Grammar*, published posthumously in 1640. It shows him niggling away at the nuts and bolts of the language, purifying that 'sterling English diction' which Coleridge praised in him, involving himself in such orthographic minutiae as the superiority of the 'serviceable *k*' over 'this halting *Q*, with her waiting-woman *u* after her'. Also among his papers were fragments of two plays: the elegiac *Sad Shepherd* and a history play called *Mortimer His Fall*. The printed text of the latter concludes curtly, 'He dy'd, and left it unfinished,' furnishing an apocryphal image of the aged maestro keeling over with the ink still wet on his quill. There is a sense of great verbal labour in Jonson, which is always contrasted with Shakespeare's agility and flow. He comments somewhat sourly on this in *Timber*: when Shakespeare is praised for having 'never blotted out line', he says, 'my answer hath been: would he had blotted a thousand'. Something of his own compositional process can be discerned in this advice to the aspiring poet:

> If his wit will not arrive suddenly at the dignity of the ancients, let him not yet fall out with it . . . Come to it again, upon better cogitation; try another time with labour. If then it succeed not, cast not away the quills yet, nor scratch the wainscot, beat not the poor desk; but bring all to the forge and file again, turn it anew . . . It is said of the incomparable Virgil that he brought forth his verses like a bear, and after formed them with licking.

John Aubrey claimed to have seen his writing chair, and reported that it 'was of strawe, such as olde women used'.

He died in August 1637, aged sixty-five, at the gatehouse in Westminster where he lived his last years with a pet fox and a drunken housekeeper. His funeral was attended by 'the greatest part of the nobilitie and gentry', and a volume of memorial odes, *Jonsonus Virbius*, was published the following year. In it his disciples, the 'Tribe of Ben', praise him as the 'great Instructor', the 'voice most echoed by consenting men'. A generation later, in his essay 'Of Dramatick Poesy', John Dryden singled him out as the 'greatest man of the last age'.

These are literary judgements. Posterity has preferred a briefer, more elusive epitaph. As his grave at Westminster Abbey was being covered, a passer-by, Sir Jack Young, noticed that the headstone was still blank. He 'gave the fellow eighteen pence' to cut an inscription. It read simply: 'O Rare Benn Jonson'.

★

Like the portraitist, Jonson's biographer has to achieve a kind of double perspective, conveying Jonson's stature as a public literary figure, yet also revealing something of the private flaws and tensions that lay behind it. It is odd how few have risen to this challenge. C. H. Herford's memoir in the eleven-volume Oxford *Ben Jonson*, published in 1925, has remained the best general account even after modern scholarship has found omissions and errors in it. Now at last we have a biography that pulls out all the right stops.* David Riggs provides a challenging and compassionate reading of the man. He gets across the barriers which have defeated others – not just the rampant egotism, but a certain sense of harshness. You feel this at the heart of the comedies: derision and punishment go with the laughter. Dryden summed it up succinctly when he said of Jonson: 'I admire him, but I love Shakespeare.' This is one way of putting it – however much you delight in his writing, you cannot quite love Ben Jonson. In fact, sometimes you're not even sure you like him.

There were plenty who didn't at the time. There is a rich store of contemporary material on him, and much of it is disparaging. The earliest and sharpest is the caricature of Jonson as 'Horace' in Thomas Dekker's comedy *Satiromastix*. This played in 1601, when Jonson was in his late twenties. Subtitled 'The Untrussing of the Humorous Poet', it gives a scurrilous portrait of Jonson in the first swagger of literary success. Dekker dwells on his ugliness – a face 'like the cover of a warming pan', a voice that 'sounds so i'th nose' – and portrays him as a seedy penny-a-liner whose only aim is to 'skrue and wriggle himself into great men's familiarity'. Dekker's purpose is to give this 'thornie-tooth'd satyricall rascal' a dose of his own medicine, but often he ends up seconding the vigour and charisma of his target, as when he bids Horace not to 'dippe your manners in too much sawce, nor at table to fling epigrams, emblemes or play-speeches about you lyke hayle-stones'.

This was one of the exchanges in the so-called 'War of the Theatres', when playhouse rivalries spilled over into a spat of

---

* David Riggs, *Ben Jonson: A Life* (Harvard University Press, 1989).

personal abuse between the authors. Shakespeare was briefly involved in this, and, according to one well-informed commentator, he gave that 'pestilent fellow' Jonson a 'purge which made him bewray his credit'. Historians have wondered what form this literary laxative took. Some suggest that Jonson is guyed as big morose Ajax in *Troilus and Cressida* ('churlish as the bear, slow as the elephant, a man in whom nature hath so crowded humours that his valour is crushed into folly'). Others say Jonson is a model for Jaques, the embittered satirist of Arden ('They that are most galled with my folly, / They most must laugh'). Riggs offers, rather unconvincingly, Malvolio in *Twelfth Night*.

The richest contemporary account of Jonson is the record of his conversations with the Scottish poet William Drummond. In the summer of 1618 Jonson walked from London to Scotland (Francis Bacon remarking drily that 'he loved not to see poesy go on other feet than poetical *dactyllus* and *spondaeus*'). He tells us nothing of the journey except that he bought a new pair of shoes in Darlington. Having been fêted in Edinburgh, he passed a few pleasant weeks in the late autumn as Drummond's guest at Hawthornden, a romantic but chilly castle perched above the North Esk River. There he bent his host's ear with anecdotes, aphorisms, jokes and libels. Drummond duly transcribed, preserving the authentic timbre of Jonson's table-talk, well seasoned and pickled. Drink, Drummond observed, 'is one of the elements in which he liveth'. The *Conversations* (first published in 1842) provide a crabby review of the current literary scene – Donne 'deserved hanging' for his metrical liberties, Shakespeare 'wanted art', John Day and Dekker were 'rogues', Samuel Daniel was 'a good honest man, but no poet' – as well as some important autobiographical material.

In Drummond, as in everyone else, there is that uncertain reaction. He is awestruck yet curiously disappointed. Jonson's flamboyance is there – 'passionately kynde and angry, careless either to gaine or keep' – but Drummond finds him a 'bragger' and a 'scorner'. He is 'oppressed with fantasie'. He would rather 'lose a friend than a jest'.

★

The achievement of Jonson's greatest comedies – *Volpone* (1606), *The Alchemist* (1610), *Bartholomew Fair* (1613) and *The Devil is an Ass* (1616) – is their openness to social realities. He harnessed the texture and parlance of Elizabethan city life –

> Deedes and language such as men doe use,
> And persons such as Comoedie would chuse,
> When she would shew an image of the times.

A certain pungency was a dramatic requisite every bit as import-ant to him as the neo-Classical notions of structural 'unity' he insisted on. As he put it in the Induction to *Bartholomew Fair*, you cannot write about a day at the fair 'without a language that savours of Smithfield, the booth and the pig-broath'. Jonson's achievement is about what comic drama can include. One of the lessons of his life, Riggs says, 'is that everything is of use'.

His early life seems in some ways the perfect apprenticeship for this. By the time he turned to playwriting in the mid 1590s, Jonson had seen the seamier side of Elizabethan life. He had grown up on Hartshorn Lane, a street-cum-sewer running between the Strand and the Thames. He had worked as a brick-layer, apprenticed to his stepfather, Robert Brett. He had fought with the English troops in the Low Countries, boasting to Drummond he had killed an enemy 'in the face of both camps'. He had married, and held a newborn daughter in his arms, and buried her six months later:

> This grave partakes the fleshly birth,
> Which cover lightly, gentle earth.

His literary apprenticeship took the form of acting in the provinces. Dekker liked to remind him of his lowly beginnings, when 'thou amblest in leather pilch by a play-wagon in the highway, and tookst mad Jeronimoes part to get service amongst the mimickes.' (This has been taken as evidence that he played Hieronimo in Kyd's *Spanish Tragedy* – a plum part – but may just mean that his eccentric behaviour persuaded the actors to take him on.) He first appears in the accounts of Philip Henslowe, owner of the Rose Theatre in Southwark, in July 1597 – a loan of £4 in 'redey mony' to 'Bengemen Iohnson, player'.

I wish he were here to pass comment on later developments at the Rose. The entombing of the theatre's remains under a 1980s office-block seems a perfect Jonsonian device. His view of Jacobean social values was a raw one. He sees a scrabbling, acquisitive society, a nexus of victims and predators. Its predominant 'humours' are greed and delusion, personified onstage by a comic cast of scavengers and speculators, legacy-hunters and gold-diggers, Meercrafts and Eithersides, Sir Moth Interests and Sir Politic Would-bes. The 'loadsamoney' ethic of the Thatcher years would hold no surprises for him.

Riggs reminds us of the courage that went into his theatrical 'image of the times'. Jonson's career has a pattern of questioning and defining the poet's public role, testing the scope of comment. This was edge-work with very real dangers attached to it. His first known work was *The Isle of Dogs*, performed by the Pembroke's Men in July 1597. The play, co-written with the pamphleteer Thomas Nashe, is lost. Its nascent comic skills cannot be judged, but its political bite is clear enough. The play was quickly suppressed by the Privy Council as 'lewd, seditious and sclandrous'. The playhouses in the London area were closed down, and Jonson and two of the actors spent ten weeks in jail in the Marshalsea. He later boasted of his obstinate silence: his 'judges' – who included rackmaster Richard Topcliffe – 'could get nothing of him to all their demands but Aye and No'. He was also plagued by prison informers, 'two damn'd villains' who tried to wheedle seditious sentiments out of him. One of these was Robert Poley, the government agent who had been present at the fatal stabbing of Christopher Marlowe in Deptford four years earlier.

This was the first of many skirmishes with the authorities. In 1603 his tragedy *Sejanus* was denounced to the Council for 'popery and treason', and in 1605 he was in prison again, for the comedy *Eastward Ho!*, co-written with George Chapman and John Marston. The trouble this time was a joke – 'I ken the man weel: he's one of my thirty pound knights' – which hit too obviously at King James's indiscriminate sale of honours, as well as mocking his Scottish accent. Punishment for this sort of thing was no joke, however. When the authors were arrested, 'the report was that they should then have their ears cut, and noses.'

Confrontation was Jonson's mode as a man and a writer. He was a fighter. His literary quarrels often flared into physical violence: he 'beat' his colleague Marston and 'took his pistol from him', and in 1598 he killed the actor Gabriel Spenser in a sword fight on Hoxton Fields. This resulted in another spell in prison, and nearly the gallows for manslaughter. While in prison he converted to Catholicism: another confrontation. For twelve years he and his wife Anne suffered the fines and petty recriminations of recusancy. Returning to the Anglican fold, 'at his first communion, in token of true reconciliation, he drank out all the full cup of wine' – so he told Drummond, anyway, and the gesture seems so typically Jonsonian that one hardly cares if it is true or not.

Sometimes the confrontation seems like truculence, literary machismo: a seventeenth-century Hemingway or Mailer. Sometimes he mocks it in himself. But it is his particular gift. Riggs champions this 'powerfully subversive streak' in him. There is courage and isolation in Jonson's story, the 'plain-speaker' in an age of political concealment. He 'comes near to us not as a father or a judge, but as a chronic transgressor who lived to tell the tale'. The price he paid for this can be seen in his turbulent life, and in the eyes of his portraits. His own motto, hand-written in his books, was from Seneca: *Tanquam explorator*. That was how he valued himself, 'as an explorer', though even here there is an overtone of confrontation, for Seneca was using *explorator* in its particular military sense of a scout or spy, so the metaphor is of the writer – and particularly the writer of comedy – venturing dangerously behind enemy lines.

8

Cardenio's Ghost

The Remnants of a Lost Shakespeare Play
[2010]

On 13 December 1727, a new play by Lewis Theobald called *Double Falsehood* was premiered at the Theatre Royal in Drury Lane. It was a romantic tragicomedy in a Spanish setting; the story was from an episode in *Don Quixote*. Theobald's statement that it met with 'universal applause' is untrue, but it certainly created a buzz. The play ran for ten consecutive performances – no mean feat in the quick-change repertoire of those days – and the first edition, published in January 1728, sold out in a few weeks. This stir of interest had little to do with Theobald's reputation as a playwright, which was rather middling: his most recent employment was as a librettist of light-operatic pantomimes. Nor was it due to the drawing power of the celebrated Barton Booth, who had been billed to play the lead role of Julio but was too ill from jaundice to appear. What drew the crowds to *Double Falsehood* was the involvement (in a manner of speaking) of another, even bigger theatrical star, for it was Theobald's remarkable claim, teasingly publicized over the previous months, that his play was based on a hitherto unknown work by Shakespeare. 'It is my good fortune to retrieve this remnant of his pen from obscurity,' he says with studied modesty. He calls it 'this orphan play' and 'this dear relick'. On the title page *Double Falsehood* is described as 'A Play . . . written Originally by W. Shakespeare; and now Revised and Adapted to the Stage by Mr Theobald'.

The forty-year-old Theobald was an attorney by training,

and a literary jack-of-all-trades by profession, but his standing as a Shakespeare expert was high. The previous year he had published an impressive book, *Shakespeare Restored*, challenging what he saw as the errors and complacencies of Alexander Pope's 1725 edition of Shakespeare, and offering many examples of his own editorial skills, particularly in the elucidation of difficult or corrupt passages. So his exalted claims for the provenance of *Double Falsehood* seemed to carry some weight. But the play's success was brief: a spate of curiosity which swiftly ran into doubts and insinuations. Writing a couple of weeks after the opening night, Theobald notes some of the objections that had been raised. Some considered it 'incredible' that a Shakespeare manuscript could have been 'stifled and lost to the world for above a century'. Some thought they discerned the 'colouring' and 'diction' of Shakespeare's younger contemporary John Fletcher, rather than Shakespeare himself, in the play. Others objected that 'the tale of this play being built upon a novel in Don Quixote, chronology is against us, and Shakespeare could not be the author.' This last, at least, Theobald was able to refute – *Don Quixote* was published in 1605, and the first English translation in 1612, and as Shakespeare lived until 1616, this left 'a sufficient interval of time for all that we want granted'.

These particular quibbles are instances of a broader, more intuitive disappointment. Today the first impression of anyone reading (or, very rarely, seeing) *Double Falsehood* is that little of it actually sounds much like Shakespeare. An eighteenth-century audience would perhaps have had lesser expectations in this respect – contemporary adaptations of Shakespeare were far more common on the stage than the originals; they were often pretty free, with interpolated heroic couplets and musical interludes, and they quite deliberately diluted some of the richness and difficulty of the original language. Nonetheless, the general blandness of *Double Falsehood*, and its many narrative defects, did not encourage those who knew their Shakespeare to believe in it as the genuine article.

And then there was the spat with Pope, initiated by *Shakespeare Restored*. The obvious agenda of that book was Theobald's desire to produce his own edition of the plays – an ambition he would realize in seven volumes in 1734 – but its more immediate result was the sharp displeasure of Pope, who was soon venting his pique against 'piddling Tibbald' in *The Dunciad*, published in May 1728, and elsewhere. In this context of rivalry the appearance of *Double Falsehood* seemed suspiciously convenient. What better way for Theobald to demonstrate his editorial expertise than to produce out of his hat this supposed lost play by the master? And, given his close knowledge of Shakespeare, as demonstrated in *Shakespeare Restored*, could he not have knocked up a pastiche himself? Thus, ironically, Theobald's Shakespearean credentials became in themselves a cause for scepticism, and the play's many echoes of canonical Shakespeare lines were seen as signs of fabrication. In his preface to *Double Falsehood*, Theobald responds with attempted nonchalance to these 'unbelievers', who 'are blindly paying me a greater compliment than either they design or I can merit' – the compliment, that is, of thinking he had written something that was actually written by Shakespeare. 'I should esteem it some sort of virtue, were I able to commit so agreeable a cheat.' But the charge of forgery stuck, particularly in the pro-Pope camp, as in David Mallet's 'Epistle to Mr Pope' (1733), which described Theobald as a thief and scavenger of Shakespearean leftovers – 'See him on Shakespeare pore, intent to steal / Poor farce, by fragments, for a third-day meal.' One obvious answer to these accusations would have been for Theobald to produce the old manuscripts he claimed to have used, but there is no evidence that anyone else ever saw them.

Though Theobald had his supporters, the consensus view through most of the eighteenth century was that *Double False-*

hood had no connection with Shakespeare. Either it was a 'cheat' or hoax cooked up by Theobald to bolster his editorial kudos; or it was genuinely an adaptation of an old play, but not one by Shakespeare. It was not until some years after his death in 1744 that scraps of evidence started to appear suggesting that Theobald may after all have been telling the truth, if not quite the whole truth. The discoverer of this new information was the great Shakespearean editor and biographer Edmond Malone. He was initially a sceptic: he thought Theobald had tricked up an old play, perhaps by Philip Massinger, with Shakespearean touches. His own copy of *Double Falsehood* survives, tartly annotated, especially where he found echoes of genuine Shakespeare – he thought the line 'Throw all my gay comparisons aside' (clearly parallel to 'lay his gay comparisons apart' in *Antony and Cleopatra*) had been 'inserted by Theobald to give a colour to the imposition he meant to put upon the publick'; another parallel was deemed 'an interpolation of Theobald's to countenance his fraud'. But Malone found reason to change his mind when he came upon an old entry in the Stationers' Company register, referring to an unknown play co-authored by Fletcher and Shakespeare. It was called *The History of Cardenio*. He must have immediately seen the link to *Double Falsehood*, for Cardenio was the name of the central character in the *Quixote* story on which the play was based (though in the play the original names are changed, and Cardenio becomes Julio). Malone published this information in 1782, in some notes he contributed to a new edition of David Baker's *Biographia dramatica*. Somewhat grudgingly he acknowledges that this unpublished *History of Cardenio* 'may possibly be the same as The Double Falsehood, afterwards brought to light by Mr Theobald'.

Over the years more evidence has mounted up, cumulative if not fully conclusive, and it is now widely accepted that *Double Falsehood* does contain some remnants of a lost play called

Cardenio, and that at least some of *Cardenio* was written by Shakespeare. These are certainly the views of Professor Brean Hammond, whose sumptuously detailed new edition for the Arden Shakespeare has been ten years in the making. The Arden series of single-play editions has been going since 1899, and this is the first devoted to a play not actually 'by' Shakespeare (a fact which earned it more news coverage than all the rest put together, which would certainly have pleased Theobald). And so *Double Falsehood* slips, as if through a side-door, into the august literary premises of the Shakespeare canon, not because it is itself a great play, or even a very good one, but because it is the nearest we can get to a Shakespeare play which has otherwise vanished.

*

We have a skeletal early history of *Cardenio*. Two performances by the King's Men are recorded in the royal Chamber Accounts for 1613. On 20 May payment was authorized for a total of twenty performances they had given, one of which is listed as 'Cardenno'. As is customary in these accounts, no authors' names are given. The list includes several Shakespeare plays, including two performances of *Much Ado about Nothing* (which the accountant calls 'Benedicte and Betteris'), plus *The Tempest*, *The Winter's Tale*, *Othello*, and probably the two *Henry IV* plays (listed as 'the Hotspurr' and 'Falstaff'). There are also four plays by Fletcher, all collaborations with Francis Beaumont, including two performances of *Philaster*. The actual dates of the performances are not specified, but it is likely some of them were part of the Shrovetide festivities around the wedding of Princess Elizabeth (the future 'Winter Queen') to the Elector Palatine on 14 February 1613. The majority of the plays are comedies or tragicomedies. *Cardenio*, judging from the Cervantes source and the Theobald adaptation, was a tragicomedy – a suitable divertimento, perhaps, for these celebrations tinged with sadness by the sudden death of the bride's brother, Prince Henry, the previous November. The King's Men performed the play again on 8 June 1613, at a courtly soirée in honour of the Duke of Savoy's ambassador, Giovanni Battista Gabaleoni, who had arrived in London a couple of weeks previously. Payment for this performance was collected a month later by Shakespeare's colleague and future editor, John Heminges – £6.13s.4d. 'for presentinge a playe . . . called Cardenna'.

Nothing further is heard of the play until 1653, when the bookseller Humphrey Moseley entered a miscellaneous group of old playscripts in the Stationers' Register, one of which – the entry spotted by Malone – was 'The history of Cardenio by Mr Fletcher & Shakespeare'. (There is a faint full stop after Fletcher, which seems to make Shakespeare an afterthought, but there is similar superfluous pointing elsewhere in the list.) This entry, dated 9 September 1653, is the only direct documentary allusion to Shakespeare's involvement in the play so far discovered.

These records, though forty years apart, are corroborative. The Moseley entry attributes the play to Fletcher and Shakespeare, and the performance dates of 'Cardenno/Cardenna' belong precisely to the period when the two authors are known to have been working together. *The Tempest*, performed in 1611, was Shakespeare's last single-authored play, but his revels were not quite ended. He wrote at least three further works (if *Cardenio* is accepted) in collaboration with Fletcher – the other two are a history play, *Henry VIII*, also called *All is True*, and a pastoral tragicomedy, *The Two Noble Kinsmen*. Fletcher was fifteen years his junior, a gentlemanly author (his father had been Bishop of London, his uncle a well-known diplomat), a writer of wit and flair, and already popular for his plays written in partnership with Beaumont. Marriage and ill-health forced Beaumont's retirement to the country in about 1613, and

Fletcher was thereafter groomed as Shakespeare's successor as chief playwright of the King's Men, a position he would hold, with prolific results, until his death in 1625. So *Cardenio* is at once a very late work of Shakespeare's – among the last things he wrote – and a new venture for his younger colleague Fletcher.

The choice of this particular story from *Don Quixote* may or may not have been Shakespeare's, but it chimes with the romance atmosphere of his late plays – a lovelorn 'knight' wandering the wilderness of the Sierra Morena; a girl living among the shepherds dressed as a boy; love-sonnets discovered in the saddle-pack of a dead mule; doleful music floating eerily amid the crags; betrayals and broken relationships moving by twists to a healing resolution. It is typical Cervantes, a romantic story told with wry deflatory humour, though the dramatists had their work cut out to condense its narrative sprawl of flashbacks, tangents and interruptions.

The story as they told it – assuming the plot of *Double False-hood* is a reasonable guide – is as follows. Julio and Leonora (Cardenio and Lucinda in *Quixote*) are lovers intending to ask their fathers' permission to marry. They are parted when Julio is summoned by letter to the court of Duke Angelo; this summons, we soon learn, has been engineered by the duke's libidinous younger son, Henriquez (Fernando), a friend of Julio who has designs on Leonora. Henriquez has already seduced and abandoned a virtuous village girl, Violante (Dorotea), and hopes to escape the consequences by hurriedly marrying Leonora – his desertion of Violante and betrayal of Julio constitute the 'double falsehood' of Theobald's title. Leonora's father is keen on this advantageous match, and she is forced to accept. She manages to smuggle a letter to Julio, who returns in time to witness the ceremony from that favourite Shakespearean vantage-point, 'behind the arras'. As the reluctant bride is about to be given away, Julio bursts from his hiding-place, but is chased off by the duke's attendants. Leonora swoons; a dagger is found on her, and a note explaining her intention to stab herself rather than become Henriquez's wife. The scene now switches to the Sierra Morena (which is actually where it begins in the *Quixote* original, with the foregoing pieced together in retrospect). Julio is a ragged refugee here, maddened by grief at the loss of his sweetheart and the perfidy of his friend: an Orlando Furioso figure. By coincidence (a busy plotter in most tragicomedies) Violante is also in the vicinity, disguised as a shepherd boy, and so is Leonora, who has taken sanctuary in a secluded convent. Through the agency of Henriquez's virtuous brother, Roderick, Leonora is sprung from the convent, and in a final scene strongly reminiscent of Shakespearean romance, Julio and Leonora are reunited, their fathers reconciled, and Henriquez accepts in an ardour of penitence his duty to marry Violante.

Composition of the play can be dated quite closely. Thomas Shelton's translation of the first part of *Don Quixote*, which includes the Cardenio story, was registered at Stationers' Hall on 19 January 1612 and published not long after. English writers were certainly aware of *Quixote* before this – Beaumont's burlesque *The Knight of the Burning Pestle* (c. 1607) is clearly indebted to it (whether Fletcher had a hand in this play is debated) – but precise phrasings from Shelton's translation are scattered throughout *Double Falsehood*, and these are likely to be part of the original text rather than cunning interpolations by Theobald. The termini for the play's composition are the publication of its source-book sometime after 19 January 1612, and its first recorded performance sometime before 20 May 1613. It is a pleasant addition to our meagre knowledge of Shakespeare in this period. Some of the time he was up in Stratford, in what one might call semi-retirement, but he is sighted in London in May 1612, giving evidence in a lawsuit involving his former landlord Christopher Mountjoy, and again in March 1613 when he signed the mortgage deed on a property in the Blackfriars.

The two performances in 1613 bring *Cardenio* close to the Shakespeare–Fletcher *Henry VIII*, which was first performed at the Globe in June 1613. It was playing there on the 29th when a burst of ordnance onstage ignited the thatched roof, and the theatre was burned to the ground: in a letter recounting this catastrophe Henry Wotton called it a 'new play'. Of the three collaborations, only *Henry VIII* was included in the First Folio of 1623. *The Two Noble Kinsmen*, based loosely on Chaucer's *Knight's Tale*, was first published in quarto in 1634. It is described on the title page as 'written by the memorable worthies of their time, Mr John Fletcher and Mr William Shakspeare'. The order of the authors' names suggests, and stylistic evidence agrees, that Fletcher wrote the lion's share of it. The same order of names, with the same likely inference, is found in Moseley's copyright entry for *Cardenio*. The exclusion of these two plays from the Folio probably reflects an editorial policy on collaborations which did not have enough Shakespeare in the mix. *Pericles*, a collaboration with George Wilkins, was also excluded, though later instated in the more capacious Third Folio of 1663–4.

The early references to *Cardenio* are bodiless – a title without a text – but it is possible one fragment of the Jacobean *Cardenio* does survive independently of Theobald's adaptation. This is a song, 'Woods, Rocks & Mountains', found in a manuscript collection of settings by the Jacobean lutenist Robert Johnson (who is not to be confused with the Tudor church musician of that name, nor indeed with the great Delta blues singer of the 1930s). Johnson is known to have composed music for King's Men productions – his beautiful settings of Ariel's songs in *The Tempest* survive. Michael Wood has ingeniously argued that the lyrics of 'Woods, Rocks & Mountains' are suggested by the wilderness setting of the Cardenio story, and have some parallels with phrases in Shelton's *Quixote*. He thinks the song was performed at the point in *Cardenio* equivalent to Act IV, Scene 2, of

Double Falsehood, where the wronged Violante sings offstage, to the accompaniment of a lute. The words of the song in *Double Falsehood* – 'Fond Echo, forego thy light strain' – are certainly Theobald's, and were ascribed to him when reprinted in musical miscellanies, but the original audiences of *Cardenio* may have instead heard her singing:

> Woods, rocks & mountaines & you desert places
> Where nought but bitter cold & hunger dwells
> Heare a poore maids last words killd wth disgraces
> Slide softly while I sing you silver fountaines
> & lett yor hollow waters like sad bells
> Ring ring to my woes while miserable I
> Cursing my fortunes dropp dropp dropp a teare & dye

As Wood notes, the second line of this song is echoed in Theobald's text, when the shepherds discuss Julio's presence in 'these wild unpeopled Mountains / Where naught dwells but hunger and sharp winds'. This would suggest the song was present in the source he was using. Perhaps he cut it because he thought the lyrics were Fletcher's rather than Shakespeare's. This may well be true – another of the songs in the Johnson collection is certainly from a Fletcher play, *The Lover's Progress* of *c*. 1623.

*

This snatch of Jacobean blues aside, we are left with the 1728 edition of *Double Falsehood* as our only text for *Cardenio* – hardly an authoritative text, something like a very late 'bad quarto', but a text nonetheless. According to the title page Theobald 'revised and adapted' the original play. One's immediate reaction is to wish he hadn't, as one would much rather have seen it before the rewrite, but a hand-wringing 'Why Oh Why?' is not the best question to ask at this point. A more useful question would be: what exactly did Theobald revise and adapt? What, in other words, was he working from when he wrote *Double Falsehood*?

In his preface to the play, responding to scepticism on this score, he gives some account of the materials he used. He claims to have in his possession no fewer than three manuscripts:

> One of the manuscript copies which I have is of above sixty years standing, in the handwriting of Mr Downes, the famous old prompter; and as I am credibly inform'd, was early in the possession of the celebrated Mr Betterton, and by him design'd to have been usher'd into the world. What accident prevented this purpose of his, I do not pretend to know; or thro' what hands it had successively passed before that period of time . . . Two other copies I have (one of which I was glad to purchase at a very good rate), which may not, perhaps, be quite so old as the former; but one of them is much more perfect, and has fewer flaws and interruptions in the sense.

This seems coherent enough. The eldest of his manuscripts dates from the mid 1660s; it had belonged to the great Restoration actor Thomas Betterton; it was in a transcription by John Downes. These men were colleagues – Betterton as star, Downes as prompter – in Sir William Davenant's troupe, the Duke's Company, whose theatre in Lincoln's Inn Fields opened in 1661; in that year Pepys saw 'Baterton' play there, and thought him 'above all that I ever saw'. That Betterton had intended to 'usher' the play 'into the world' – in other words, stage it – is plausible, since he and Davenant produced versions of the other Shakespeare–Fletcher plays at this time – *Henry VIII* in 1663 and *The Two Noble Kinsmen* (retitled *The Rivals*) in 1664. A production of *Cardenio* with Betterton in the title role would be a natural follow-up to these, but for one reason or another did not happen. Theobald also says that his Restoration manuscript had certain 'flaws and interruptions', some but not all of which were ironed out in one of the more recent manuscripts he had. These could be physical flaws – missing or damaged pages – but more probably he means that the text itself was in some way defective. 'Interruptions' might signify awkward transitions and inconsistencies in the narrative, and indeed *Double Falsehood* has a good many of these.

To cut a long bibliographical story short, it seems likely that Theobald's manuscripts were not preserved copies of the Jacobean *Cardenio*, but copies of a Restoration adaptation of it by Sir William Davenant. This idea was proposed back in 1969, in an influential essay by John Freehafer, and is enthusiastically pursued in Hammond's introduction to the Arden edition. In this reading *Double Falsehood* is an adaptation of an adaptation: two degrees of separation from Shakespeare (or three if one counts the Fletcherian 'colouring' which suffuses much of the play, as spotted by those first sharp-eyed critics in the 1720s). We have a parallel to this putative Restoration version of the play in the form of Davenant's reworked version of *The Two Noble Kinsmen*. Hammond sums up somewhat bleakly the drastic surgery which the *Kinsmen* underwent before emerging onstage in 1664 as *The Rivals*. Davenant's 'main objective as an adapter was domestication', he finds. He 'removed all the elements of ritual, mythology and medievalism'; replaced the tragicomic climax of the original with a 'banal test of virtue written in heroic couplets'; reduced the number of principal parts to the Restoration norm of nine; shortened the action by amputating most of the first and last acts; added a comic subplot and some songs; changed the names of the main characters; and – as well he might after this thorough makeover – gave it a new title. Something along these lines may have been done to *Cardenio* in the 1660s, including the new title, under which it would eventually appear in 1727.

This need not become an exercise in blame-shifting.

Davenant, here summarized as an artless bodger, was actually a
good poet – rather better than Theobald – and a committed
Shakespearean: his adaptation of *Macbeth* (1664) contains what
are thought to be some genuine Shakespeare lines omitted from
the Folio edition; so we need not be entirely gloomy about his
intervention. But certainly this double provenance would
explain much that is unsatisfactory about the structure of *Double Falsehood*: it inherits the 'flaws and interruptions' of another
author's cuts. It would also explain Theobald's reluctance to
show anyone the original manuscripts (or indeed to include the
play in his own later edition of Shakespeare). He knew the copy
he was working from was already adulterated material. The play
was 'written originally by W. Shakespeare' – as he says on the
title page, and no doubt genuinely believed – but he did not
actually have a copy of W. Shakespeare's play, only a doctored
Restoration version of it. He does not tell us this. He implies
throughout that he is working from some kind of Shakespearean original – a 'remnant of his pen', a 'relick' – albeit in a flawed
transcript. If that constitutes a 'cheat', he was guilty of it.

★

For the hunter after *Cardenio* – and few venture into the thickets
of *Double Falsehood* for any other reason – all this sounds like bad
news. The original text remains tantalizingly out of reach. It
survived for a while – the manuscript copyrighted by Moseley
in 1653; the manuscript adapted by Davenant in the 1660s – but
it did not survive intact into the eighteenth century. Nor, unfortunately, is it likely to turn up now, though a pair of post-Dan
Brown novels – J. C. Carrell's *The Shakespeare Secret* and Jean
Rae Baxter's *Looking for Cardenio* – have turned on this possibility, and there has also been an unconvincing attempt by Charles
Hamilton to prove that it survives as the anonymous playscript
known as *The Second Maiden's Tragedy*, which is more generally

(and more sensibly) attributed to Thomas Middleton. There is no sign that Theobald had any specific knowledge of the earlier *Cardenio* text, records of which re-emerged after his death. (He did know it was late Shakespeare – written, as he puts it, 'in the time of his retirement from the stage' – but that was something he could easily have deduced from the date of Shelton's *Quixote*.) Most tellingly, he did not know the original title of the play: in all his writings on the subject, he never once mentions the name of Cardenio. This strongly argues that he only knew the later, retitled version.

But, though he lacked information about the old play, Theobald obviously knew it had once existed, and perhaps there is a crumb of comfort somewhere in this narrative of attenuation and loss. Eighteenth-century adaptations of Shakespeare are invariably, and detrimentally, a movement away from the original, but in this case the adapter was trying to get back to the original. It is worth remembering just how good Theobald was in more conventional areas of Shakespeare editorship. Though harshly criticized by Dr Johnson, his stock is high among modern editors and experts. According to Gary Taylor he was 'one of the finest editors of the last three centuries', while Brian Vickers accounts him 'the best all-round editor of Shakespeare in his period or any other'. In *Shakespeare Restored*, Theobald set out his stall as a new kind of editor – scholarly, specialist, always ready to grapple with the textual corruptions endemic in the First Folio and other early texts. An editor, he wrote, must endeavour to 'restore sense', and by 'reasonable emendation to make that satisfactory and consistent with the context which before was so absurd, unintelligible and intricate'. An example of this is his famous emendation of a sentence from the Hostess's speech in *Henry V*, describing Falstaff on his deathbed. As printed in the Folio it read: 'For his Nose was as sharp as a pen, and a Table of greene fields.' Theobald proposed that 'a Table'

should read 'a babled' – i.e. 'he babbled', with the familiar
Shakespearean elision for the pronoun, pronounced like the *a* in
'a-hunting'. Thus he rescued a line of great poignancy from the
garbled reading set down by one of the Folio's compositors a
century earlier.

This idea of the editor as a 'restorer', a recoverer of obscured
nuggets of Shakespearean text, carries over into his rather different project on *Double Falsehood*. We can at least feel that
Theobald knew what he was doing, and that his version would
have salvaged as much of the Jacobean original, and removed
as many of the Restoration accretions, as he could. However,
he is also likely to have 'reconstructed' material he thought had
been cut or rewritten, thus muddying the text with pseudo-
Shakespearean additions, including those half-quoted lines from
other plays which aroused the suspicion of Malone and others.

It is broadly agreed that Shakespeare's hand is more discernible in the first two acts of *Double Falsehood*, though we have no
idea how the original collaboration with Fletcher might have
worked, and this is not at all a watertight division, just a general
consensus between old-style connoisseurs who think they can
'spot' an author's style, and new-fangled stylometrists who use
complex statistical sampling to create an author's 'lexical finger-
print'. The play opens with a melancholy Duke talking of
mortality, which makes one think of Duke Orsino in *Twelfth
Night*, or the funereal opening of *All's Well*, and it is done with
typically Shakespearean casualness, dropping us straight into
the play in the middle of a conversation:

   Roderick My gracious father, this unwonted strain
    Visits my heart with sadness.
   Duke   Why, my son?
    Making my death familiar to my tongue
    Digs not my grave one jot before the date.

We are then swiftly apprised of the distinction between the duke's two sons – the good Roderick, 'who, with my duke-doms, heirs my better glories'; and the wayward Henriquez, 'thy irregular brother', who is a 'truant to my wishes and his birth', and whose 'taints of wildness hurt our nicer honour, / And call for swift reclaim'. The scene is sleekly written, has the hall-marks of rapidity and economy, and shows some distinctive linguistic touches, such as the use of 'heir' as a verb, quoted above; also 'spreads me with blushes'; 'hot escapes of youth'; 'bosom'd trust'. In the following scene we first meet Julio, who in the original was Cardenio, the Quixotic lover and outcast. The dialogue between him and his father is rather flat, but the tempo picks up with the arrival of Leonora. In a brief soliloquy before her entrance, Julio voices his fear that her love for him is cooling:

> I do not see that fervour in the maid
> Which youth and love should kindle. She consents,
> As 'twere, to feed without an appetite.
>   . . . This affection
> Is such a feign'd one as will break untouch'd,
> Die frosty ere it can be thaw'd; while mine,
> Like to a clime beneath Hyperion's eye,
> Burns with one constant heat . . .

Leonora in turn fears that Julio's impending visit to court will seduce and distract him: it will 'banish my image' from his mind,

> And I be left, the scoff of maids, to drop
> A widow's tear for thy departed faith.

These lines certainly could be Shakespeare, as could various others in Act I, for instance Henriquez's rhapsody about the lowly but beautiful Violante, as he stands beneath her balcony with his musicians, which begins, 'This maid, / For whom my

sighs ride on the night's chill vapour, / Is born most humbly . . .'
One is cherry-picking, obviously. These are high points; around
them is a more level terrain across which the verse moves at an
amiable iambic jog-trot which seems at best 'Shakespeare lite'.

The opening of the second act is interesting in a different
way, because it exemplifies those 'flaws and interruptions' in
Theobald's source. It introduces two bluff countrymen, Fabian
and Lopez, who never appear again, and are perhaps a relic of an
excised subplot; it has Henriquez abruptly announcing that he
has raped Violante ('By force alone I snatch'd th'imperfect joy')
in a way that suggests an earlier scene is missing; and it prints as
prose some lines which scan as regular pentameters. Here is
Henriquez agitatedly mulling over what he has done:

> Was it a rape then? No. Her shrieks, her exclamations then had
> drove me from her. True, she did not consent: as true, she did
> resist; but still in silence all. 'Twas but the coyness of a modest
> bride, not the resentment of a ravish'd maid. And is the man yet
> born, who would not risk the guilt to meet the joy? The guilt!
> That's true. But then the danger, the tears, the clamours of the
> ruin'd maid, pursuing me to court. That, that, I fear will (as it
> already does my conscience) something shatter my honour.
> What's to be done?

I give this in Theobald's prose, though Hammond restores part
of it ('Twas but . . . That's true') to verse. How good is it? Is it
genuine Shakespeare, or an efficient pastiche of Hamlet-style
self-interrogation? And if the latter, is it pastiche by the co-
worker Fletcher or by one of the later adapters? Reading *Double
Falsehood* – or rather, trying to read *Cardenio* – you become giddy
with options, doubts, voices that fade in and out like bad radio
signals.

There is one brief passage towards the end of the first act

which even the doughtiest sceptic has to admit sounds convincingly Shakespearean. It is a put-down, essentially, or anyway a frankly phrased dismissal. The long-suffering Violante has had more than enough of Henriquez's insistent romantic attentions. She looks down at him, this importunate upper-class dandy serenading under her balcony. 'Home, my lord!' she says firmly. And then this –

> What you can say is most unseasonable; what sing,
> Most absonant and harsh. Nay, your perfume,
> Which I smell hither, cheers not my sense
> Like our field-violet's breath.

Of the five English writers whose 'lexical fingerprints' can be found on this hybrid playscript – Shelton, Fletcher, Shakespeare, Davenant, Theobald – there is surely only one who could have written this particular piece of it. 'Absonant', with its hard neologistic consonants; the 'perfume' wafting up from the overbred gallant or oversexed stallion below; the country-girls' sweet possessive, '*our* field-violet' (compare *The Winter's Tale*, 'our carnations and streak'd gillyvors'); the lilting rhythm running on through the line-breaks. The ghost of Shakespeare's *Cardenio* is only fitfully raised in Theobald's third-hand eighteenth-century redaction, but we should be grateful to him for even its briefest apparitions. Perhaps the play's tenuous survival is in part a measure of its original middling quality. It is 1613, and the maestro is tiring, or coasting, or not quite what he was – it is mostly Fletcher's show. But here, for a few moments of stage-time, he rolls out this gorgeous four-line riff which touches us and lifts us. This piece of late Shakespearean verse, like some others of comparable quality in *The Two Noble Kinsmen*, is in essence valedictory: the magical stuff he could always produce, and can still produce if he chooses, which increasingly he does not.

9

'The Life etc'

Shakespeare's First Biographer

[2009]

Nicholas Rowe's *Some Account of the Life &c of Mr. William Shake-spear* was written as a preface for his handsome new edition of the plays, published in six volumes in 1709. It is often described as the first biography of Shakespeare. There have been many hundreds of them since – longer, weightier, more probing and indeed more factually accurate – but three centuries after its appearance Rowe's brief biographical sketch still deserves to be taken seriously. The title is not exactly snappy but I rather like it. 'Some account of the life etc' seems a good enough summary of what a biography is, the 'etc' encompassing all that other stuff which makes it something more than a mere chronology of a person's life.

Rowe was writing nearly a century after Shakespeare's death (1616), beyond the arc of living memory and first-hand testimony, and with little in the way of printed sources to draw on. There was some vaguely biographical material in the introduction to the First Folio (1623), edited by Shakespeare's former colleagues, John Heminges and Henry Condell; and a scattering of comment and anecdote in collections such as Ben Jonson's *Timber* (1640), Thomas Fuller's *Worthies of England* (1662), John Dryden's *Essay of Dramatic Poesy* (1668) and Gerard Langbaine's *Account of the English Dramatick Poets* (1691). The researches of John Aubrey, an expert though not always reliable sniffer-out of information, had turned up some interesting details, but they remained in an unedited bundle of manuscripts, and there is no sign that Rowe had any knowledge of them.

These are the antecedents of Rowe's *Account* – disjointed bits of biographical information and tradition: '*tamquam tabulata naufragi*' ('like the fragments of a shipwreck'), in Aubrey's vivid phrase. Rowe is the first to attempt to put them together, to produce a fuller narrative 'account' rather than just individual items – indeed, the word 'account' conveys this, carrying across its financial meaning to suggest a metaphorical reckoning up of a man's life.

The appetite which Rowe sees himself as satisfying was to some extent a new one. How 'fond' people are, he says, 'for any little personal story of the great men of antiquity, their families, the common accidents of their Lives, and even their shape, make and features . . . How trifling soever this curiosity may seem to be, it is certainly very natural.' Nowadays we take this curiosity for granted, but at the beginning of the eighteenth century the art of biography was still in its infancy. Its first heyday would come some decades later, with such works as Samuel Johnson's *Lives of the Poets* (1779–81) and James Boswell's great *Life* of Johnson (1791). It is from this later period, and from this literary circle, that we have the first full-length, scholarly biography of Shakespeare – Edmond Malone's, compiled over decades, and posthumously published in 1821.

Rowe's biography is no match for Malone's, but it is an important fingerpost towards it – important as a gathering of data and impressions into a more rounded portrait, and important also because of the style and panache with which it is written. This is not some formulaic panegyric of a great man, but something more relaxed, conversational, accessible. Rowe was in his mid thirties when he wrote it – a literary man about town; a friend of the poet Pope, who spoke warmly of his 'vivacity and gayety of disposition'. He was, like his subject, a professional playwright (and his edition of Shakespeare was itself a professional undertaking: the publisher, Jacob Tonson, paid him

£36.10s. for it). He wrote a series of mellifluous tragedies, one of which, *Jane Shore* (1714), was avowedly an imitation of Shakespeare. His most popular play, *The Fair Penitent* (1703), features a serial seducer, the 'haughty, gallant, gay Lothario', whose name remains in the language long after the play has been forgotten.

It would be hard to argue that Rowe was anything but a minor author, but he was admired by Dr Johnson, who included him in his *Lives of the Poets*, and who praised the 'suavity' of his style. He was talking of Rowe's plays, but suavity is precisely right as a description of the brisk, fluent tones of the *Account*.

*

Rowe's literary career suggests an important aspect of this pioneering biography – it is a life of Shakespeare written by a man of the theatre, and drawing on theatrical knowledge and traditions about Shakespeare. An example of this is the casually proffered information that Shakespeare played the part of the Ghost in early productions of *Hamlet*. This wonderful nugget is unique to Rowe, but ties in with another early tradition, that Shakespeare played Adam in *As You Like It*. These are smallish parts, and old-man parts, such as a busy, prematurely balding actor-writer might give himself.

A further aspect of this theatrical context is the contribution made by the veteran actor Thomas Betterton, a colleague of Rowe's who had recently played the title role in his *Ulysses* (1705). 'I must own a particular Obligation to him,' Rowe writes, 'for the most considerable part of the passages relating to his [Shakespeare's] Life . . . his Veneration of the Memory of Shakespear having engag'd him to make a journey into Warwickshire, on purpose to gather up what Remains he could.' Up in Stratford, Betterton consulted the parish registers and other 'Publick Writings relating to that town'. This is admirable sleuthing by the standards of the day, though in some respects

rather carelessly done. It is as well to note now the faulty information which found its way into the *Account*. Shakespeare was
not one of ten children but one of eight; and he did not have
three daughters, but two daughters and a son. Betterton apparently missed the burial entry for Shakespeare's son, Hamnet,
who died in 1596, at the age of eleven. But he did note the details
of Shakespeare's marriage, and Rowe is the first biographer to
identify the poet's wife – 'the daughter of one Hathaway, said to
have been a substantial Yeoman in the Neighbourhood'.

Betterton is not to be censured, however, for the apparent
vagueness about Shakespeare's birth-date, which Rowe gives
only as 'April, 1564', rather than the traditional 23 April. In this
he is more correct than many later biographers. The idea that
Shakespeare was born on St George's Day is a jingoistic conveni-
ence which was mooted later in the eighteenth century and
swiftly became a pseudo-fact. The only documentary fact is that
Shakespeare was baptized on 26 April 1564. The actual day of his
birth is unknown. Thomas de Quincey (who was almost as
much of a connoisseur of Shakespeare as he was of opium)
plausibly suggested that the wedding day of Shakespeare's
granddaughter Elizabeth, 22 April, was chosen in memory of
his birthday.

Betterton typifies this lineage of playhouse tradition which
lies behind the *Account*. In *Roscius Anglicanus* (1708) John Downes
praised him for his performance in the title role of Shakespeare
and Fletcher's *Henry VIII* – 'the part of the King was so rightly
and justly done by Mr Betterton, he being instructed in it by Sir
William [Davenant], who had it from old Mr Lowen, that had
his instructions from Mr Shakespeare himself' – a genealogy
akin to the studio lineages of Italian Renaissance painting.
Betterton also appears as an early owner of the 'Chandos portrait' of Shakespeare, now in the National Portrait Gallery.
According to the historian George Vertue, writing in 1719, the

then-owner of the painting, a barrister named Robert Keck, 'bought [it] for forty guineas off Mr Batterton who bought it of Sir W. Davenant'.

Betterton, born in about 1635, had no personal knowledge of Shakespeare, but he was steeped in the texts as a performer. As Rowe says, 'No man is better acquainted with Shakespear's Manner of Expression, and indeed he has study'd him so well, and is so much a Master of him, that whatever Part of his he performs, he does it as if it had been written on purpose for him.' The actor who becomes a 'Master' of Shakespeare – an expert – is a kind of prototype for the biographer, whose mastery of his subject is also to some extent mimetic.

*

Among Rowe's notable 'firsts' is his recounting of the story of the young Shakespeare poaching deer from the estates of a Warwickshire grandee, Sir Thomas Lucy of Charlecote. Sometime after his marriage, Rowe says, Shakespeare fell into 'ill Company'. (He married in 1582, so this was in his late teens or early twenties.) Among this company were 'some that made a frequent practice of Deer-stealing', and they 'engag'd him with them more than once in robbing a Park that belong'd to Sir Thomas Lucy', for which he was 'prosecuted by that Gentleman'. This is one of those stories which sounds like pure folklore, part of the Shakespeare 'mythos', yet it has proved tenacious and even today has its heavyweight proponents. It received an added boost in the 1790s, when Malone found an independent manuscript account, written in the late seventeenth century by an obscure parson named Richard Davies, who said: 'Shakespeare was . . . much given to all unluckiness in stealing venison & Rabbits particularly from Sr [—] Lucy who had him oft whipt.' This manuscript was hidden away in the archives of Corpus Christi College, Oxford, and it is extremely unlikely that Rowe had read it.

That the story exists in two independent early versions is, of course, no guarantee that it is true, but shows at least that there *was* a story. Rowe did not invent it. He goes on to note a compelling echo of the case in some badinage from *The Merry Wives of Windsor* (c. 1597), where the foolish Justice Shallow accuses Falstaff of poaching from his estates – 'You have . . . kill'd my deer and broke open my lodge' – and intends to prosecute him for it. Can it be coincidence, Rowe asks, that this Shallow is also said to 'give a dozen white luces in the coat' – in other words, to have a family crest featuring luces (young pike), which was precisely the punning heraldic device used by the Lucys of Charlecote? No commentator on the *Merry Wives* has found a better explanation, and even great modern biographers like E. K. Chambers and Samuel Schoenbaum – hard-nosed documentary empiricists – have felt that the poaching episode as recounted by Rowe has 'the ring of truth'.

Rowe makes much of this episode – a scoop of sorts – but there is not a whisper of that tediously winsome romanticizing of it found in later, especially Victorian, versions. It is these which provoke scepticism, not the bare bones of the story, which was probably picked up by Betterton in Stratford, where the Lucys were well known and not especially popular. Throughout Rowe's *Account* there is this judiciousness in his use of biographical material. He states, but does not over-egg, Shakespeare's middling origins, his lack of higher education, his writing by the 'mere Light of Nature', and so on.

A good deal of Rowe's preface is devoted to critical comment, some of it bearing the imprint of eighteenth-century prejudices which today sound quaintly antiquarian. Few, for instance, would agree with his dismissal of tragicomedy as 'the common Mistake of that Age', since we now value those teasing mood-shifts and plot-twists which the genre brings. But then, to be fair, Rowe does not quite agree with his dismissal either.

He registers the view, but then adds, 'tho' the severer Critiques among us cannot bear it, yet the generality of our Audiences seem to be better pleas'd with it than with an exact Tragedy.' Similarly, he is sanguine – as many of those 'severer' critics were not – about the poet's supposed ignorance of the Classics. A better knowledge of them might have added more 'Correctness' to his style, he thinks, but might also 'have restrain'd some of that Fire, Impetuosity, and even beautiful Extravagance which we admire in Shakespeare'.

Some of Rowe's commentary on individual plays seems rather fluffy, but one must set this against the more important precision of his work as an editor. The *Account* introduces the first new edition of Shakespeare's plays since the First Folio. It appeared at a time when the plays were routinely primped, pol-ished, bowdlerized, rejigged and retitled to accord to Augustan ideas of theatrical 'decorum' – Nahum Tate, who rewrote *King Lear* with a happy ending, is the most notorious of these tinker-ers, but there were many others. Rowe's edition returns the reader to the original, difficult, sometimes rough-hewn master-pieces which Shakespeare wrote. It is hardly an adventurous edition, by later standards – essentially just a cleaned-up version of the Folio text, with some of the more obvious textual corruptions emended. Rowe does not have the inspired inter-pretative touch of later eighteenth-century editors like Lewis Theobald and George Steevens, nor the encyclopaedic know-ledge of Elizabethan–Jacobean literary history which Malone brings to bear. But his clear, sensible, well-printed presentation of Shakespeare's text is an important step towards those more sophisticated editions.

The cheerful, nonchalant quality of the *Account* sometimes tends towards the slapdash, as at the end, where he signs off – or, rather, peters out – with a glancing reference to 'a book of [Shakespeare's] Poems publish'd in 1640'. Having only recently got hold of a copy, he adds, 'I won't pretend to determine whether it be his or no.' The edition he refers to, edited by John Benson, is indeed genuine; it has some faults, and some misleading titles, but it contains almost all Shakespeare's sonnets, and did them some service in that the only previous edition of them (1609) had fallen into obscurity. There may be some commercial in-fighting behind Rowe's casual dismissal, as a few months later an edition of Shakespeare's poems, based on the 1640 text, was issued by a rival publisher. But, whatever the reason, it seems a pity that Shakespeare's first biographer turned away from this gold mine of psychological insights into his subject. It makes one wonder what other sources he failed to follow up, what other questions he chose not to 'determine'.

For all its faults Rowe's biography has remained durable and readable. There is a modern tendency to dismiss the early biographers as purveyors of unverifiable anecdote and gossip. This seems an arrogant view of writers so much closer to Shakespeare in time, and in cultural context, than we are; writers who simply knew things which we now have to burrow laboriously through ancient archives to rediscover. Dr Johnson notes this point when he describes Rowe's *Account* as 'a Life of the author such as tradition, then almost expiring, could supply'. This is what one celebrates 300 years on – Rowe's timely intervention to rescue a sense of Shakespeare the man, and to preserve some fragments of the shipwreck which might otherwise have been lost for ever.

Cipher Wheels

The Shakespeare Authorship Controversy
[2010]

Here is a Trivial Pursuit-style question. What, aside from their fame, did Mark Twain, Helen Keller, Henry James, Sigmund Freud, Charlie Chaplin and Orson Welles have in common? The answer is, they all believed that the plays and poems attributed to William Shakespeare were really written by someone else. The first three belong to the classic 'Baconian' era of the late nineteenth and early twentieth centuries, when claims for Sir Francis Bacon's authorship were uppermost, and were argued most vociferously in America. Freud and Welles were more modern 'Oxfordians', believing the true author to be Edward de Vere, seventeenth Earl of Oxford, as first proposed by J. Thomas Looney in 1920. Chaplin was a floating voter, or generic 'anti-Stratfordian'. He did not know who wrote the plays, he explained in his 1964 autobiography, 'but I can hardly think it was the boy from Stratford. Whoever wrote them had an aristocratic attitude.'

These are essentially celebrity endorsements: none of these people, with the possible exception of Freud, could be called a Shakespeare scholar. It is an impressive list but also a very elderly one. One could continue it through to the present day (Malcolm X, Enoch Powell, Derek Jacobi, Mark Rylance, Jim Jarmusch . . .), but those big names take us back to the heyday of the authorship controversy, when the anti-Stratfordian cause seemed something daring and even excitingly modern in its challenge to traditional (and, from the American point of view, English) orthodoxy. And if to many it also seemed barmy, it was a flamboyant, newsworthy sort of barminess. Some of the front-line Baconian theorists were themselves minor celebrities, eccentric exemplars of the epoch's passion for discovery, on a par with inventors and spiritualists and staring-eyed explorers in search of lost cities.

One such oddball was the wealthy Detroit physician Orville Ward Owen, author of the six-volume *Sir Francis Bacon's Cipher Story* (1894), who gained his knowledge of Bacon's authorship, and much else besides, by means of an enormous spooling mechanism dubbed 'The Cipher Wheel' (see Plate 7). This consisted of two wooden cylinders and a thousand-foot long strip of canvas, on to which were pasted the complete plays of Shakespeare, together with some works by Marlowe, Spenser and others which Bacon might also be expected (in Dr Owen's view) to have written. The big wheels turned, certain keywords were highlighted, phrases adjacent to them were read off and dictated to a stenographer, and so the 'cipher story' slowly unfolded. Later Owen was to be seen in Gloucestershire, with yet heavier machinery, dredging a stretch of the Wye near Chepstow Castle in search of certain caskets full of manuscripts to which Bacon's messages had directed him. On his deathbed in 1924, a 'penniless invalid', Owen said he had ruined his health, wealth and reputation on the Baconian quest. Stay away from it, he warned: 'you will only reap disappointment.'

Despite the failure of early cipher-hunters like Owen, Elizabeth Wells Gallup and Ignatius Donnelly to find anything meaningful, the idea that Shakespearean texts contain coded messages of authorship remains central. The *Sonnets*, with their apparently confiding, first-person tone, have proved fertile ground. Oxfordians find anagrams of 'Vere' *every*where, especially in the line from Sonnet 76, 'Every word doth almost tell my name'. In the infamously puzzling dedication to the first edition of 1609 – ostensibly written by the publisher, Thomas

Thorpe – the author is styled 'our ever-living poet'. Oxfordians point out that the first three words are (almost) an anagram of one of Oxford's mottos, *Vero nil verius* ('Nothing truer than truth'). Yet the same dedicatory text, when examined by Brenda James in *Henry Neville and the Shakespeare Code* (2008), reveals an entirely different secret, achieved by putting the 144 letters of the dedication into a 12 × 12 matrix, and juggling them around according to certain cryptographic rules, whereupon there emerges first the encouraging message, 'The wise Thorp hid thy poet', and then the all-important name of the poet: not Oxford but 'Nevill'. They cannot both be there, and this is an instance of a general problem with the anti-Stratfordian case nowadays, for Sir Henry Neville is only the latest entry in a crowded field of contenders for the authorship, which also includes Christopher Marlowe, Fulke Greville, Roger Manners, fifth Earl of Rutland, and the conveniently initialled William Stanley, sixth Earl of Derby. Things were easier in the old duopoly of Bacon and Oxford: you might not be able to hear the signals but at least you knew who was supposed to be sending them.

The idea of concealed words and names – anagrams, acrostics, *à clef* puns – at least has some historical authenticity, for the Elizabethans loved this sort of thing. Such word-games are more likely to appear in poems than stage-plays, where they are harder to catch, but the dementedly pedantic Holofernes in *Love's Labour's Lost* constructs something very like a crossword clue about a wounded deer ('Of one sore I an hundred make by adding but one more l', etc.) which may also be a concealed personal allusion. So those Oxfordian anagrams are not in themselves fantastical, though they are often imperfect – for instance, 'our ever-living' only becomes '*vero nil verius*' by changing the last *g* to an *s* – and tend to require a prior belief-system to make them seem significant. The more extensive and deeply embedded codes – those lurking Bilateral Ciphers and King's Move Ciphers and Transformation Codes – seem totally implausible, and bring with them the depressing idea that the whole purpose of the texts was to be a vehicle for the secret message, the actual choice of words being primarily dictated by what Brenda James calls the 'mathematically determined lay-outs' of the code.

Of course there is another reason why coded messages loom so large in the quest to prove that someone else wrote the works of Shakespeare. They are required precisely in the absence of any overt messages – otherwise known as historical evidence – to that effect. It is one of the many weaknesses of the anti-Stratfordian case that not a whisper is heard of any such suspicion until the mid nineteenth century. In the crowded, intimate, gossipy world of the Elizabethan and Jacobean theatre, in the letters and diaries and epigrams of Shakespeare's contemporaries, in the *ad personam* jibes that were flung about 'like hailstones' in the so-called War of the Theatres at the turn of the century, no one makes any allusion to this incredible sleight of hand being perpetrated, year after year, play after play, by the most popular writer of the day.

*

James Shapiro is too expert and perhaps too courteous a scholar to descend into a cantankerous cataloguing of the flaws in the anti-Stratfordian argument. He certainly thinks the argument is wrong, as his new study of the controversy* makes clear, and he offers precise reasons why William Shakespeare of Stratford is really the only cogent candidate for authorship. But his purpose is not, or not primarily, to refute. He is interested, he says, 'not in what people think – which has been stated again and again in unambiguous terms – so much as why they think it'. The book is precisely about the question posed in the subtitle, 'Who wrote

---

*James Shapiro, *Contested Will: Who Wrote Shakespeare?* (Faber, 2010).

Shakespeare?', but while most other books on the subject are
about the answer to that question, this one is about the question
itself. Who asked it, and when did they ask it, and most of all
why did those particular people ask it at those particular times?
This is essentially a historiographical study of the controversy,
looking at the cultural contexts of its emergence and evolution,
and at the lives, circumstances, agendas and pathologies of those
who have contributed to it. It is also unlike most other books on
the subject because it is a pleasure to read. Like its predecessor,
1599: A Year in the Life of William Shakespeare (2005), it is briskly
paced, cleverly detailed, elegantly argued, and never forgets
that, for all the complexities and quiddities of the material, the
writing of history is essentially the telling of a story (or, in this
case, the story of a story).

Shapiro begins by dropping a small chronological bombshell
behind anti-Stratfordian lines. This is his contention that a key
document, long advanced as the earliest expression of doubts
about Shakespeare's authorship, is a forgery. The document is a
small, bound manuscript copy of a pair of lectures delivered to
the Ipswich Philosophical Society in the early months of 1805
by one James Corton Cowell. In the first lecture, 'Some Reflec-
tions on the Life of William Shakespeare', Cowell proceeds to
'unfold a strange and surprising story', the upshot of which was
that Shakespeare's plays had been written by Bacon. This
unheard-of idea was met with 'cries of disapproval and execration'. In the second lecture Cowell reveals that the originator of
this theory was an aged Warwickshire scholar, Dr John Wilmot,
rector of Barton-on-the-Heath, who had scoured the archives
of Stratford and 'covered himself with the dust of every private
bookcase for fifty miles around', without finding any record or
relic of Shakespeare the writer, and who had begun – some
twenty years previously, thus around 1785 – to formulate the
theory of pseudonymous authorship by Bacon.

The Cowell lectures, often mentioned but seldom read, give the anti-Stratfordian tradition a toehold in the eighteenth century, a touch of much needed venerableness. But Shapiro's keen eye notes what seem to be anachronisms. When Cowell refers to Shakespeare having taken up 'the very unromantic business of a money lender and dealer in malt', he displays a casual knowledge of biographical information unavailable in 1805 – the malt-dealing evidence was not discovered until the early 1840s. Shapiro also questions this usage of 'unromantic' as early as 1805. Another oddity is that Cowell gives an erroneous location for Barton-on-the-Heath, where he supposedly had his revelatory discussions with John Wilmot. Shapiro's conclusion is that 'Cowell', of whom nothing else is known, is a fiction; and that his supposed lectures are a clever pro-Baconian fabrication, probably dating from the early twentieth century, not long before the manuscript was discovered in the Durning-Lawrence Library at the University of London and announced to the world in the *TLS* in 1932.

But though the evidence of authorship-doubts in the eighteenth century is questionable, Shapiro traces the cultural roots of the controversy back to that time. It was at this period that Shakespeare began to be 'regarded as a deity', an elevation which was a 'crucial precondition for all subsequent controversies about his identity'. A key figure in this was the actor David Garrick, whose declamatory 'Ode to Shakespeare' – 'Tis he! 'Tis he!/The god of our idolatry!' – was the centrepiece of the bicentennial Stratford Jubilee of 1764. After his death Garrick was eulogized by Cowper as 'great Shakespeare's priest', who had 'called the world to worship on the banks/Of Avon'. The fine but faintly preposterous painting by George Romney, *The Infant Shakespeare Attended by Nature and the Passions* (*c.* 1792), makes clear allusion to the Christ-child of traditional Nativity paintings. This deification, though in itself merely rhetorical, promoted an idea of Shakespeare which set him apart from the normal, flawed, mortal race of men. So too did the increasing tendency to read his plays and poems as a kind of autobiography, a mirror held up not just, as Hamlet says, to 'Nature', but to particular aspects of Shakespeare's own life and personality.

So there begins to arise a disparity: on the one hand, this inferred biography of almost superhuman cultivation and profundity; on the other, the then-known facts of his life, which were few and uninspiring. By the mid nineteenth century, when documentary researchers like J. O. Halliwell-Phillipps were stacking up new records of Shakespeare's financial and property dealings, not to mention his hounding of debtors and hoarding of grain, this disparity had developed into an 'unbearable tension . . . between Shakespeare the poet and Shakespeare the businessman; between the London playwright and the Stratford haggler; between Shakespeare as Prospero and Shakespeare as Shylock; between the kind of man revealed in the autobiographical poems and plays, and the one revealed in tax, court and real estate records; between a deified Shakespeare and a depressingly mundane one. Surely he was either one or the other.' This was the tipping point. 'It was only a matter of time before someone would come along and suggest that we were dealing not with one man but with two.'

That someone proved to be a 44-year-old American woman called Delia Bacon – minister's daughter, former schoolteacher, failed playwright – who in the spring of 1845 took rooms in a hotel in New Haven, Connecticut, and began to devote herself to a bold new theory of Sir Francis Bacon's secret authorship (new, that is, if one accepts that the Cowell lectures are a fake). An important influence on her was the deconstructionist scholarship of the 'Higher Criticism' – close-focus lexical studies of biblical and Classical texts, which had proved that the Homeric epics were the product of multiple authors. More serendipitous was her acquaintance with the inventor Samuel Morse, then developing his famous code: it was he who alerted her to Bacon's considerable interest in cryptography. That she was Bacon's namesake no doubt helped: almost inevitably, she came to believe she was related to him. She finally published her theories in an anonymous essay, 'William Shakespeare and his Plays: An Enquiry Concerning Them' (1856), and then the following year in a rambling tome, *The Philosophy of the Plays of Shakspere Unfolded*. The secret was out, but it had taken its toll; she died in a mental hospital two years later.

The Baconians held sway for over sixty years, but by the time Orville Ward Owen was dredging for manuscripts at Chepstow their days were numbered. In 1920 the Oxfordian claim was launched with the publication of *'Shakespeare' Identified* by J. Thomas Looney. (The cheap but cherished jibe about the appropriateness of his name is forestalled by Shapiro, who says it is correctly pronounced to rhyme with 'boney'.) A shadowy Tyneside churchman, Looney was a leading figure in the Church of Humanity, which was based on the 'Positivist' teachings of Auguste Comte, and which sounds like an Edwardian version of Moral Rearmament. Nostalgic for a lost world of social coherence, and tending to a grating note of crypto-fascism, Looney was convinced the author of the plays was an aristocrat, someone 'linked more closely to the old order than the new', and not at all 'the kind of man we should expect to rise from the lower middle-class population of the towns'. The seventeenth Earl of Oxford, born in 1550, had impeccably blue blood, and was even a poet, though his known output is a slender selection of rather facile love-poems. Much else about him was unknown in 1920 – or if known quietly ignored – and it is ironic that Looney's chosen chevalier of the 'old order' should turn out to be one of the nastiest Elizabethans on record: shrill, violent, unstable and pathologically extravagant. He slapped Sir Philip Sidney on the tennis court and called him a 'puppy'. He killed an unarmed man, a cook named Brincknell, and got off on a plea that Brincknell had committed suicide by 'running upon' his sword. He ditched his wife and daughter for the court beauty Anne Vavasour, then ditched her too when she became pregnant. Among his contemporaries he was a byword for preening vanity (see Gabriel Harvey's 1579 caricature, *Speculum Tuscanismi*), and he was accused of blasphemy and buggery (see allegations *passim*, not nececessarily true but indicative of his reputation). Anyone remotely tempted by the idea he was Shakespeare should read Alan Nelson's trenchant biography, *Monstrous Adversary* (2003).

Shapiro is very good at teasing out the underlying or unconscious motives of Shakespeare-denial, and one of the most interesting back-stories concerns the Oxfordian convert Sigmund Freud. Fascinated by Shakespeare from childhood, Freud became even more so when he began to formulate his Oedipal theory, partly drawn from his own ambivalent feelings on the death of his father in 1896. It was, of course, Sophocles' *Oedipus Rex* which furnished the name for this 'universal event in early childhood', but in some ways *Hamlet* was even more important. *Hamlet*, he wrote, 'has its roots in the same soil as *Oedipus Rex*', but while in *Oedipus* the fantasy of patricide 'is brought into the open', in *Hamlet* it 'remains repressed, and – just as in the case of a neurosis – we only learn of its existence because of its inhibiting consequences'. Hamlet's failure to avenge his father's murder results from 'the obscure memory that he himself had contemplated the same deed against his father out of passion for his mother'. What clinched it for Freud was that, according to the then-accepted chronology, Shakespeare wrote the play in the immediate aftermath of his own father's death in 1601. It was as if Shakespeare was right there on the couch, telling him (via the text of *Hamlet*) about this strange dream he'd had of his dead father. 'It can of course only be the poet's own mind which confronts us in *Hamlet*,' Freud states confidently in *The Interpretation of Dreams* (1900).

It was with some consternation, therefore, that Freud later learned of a new document which cast doubt on this dating of *Hamlet*. This was a marginalium by the pamphleteering Cambridge don Gabriel Harvey – ironically one of Oxford's early detractors – and its phrasing seemed to show that *Hamlet* was on stage during the lifetime of the Earl of Essex. The latter was executed in February 1601, so by this reckoning the play was written and staged before the death of John Shakespeare in September 1601, and was not, after all, a personal key to the poet's mind in the trauma of bereavement. To state baldly what Shapiro pursues more suggestively, the emergence of Oxford as the new putative author of *Hamlet* was a godsend for Freud. It was not ideal that his father had died back in 1562, when Oxford was twelve, but it was better than an inconveniently living father; and it was definitely an added bonus that his mother had remarried not long afterwards. Freud had never been much convinced by the Baconian thesis, but his button-holing enthusiasm for Oxford is well documented – 'Does Smiley [one of his patients] really still believe those plays were written by that fellow at Stratford?' – and continued till his death.

The authorship controversy is ultimately a sorry story, with its core of undiluted snobbery, its self-generating conspiracy theories, its manipulated evidence, its reductive view of plays and poems as fiendishly difficult crossword puzzles. The call for an 'open debate' which echoes through Oxfordian websites is probably pointless – there is no common ground of terminology between 'Stratfordians' (as they are reluctantly forced to describe themselves) and anti-Stratfordians. As the director of the Folger Shakespeare Library, Gail Kern Paster, recently put it, 'To ask me about the authorship question . . . is like asking a palaeontologist to debate a creationist's account of the fossil record.' With this inquisitive and open-minded account of the controversy, James Shapiro has done a service to both camps, and indeed to that mysteriously talented glover's son from the Midlands who is at the heart of it all.

II

Conversing with Giants

Antonio Pigafetta in the New World
[1998]

There are stories about giants in just about every language in the
world, but this one is different. The earliest surviving version
of it is found in manuscript copies, in both French and Italian,
dating from the early 1520s. It begins as follows:

> One day, quite unexpectedly, we saw a giant. He was on the
> shore of the sea, completely naked, dancing and leaping and
> singing, and as he sang he poured sand and dust over his head.
> The Captain sent one of the sailors over to him. He told the
> sailor to sing and leap like the giant, so as to reassure him and
> show him friendship. This the sailor did, and presently led the
> giant to a little island where the Captain was waiting. When the
> giant stood before us he began to be astonished and afraid, and
> he raised one finger upwards, thinking that we came from
> heaven. He was so tall that the tallest of us only came up to his
> waist, and his body was very well built. He had a large face
> painted red all over, and his eyes were painted yellow, and there
> were two hearts painted on his cheeks. He had only a little hair
> on his head; this was painted white. When he came before the
> Captain he had clothed himself in the skin of a certain beast,
> very skilfully sewn. This creature has the head and ears of a
> mule, a neck and body like a camel's, the legs of a deer, and the
> tail of a horse. There is a great quantity of these creatures here.
> The giant's feet were also covered with the skin of this animal,
> made into shoes . . . The Captain had food and drink brought to

the giant, and then the men showed him some things, among
them a steel mirror. When the giant saw his likeness in it, he was
greatly terrified, and leapt backwards, and in doing so knocked
down three or four of our men.

There are further incidents, to which I will return, but perhaps
certain details have already suggested what is special about this
story, what makes it different from Odysseus' encounter with
the Cyclops or Jack's adventures up the beanstalk. The difference is that this is not a legend or fairy tale; it is an encounter
that really happened. It occurred at a specific time and place, and
was witnessed by several other people besides the narrator. This
is, in other words, a piece of travel-writing. It belongs to a genre
that might be called – to borrow the title of another sixteenth-
century travel-book – 'News out of the New World'. This does
not necessarily dispose us to believe the story. Travel-writers
often exaggerate and sometimes lie, and when they have been at
sea for nearly a year they may perhaps be expected to do
both. An encounter with a giant certainly makes for good
copy – perhaps suspiciously so.

But on the question of belief I reserve judgement. What
interests me is precisely the ambiguity of the story. It is a true
report that sounds like a fairy tale; it is a fairy tale that real
people have experienced.

*

The author of this account was a young Italian gentleman called
Antonio Pigafetta: an unsung hero of early sea travel. He was a
member of the expedition commanded by the Portuguese
adventurer Fernão de Magalhães, better known as Magellan, an
expedition famous for achieving the first circumnavigation of
the world. The incident he is describing took place around the
beginning of June 1520, on the coast of what is now Argentina.

Magellan himself is the 'Captain' referred to in Pigafetta's account.

Little is known of Pigafetta's early life. He was born in the northern Italian town of Vicenza, probably in the year 1486. He may have seen some military service against the Turks – he compares the arrows of the 'giant' to Turkish arrows – but the first certain knowledge we have of him is in early 1519, when he turns up in Barcelona in the service of another Vicentino, Monsignore Francisco Chiericati, a churchman and politician who was then the Protonotario, or papal ambassador, to the court of the Spanish king and Holy Roman Emperor, Charles V.

There Pigafetta first learned of the 'small armada of five ships' being prepared by Magellan in Seville, and of its daring intention to sail not just to the New World of America, as others had done since the pioneering voyages of Columbus and Vespucci in the 1490s, but beyond it, in search of a new route to the spice-rich islands of the East Indies. He promptly set off for Seville and signed up for the expedition. He describes this decision with a characteristic mix of awe and nonchalance:

> I knew the very great and awful things of the ocean, both from my reading of books and from conversing with certain learned and well-informed people who attended on my master the Protonotario. So now I determined to experiment, and to see with my own eyes some part of those things.

In contemporary documents Pigafetta is described as '*criado del capitán*': he is Magellan's aide or assistant. He is also described as a '*sobresaliente*', or supernumerary. He was not, in other words, a regular member of the crew. He was not primarily a sailor at all, though he was a scholar of sorts, well grounded in the mathematics and astronomy of the day: among his extant writings is a learned treatise on the computation of longitude. He was also a political servant, and is careful to note that his decision to join

Magellan's fleet was done 'with the favour' of both the Protonotario and the Spanish king.

What these terms and contexts add up to is this: Pigafetta was,
probably for the first time on a voyage of this sort, specifically
there in order to write about it. He was the observer, the chron-
icler, the reporter. His 'desire', and that of his masters, was 'that
it might be said I had performed this voyage, and had seen well
with my own eyes the things hereafter written'. The account he
produced – drily entitled, in the French manuscript from which
I am quoting, *Navigation et descouvrement de la Indie supérieure* – is
mostly a fulfilment of this aim. It is lucid, factual, and demonstrably based on a journal or logbook kept throughout the voyage.

If his meeting with the 'giant' seems to us an exaggeration or
a lie, it was surely not intended to be so. Was it something more
like a hallucination, something so powerfully imagined that it
seemed to be real?

*

The mariner bound for the New World faced many dangers.
There were the tempests and twenty-foot waves of the Atlantic; the diseases and brutalities of life aboard ship; the threat of
piracy or enemy action. There were the man-eating fish with
teeth like saws which the Spanish sailors called *tiburón*. There
were the periods of privation when men ate sawdust and oxhide,
and dead rats fetched half a ducat apiece. These, perhaps, were
some of the 'great and awful things' envisaged by Antonio
Pigafetta as he boarded Magellan's flagship, the *Trinidad*, in
August 1519. Most of them he would come to experience in the
course of his three-year journey round the world. But no less
pressing were the dangers of the imagination, the tricks of the
mind, the visions that came when darkness fell and the sea was
calm and he lay in his little cabin with his nostrils filled with the
bonfire-smoke of *estrenque*, the faggots of dried esparto grass

they burned on the poop as a beacon to the other vessels of the fleet, straggling along somewhere out there on the Ocean Sea.

For the ancient world, to which Pigafetta still partly belonged, the sea was a place peopled with apparitions: the sirens, mermaids, monsters and gods of Classical mythology. In the Bible, too, the sea is associated with visions – 'They that go down to the sea in ships, that do business in great waters, these see the works of the Lord and His wonders in the deep' (Psalm 107). In the early Christian tradition these sea visions are elaborated into a darker idea of the 'deep' and its contents. St Augustine says the sea is 'the element subject to the devil'. It is a 'gloomy abyss', the remains of the original pit of hell, and is inhabited by demons. This is already some way towards the interpretations of modern psychoanalysis, in which the sea is thought of as a symbol or archetype of the unconscious. Jung refers to the visions associated with the sea as 'invasions by unconscious contents'.

To a man of learning like Pigafetta this lent a magical dimension to that long and arduous sea-crossing, and some of it surfaces into his narrative. In the midst of a storm, he writes,

> The body of St Anselm appeared to us . . . in the form of a fire lighted at the summit of the mainmast, and remained there near two hours and a half, which comforted us greatly, for we were in tears only expecting the hour of our perishing. And when that holy light was going away from us, it gave out such brilliance in our eyes that for nearly a quarter of an hour we were like people blinded and calling for mercy . . . It is to be noted that whenever that light which represents St Anselm shows itself and descends on a vessel in a storm at sea, that vessel is never lost. Immediately this light departed, the sea grew calmer, and then we saw various kinds of birds among which were some that had no fundament.

This is not a hallucination – he is describing the electrical phenomenon known as St Elmo's Fire – but the language tends

towards the visionary, and ends with this decidedly odd seabird
that lacks an anus.

One has a sense of mental disorder here. Already the strange
but true – 'There are also fish that fly' – begins to mingle indis-
tinguishably with the strange but not quite true. The grasp on
what is possible grows weaker. And then, on St Lucy's Day, 13
December 1519, after nearly four months at sea, the fleet touched
land on the coast of Brazil, and they were in the New World,
where just about anything was possible.

At first they were in territory already explored and margin-
ally settled by Europeans. Some of the crew had been there
before. They were careful to avoid the settlers, who were Portuguese (Magellan had deserted the Portuguese in favour of Spain,
and his expedition was designed to break their monopoly over
the East Indian spice-trade). But after the hazards of the crossing
this was paradise. The climate was sweet, the land abundant, the
natives amiable. They dined on tapir meat and 'a fruit named
battate [sweet potato] which has the taste of chestnut and is the
length of a shuttle'. A sense of relief and assurance is reflected in
Pigafetta's text, which is busily reportorial at this point.

But as they moved slowly south, away from 'the equinoctial
line', or equator, in search of the desired passage to the Pacific
Ocean, they began to enter the kind of unknown and topo-
graphically hostile landscape which is the real stuff of the New
World experience. *Hic finis chartae viaeque*: here ends the map,
here ends the known way.

By the end of March 1520, more than four months after their
first landfall, the fleet was coasting down along the grey, wind-
whipped tundra of what is now called Patagonia. They saw
penguins, which Pigafetta calls 'sea geese', and walrus ('sea
wolves'). The weather was worsening, the companies were restless. Here, at a location which Pigafetta accurately estimated as
'forty-nine degrees and a half in the Antarctic heavens' (i.e. 49°

1. Thomas Coryate hitches a ride. Title-page of the first edition of his newsletters from India (1616).

2. John Aubrey at forty, in a pencil and chalk portrait by William Faithorne the Younger (1666).

3. The alchemist and clairvoyant Edward Kelley. This engraving by Franz Cleyn (1659) is the earliest surviving portrait.

4. Křivoklát Castle in the Czech Republic, where Kelley was imprisoned in 1591.

5. Dynastic harvest. William Brooke, tenth Baron Cobham, and his family, painted in 1567.

6. A grim-looking Ben Jonson, in the engraving by Robert Vaughan from the mid 1620s.

7. Decoding Shakespeare. Baconian devotee Dr Orville Ward Owen's 'cipher wheel', photographed in Detroit in the 1890s.

8. Castle ruins above La Petrella Salto, scene of the Cenci murder in 1598.

9. 'A fallen angel'. Seventeenth-century painting attributed to Guido Reni, long thought to be a portrait of the glamorous murderer Beatrice Cenci.

10. The 'Manfred portrait', discovered in an attic in 1981, and claimed to be an unknown portrait of Lord Byron.

P.S. On the road down I began a little book of our conversations, &c. mine & the statue's. You shall see it when I come back. I have been *here a month yesterday.

My dear Sir,

Tuesday

Here, without loss of time, in order that I may have your opinion upon it, is little Yes & No's letter in answer to my last. You are to understand I had particularly desired her to transmit me no more letters, & I have been obliged to send off sixteen pounds in consequence of three she sent me.

London Feb 26

Sir,

I should not have disregarded your injunction, not to send any letters which might come for you had I not promised the Gentleman who left the inclosed to forward it the earliest opportunity as he said it was of consequence.

Mr. Patmore called the day after you left town. My Mother and myself are much obliged by your kind offer [of tickets for the play] but must decline accepting it. — All my family send their best respects to you in which they are joined by

yours truly

A Book intitled Somer's

variety of English men ———— Lyies has been left. Likewise your child of the Fight for Mr. S.Colburn.

11. 'Little Yes & No's letter'. William Hazlitt to P. G. Patmore, 5 March 1822, forwarding a copy of one of Sarah Walker's letters to him, here reproduced for the first time.

12. Bet Rimbo. The house in Harar, Ethiopia, where the poet Arthur Rimbaud is said to have lived, seen here in 1994 before restoration.

13. Joseph Lis alias Silver, photographed by the Paris police in 1909.

14. The colossus. Poet, boxer and provocateur Arthur Cravan, Paris, c. 1910.

15. In the hermit's cell. The author visiting Alexander Laime on the Carrao River, Venezuela, 1992.

16. The last picnic. Jim Thompson (*left*) photographed in the Cameron Highlands of Malaysia, a few hours before his disappearance on 26 March 1967.

17. Grip the raven at rest in Philadelphia.

30' S), they found shelter in a wide inlet which they christened Puerto San Julián, after the patron saint of hospitable welcome. They decided to winter there. For two months they saw no one at all. Then one day, around the beginning of June, 'quite unexpectedly', they met the giant.

★

Let us try to separate the elements of truth and fable in this encounter.

The 'giant' was almost certainly a Tehuelche or Tcheulchi, one of the nomadic tribes of Patagonia. They were, and are, a very tall race. Bruce Chatwin describes them as a 'race of copper-skinned hunters whose size, strength and deafening voices belied their docile character'. And that extraordinary hybrid creature of the region whose skins the giant wears – described by Pigafetta as part mule, part camel, part deer and part horse – is also real. It is recognizably enough a guanaco, a smaller cousin of the llama which is still found in the area.

This much is true. The difficulty arises precisely with the description of the man as a 'giant'. This is not just a loose description, since Pigafetta specifically says that the tallest of the Europeans 'came only to his waist'. Nor is he alone in this perception. A fragmentary logbook kept by an unnamed Genoese mariner on the voyage says: 'There were people like savages, and the men were from nine to ten spans high.' A span, the width of an outstretched hand, is generally taken as nine inches: the giants were therefore reckoned by this observer to be as much as seven and a half feet tall. This is certainly an exaggeration, as later travellers were relieved but disappointed to find. In 1698 a French explorer, François Froger, wrote of 'the famous Patagons' – 'Some authors avouch [them] to be eight or ten feet high . . . however, the tallest of them was not above six feet high.' The *Guinness Book of Records* states: 'The Tehuelche of

Patagonia, long regarded as of gigantic stature (i.e. 7–8 ft), have in fact an average height (males) of 5 ft 10 in.'

It would be easy to say that Pigafetta and the Genoese pilot were exaggerating and leave it at that. But this seems uncharacteristic of Pigafetta. I would say that the exaggeration is something intrinsic to the occasion, rather than supplied later for literary effect or personal vainglory. The magnification of the Tehuelche into a giant occurs right there and then, in the impact of that first meeting. The emptiness of the landscape, the lack of visual comparison, would also be a factor.

Pigafetta really thought that he was dealing with a giant, really felt he was a waist-high pygmy beside him. That was how it seemed to him and to others. It was a kind of collective mirage conjured up out of the freezing deserts of Patagonia.

*

We have to imagine what it was like to deal with these experiences, thousands of miles away from all that was familiar. The sheer novelty of the New World – its people, its creatures, its flora – was challenging in a way we find hard to appreciate today, when so much is already prepared in our minds, already mapped out, the impact of difference softened to a pleasant notion of the picturesque.

How did the traveller deal with all this strangeness? He did so by finding some kind of precedent: an illusion, at least, of familiarity. And since there was often no actual precedent within his experience, he resorted to other sources – to the reservoir of travellers' tales, partly printed, partly oral; and to the folk stories and legends of his European culture. In this way much of the 'discovery' of America involved an importing of images and ideas and indeed fantasies from Europe. Like the sea itself, *terra incognita* became a place of wonders, an 'invasion of unconscious contents'.

There are many instances of this in the writings of Columbus and Vespucci. Columbus's obsession with cannibals derives in part from his avid reading of early travel-writers like Marco Polo and Sir John Mandeville, whose accounts abound in *anthropophagi*, or man-eaters. Columbus actually invented the word 'cannibal' himself – it was a mishearing of the tribal name 'Carib' – but it was inspired by an idea, a fear, he brought with him. The word first appears (as '*Caniba*') in a journal-entry dated 23 November 1492. Columbus also reported the existence of a tribe of 'dog-faced men' on one of the Caribbean islands. These, too, were an echo of Marco Polo, who wrote of certain supposed inhabitants of the Andaman Islands: 'They have heads like dogs, and teeth and eyes like dogs; for I assure you that the whole aspect of their faces is that of big mastiffs. They are a very cruel race: whenever they can get hold of a man who is not one of their kind, they devour him.' This adds – via Latin *canis*, dog – to his idea of the Caniba or Carib as monstrous subhuman creatures.

Another spectre conjured up in the New World is the Amazon. On his first voyage Columbus heard of certain female warriors inhabiting the island of Matinino (Martinique). As he understood it, they lived without men, they fought with bows and arrows, and they wore armour ('plates of copper'). He called them, naturally enough – though obviously without any input from his Arawak informants – 'Amazons'. The Amazons, it is well known, belong to Greek mythology. They were depicted as a tribe of warrior women who had swept down from the hills of Scythia to occupy various Hellenic sites, notably the Isle of Lesbos. They shunned men, except once a year for the purposes of procreation; they killed male offspring; they cut off their right breasts to facilitate the pulling back of the bowstring (hence their name, from Greek *a mastos*, 'without breast'). These formidable women are to be found in all sorts of Classical and medieval sources. They encode, not very opaquely, a whole range of male sexual fears and fantasies. Columbus himself gives a long and rather erotic gloss on the subject in his commentary on the *Historia rerum* of Aeneas Sylvius. And here, on this first voyage, he imports them wholesale into the New World.

On his second voyage, in 1493, Columbus actually encountered armed Carib women on the island of Guadeloupe. They were suitably fierce, but otherwise shared none of the characteristics of the Classical Amazons. They did not live without men, nor did they cut off their breasts. But by then the connection was made, the legend was alive. It circulated, it gripped the imagination, and when, fifty years after Columbus, Francisco de Orellana encountered female warriors in the hinterlands of Peru, it was natural that he too should believe they were Amazons, and equally natural, in this nameless continent, that the river he was travelling down should thereafter be called the Amazon.

The cannibal, the dog-faced man, the Amazon dominatrix: these are some of the chimeras that haunt the traveller in the New World. (The cannibal is not quite a chimera, of course, but the practice of cannibalism was certainly not rife in the Caribbean in the way it was painted to be.) The reader of Amerigo Vespucci's *Lettera delle isole novamente trovate*, meanwhile, would learn that there were also dragons in the New World. Vespucci had seen one being captured and cooked by Brazilian Indians: 'Their feet are long and thick, and armed with big claws; they have a hard skin and are of various colours; they have the muzzle and aspect of a serpent, and from their snouts there rises a crest like a saw which runs along the middle of the back as far as the tip of the tail.' This dragon, whose 'appearance was so foul that we marvelled at its loathsomeness', was in reality an iguana.

There is a common thread to these New World prodigies.

They seem to represent an unconscious fear of being devoured, swallowed up, a fear of disappearing into the mysterious other-ness of the New World. The traditional giants of legend and fairy tale have also this devouring aspect: 'I'll grind his bones to make my bread.'

★

Like those earlier travellers, Antonio Pigafetta set off on his journey into the unknown with certain preconceptions about what he would find. He knew of the 'great and awful things of the ocean', he tells us, both from his 'reading of books' and from conversing with 'well-informed people'. We cannot be certain what he had read – the only text he actually mentions in his narrative is Aristotle's *De coelo et mundo* – but it seems likely he knew the writings of the Florentine explorer Amerigo Vespucci, such as the *Lettera* quoted above on the subject of Brazilian 'dragons'. Vespucci was an influential figure, though now some-what discredited – he is commemorated in the name 'America', though only on the basis of his spurious claim to have landed on the American mainland in 1497, a year before Columbus's actual arrival there. He was, like Pigafetta, a man of some culti-vation and social standing. The family had been well known in Medici Florence; his sister-in-law Simonetta was the swan-necked beauty who modelled for Botticelli's *Birth of Venus*.

Vespucci's *Lettera*, which was published in Florence in about 1505, may indeed be a source of Pigafetta's giants (in the sense that Marco Polo was the source of Columbus's cannibals), for one of its more memorable episodes was an encounter with 'giants' on the island of Curaçao. Vespucci and his companions first saw five women 'so lofty in stature that we gazed at them in astonishment'. They were 'taller than a tall man'. The travellers were tempted to capture them and 'carry them to Castille as a prodigy', but were scared off by the emergence of a group of men who were even bigger. These men 'went entirely naked'. They were 'so well-built that it was a famous sight to see them, but they put us into such uneasiness that we would much rather have been back in our ships'.

Vespucci concludes: 'I call that island the Isle of Giants, because of their great size.' The legend '*Gigantes*' was duly appended to Curaçao in various early sixteenth-century maps. It is not hard to see Pigafetta's experiences in Patagonia as an echo, a confirmation of what he has read in Vespucci's *Lettera*. He has anticipated the presence of giants in the New World, and suddenly, with a lurch of fear in his stomach, he sees one.

There is another book to be considered, one that may hold a key to the name of the region, Patagonia. According to Pigafetta it was Magellan himself who coined this name: 'The Captain named this kind of people Pathagoni'. The customary interpretation is that *patagón* is intended to mean 'big foot' (from Spanish *pata*, a foot or paw), and that it relates to the footwear of the natives: huge galoshes of guanaco hide packed with straw. But there is another possible derivation, which is that the 'giants' of the region reminded Magellan of a creature that featured in a popular romance, *Primaleon of Greece*. In this, the hero Primaleon sails to a faraway island where the natives eat raw flesh and wear animal skins. They live in fear of a huge half-human monster 'with a head like a dog' in the interior of the island. Primaleon heroically vanquishes it, and carries it back to his homeland, 'Polonia', where it is civilized by the kind attentions of Princess Zephira. This giant monster with the bestial features is called the 'Great Patagon'.

A Spanish edition of *Primaleon* was published in 1512, seven years before Magellan's departure. Its imagery has a strong tinge of the New World about it. Is this the source of Magellan's name for the giants of San Julián – another of these imagined precedents which the traveller reaches for when faced with the extraordinary?

★

There was a period of nearly three months between the first sighting of the Tehuelche giant and the fleet's departure from San Julián. During this time Pigafetta came to know two of the giants quite well. They were baptized and given Christian names (Juan and Pablo) and were kept on board ship. They continue to seem like fairy-tale giants – 'they ate a large basketful of biscuit, and rats without skinning them, and they drank half a bucket of water at one go' – but also they begin to emerge as human characters. Of Juan, Pigafetta says:

> He was a gracious and amiable person, who liked to dance and leap. When he leaped he made holes in the ground where he landed to the depth of a palm. He was a long time with us . . . This giant pronounced the name of Jesus, the Paternoster, the Ave Maria, and his own name as clearly as we did. But he had a terribly strong and loud voice.

Over the weeks and months of the bitter Patagonian winter Pigafetta observed them, and conversed with them, and learned something of Tehuelche society and culture:

> They have no houses, but have huts made of the skins of the animals with which they clothe themselves, and they go hither and thither with these huts of theirs as the Egyptians [i.e. gypsies] do . . .
>
> When they go hunting they wear a cord of cotton around their heads from which they hang their arrows, and they tie up their genitals inside their bodies on account of the severe cold . . .
>
> They eat a certain white powder made of roots [probably a form of manioc]. Sometimes they eat thistles . . .

When these giants have a stomach ache they do not take medicine, but put an arrow, about two foot long, down their throats, and then they vomit up a green bile mixed with blood . . . When they have a headache they make a cut across the forehead and also on the arms and legs, to draw blood from several parts of their bodies. One of the two who were in our ship told me that the blood did not choose to remain in the place of the body where the pain was felt.

Of their pagan religion he relates:

He [Pablo] told us, by signs, that he had seen devils with two horns on their heads, and long hair down to their feet, who breathed fire out of their mouths and their rumps. The greatest of these devils is called in their language Setebos.

This explains an earlier comment about the giants: 'They began to be enraged, and to foam like bulls, crying out very loud, *Setebos.*' There is a literary reverberation here, for this sentence appears in Tudor English ('They roared lyke bulles, & cryed uppon theyr great devill Setebos') in Richard Eden's *History of Travayle in the West and East Indies* (1577), which includes an abbreviated translation of Pigafetta's narrative. Here it was read by Shakespeare, and used for his own version of the New World native, Caliban in *The Tempest*, who cries: 'O Setebos! These be brave spirits indeed.' Thus Caliban, who is anagrammatically a cannibal, is also in some measure a Patagonian; and thus the reality of this encounter on the shores of Argentina merges back into the fictional world from which it partly arose.

Towards the end of Pigafetta's stay in San Julián, there comes a moment of great poignancy, a reaching out across the huge cultural differences between Europe and the New World, across this curiously blurred frontier between the real and the fictional. The giant called Pablo has fallen sick. He is in a cabin of the ship. Pigafetta is there with him:

> He asked me for *capac*, or bread, for this is the name they give to
> that root which they use for bread; and for *olla*, or water. And
> when he saw me write these names down, and afterwards ask
> him for other names, he understood what I was doing with the
> pen in my hand.

At this moment the relationship between them seems at last to
become whole. The point of view changes. Suddenly we see
Pigafetta through the giant's eyes: a small, dark-eyed, rather
earnest man with this curiously plumed implement poised above
the paper.

This moment of illumination enabled Pigafetta to produce a
brief but impressive dictionary entitled, in the French manuscript, 'Vocables des Geans Pathagoniens'. This is a list of ninety
words and phrases in 'Patagonian' – a lexicon quite unpreced-
ented in the European literature on the New World at this date.
About half of the words translated are parts of the body, always
easy to establish on a point-and-tell basis. After the anatomy is
exhausted, the list moves on: to fire, smoke, ice, wind and stars;
to fish, dog, wolf, goose (i.e. penguin) and oyster. Pigafetta
notes the guttural tone of the language – the words are 'pronounced in the throat' – but perhaps the keynote of this lexicon
is not the strangeness of the sounds but the communality of the
world they describe: a sense of what is shared by these two men.

Pigafetta concludes: 'All these words were given to me by this
giant,' and one is touched by his brusque acknowledgement of
this gift he has received from a monster who turns out, after all,
to be a man not much different from himself.

*

There follow the maritime adventures which have earned this
voyage its place in history – the discovery of the southern passage into the Pacific now called the Strait of Magellan; the long
months of privation as they drifted on westwards towards the

Spice Islands; the death of Magellan in a skirmish with natives
in the Philippines; and, on 6 September 1522, the final return to
Seville of a single ship, the *Victoria*, and just eighteen of the 240
men who had set out three years earlier.

Among these survivors was the resourceful reporter Antonio
Pigafetta. At Valladolid he presented to the Spanish king 'neither gold nor silver, but things much more precious in the eyes
of so great a sovereign'. Chief among these was 'a book written
by my hand of all the things that had occurred day by day on
our voyage'. This original journal is lost. The early manuscripts
that do survive – three in French and one in Italian – are essentially a paraphrase of it: 'I have reduced into this small book the
principal things, as well as I could.'

In 1523 he was fêted at a grand reception in Venice. He was
also admitted into the Order of the Knights of Rhodes, and
signs himself thereafter with a flourish, 'Antonio Pigafetta
Cavaliere'. The following year he received permission from the
Venetian Senate to have his account of the voyage printed, but
he does not seem to have done so. The aftermath of his great
adventure is obscure; one perhaps discerns a note of exhaustion.
He died in about 1535, not yet fifty years old.

His house in Vicenza still stands, on the sloping street that was
then called Via della Luna and is now Via Pigafetta. It is a tall and
very handsome house, with a smart dress-shop on the ground
floor. On the façade, either side of the arched Romanesque
doorway, runs an inscription. It has faded over the years, and is
anyway easily missed because it is carved at knee height. According to local tradition it was Antonio himself who had it done.
One might expect it to record something grand and triumphal
about the circumnavigation, about the great and awful things of
the ocean, about going to the uttermost ends of the earth and
back again. But all it says, in slightly ungrammatical French, is:
'*Il nest rose sans espine.*' There is no rose without a thorn.

If there is some deeper resonance in this it escapes me. Perhaps the resonance lies precisely in its simplicity: he had travelled so far to discover this small truth. Or perhaps local tradition is wrong, and this is just a family motto put there by some other early Pigafetta — one who had a smattering of courtly French but had never conversed with giants in Patagonia.

12

'Sneezing . . . Yawning . . . Falling'

The Notebooks of Leonardo da Vinci
[2005]

Leonardo da Vinci is famous for the great variety of his accomplishments – painter, sculptor, inventor, anatomist, engineer, architect, mathematician, musician, and so on – but he is not often remembered as a writer. He was actually a very prolific writer. His surviving papers run to over 7,000 pages (though some of them very small pages), and this is only a part, perhaps about two thirds, of his total output. A few hundred of them are sketches or drawings with no verbal content, and the rest is the mighty hoard of Leonardo's manuscripts and notebooks, unpublished during his lifetime, and jealously preserved after his death in 1519 by his former secretary, Francesco Melzi. They range from complete treatises to scribbled fragments, and all are written in that curious right-to-left 'mirror-script' which makes the intrinsically difficult business of reading them even harder. An early reader compared it to Hebrew – 'he wrote according to the custom of the Jews.'

Leonardo is the writer of these pages, but in most of them he is not a writer in a literary sense. Rather, he is a writer-down of things: a recorder of observations, a pursuer of data, an explorer of thoughts, an inscriber of lists and memoranda. Though he makes some brief excursions into consciously literary forms, the overall tone of his writing is terse, colloquial, practical, laconic. In painting he is a master of nuance, but as a penman he tends to the workmanlike. At its best his writing has a marvellous uncluttered clarity. Beyond the orthographic veil of his script one arrives at what Giorgio Nicodemi called his 'serene and accurate habits of thought'. There are many beautiful sentences in the notebooks. '*Infra 'l sole e noi è tenebre, e pero l'aria pare azzurra*' ('Between the sun and us is darkness, and yet the air seems blue') is a beautiful sentence, but it is not literary style that makes it so. The words are pared back to the quick; it is a statement of lucid simplicity into which complex scientific questions are folded. Conversely, when he tries to be florid and clever – in certain descriptive passages of floods, tempests, battles; in certain brochure-like letters to potential patrons – the results are pretty turgid. If one is thinking of actual literary compositions Leonardo is at his best when writing to entertain: his Aesopian fables, which have that same splendid spareness of diction; his spoof newsletters and riddling mock-prophesies. These are dilettante works, composed for the amusement of the Sforza court in Milan, but they are full of interesting, sometimes eerie, resonances.

This most voluminous writer had a very ambivalent attitude to language and its uses. In a well-known comment Leonardo described himself as an '*omo sanza lettere*', an 'unlettered man'. Specifically he meant that he had not been taught Latin; that he was not a university man schooled in the gentlemanly 'liberal arts' (so-called precisely because they were not bound to the necessity of learning a trade). He had followed instead the course of apprenticeship, an education which took place in a commercial workshop, which taught artisan skills rather than intellectual ones, and which was conducted in Italian rather than Latin. His description of himself as 'unlettered' is in part a sardonic celebration of this more practical form of learning. It occurs in a fragmentary essay whose chief theme is a vigorous disparagement of the 'lettered' – the academics and experts, the *ipse dixit* commentators and abbreviators. They are 'trumpeters and re-citers of the words of others'; they are 'pumped up' with second-hand information. He, the unlettered man, cannot quote the scholarly authorities as they do, 'but I will quote something far greater and more worthy: experience, the mistress of their masters'. There is a touch of social defiance in this. His lack of formal education, his underprivileged beginnings as an illegitimate son in the rural backwater of Vinci, are being turned into a strength. His mind is free of the lumber of precepts; intellectually he is a self-made man.

Though precociously brilliant in the visual arts Leonardo was a late starter as a writer. Some isolated folios survive from the 1470s, when he was in his twenties, but the earliest extant notebooks – the first evidence of a systematic programme of writing – date from the later 1480s, when he was in Milan. One sees the development in the handwriting itself. The early fragments are looped and curlicued and somewhat effortful (a 'notarial' hand, some think, suggestive of training under his notary father, Ser Piero da Vinci). In the Milanese notebooks the orthography is more marshalled and compact, though it is not yet the dense, minimal script of the last years.

There is often a sense with Leonardo that words are something to be mistrusted: first-hand 'experience' ('*sperientia*', which can also be rendered as 'experiment') is all. Beside one of his anatomical drawings of a heart is a block of text which looks like an explanatory caption but which actually reads:

> O writer, what words of yours could describe this whole organism as perfectly as this drawing does? Because you have no true knowledge of it you write confusedly, and convey little understanding of the true form of things . . . How could you describe this heart in words without filling a whole book? And the more minutely you try to write of it the more you confuse the mind of the listener.

Here language itself is associated with lack of clarity. Words get in the way; they equivocate and tangle things up. The riddles and rebuses he cooked up for the Milanese courtiers express a similar idea: that writing is mere trickery, a party-turn. Vasari makes much of Leonardo's lively and witty conversation (though he was too young to have heard it himself), but I have also an opposite impression: a man prone to long, discomfiting silences, a solitary who loved the company of animals. 'Man has great power of speech, but what he says is mostly vain and false; animals have little, but what they say is useful and true.'

In a sense Leonardo's rather prickly relationship with language is a boon for the biographer. Lacking in verbal artifice, well carpentered but seldom much polished, his manuscript writings are a way to get closer to him. His paintings are meticulous and inscrutable, and do not offer much in the way of personal revelation, but in the notebooks we hear him. We hear his speech patterns in the sentences; we catch the timbre of his voice in the rough vernacular spellings of fifteenth-century Tuscan.

Even within the private ambit of the notebooks Leonardo includes little personal material, but the nuggets are there. In a folio on the aerodynamics of bird-flight, squeezed unceremoniously into a corner, we find the famous note about his 'first memory' (or, as Freud preferred, fantasy): 'It seemed to me, when I was in my cradle, that a kite came to me, and opened my mouth with its tail, and struck me several times with its tail inside my lips.' There are other enigmatic fragments ('If freedom is dear to you, do not reveal that my face is the prison of love'), and aphoristic reminders ('Do not be a liar about the past'), and occasional little confessions, as this about lazing in bed: 'In the morning, when the mind is composed and rested, and the body is fit to begin new labours, so many vain pleasures are taken by the mind, imagining to itself impossible things, and by the body, taking those pleasures which often cause a failing of life' (he appears to be talking about masturbation). And there are passages where he taps into his own dream-life, as in the prophecy entitled 'Of Dreaming': 'You will speak with animals of every species and they will speak with you in human language. You will see yourself fall from great heights without harming yourself.'

Leonardo once said that a painting should show 'mental events' ('*accidenti mentali*') through the physical gestures of the figures in it, and I think of this phrase when I read his manuscripts, which are precisely filled with 'mental events', large and small, rigorously annotated, together with a rich mix of ephemera – jokes, doodles, snatches of poetry (Ovid, Horace, Dante), drafts of letters, household accounts, paint recipes, shopping lists, bank statements, and so on – which in some ways tell us more about him than those great works of art and science for which he is famous.

*

Leonardo's manuscripts survive in two forms – in bound collections, compiled after his death, and in notebooks, which are more or less intact from the time when he owned them. The most famous of the great miscellaneous collections is the Codex Atlanticus, in the Biblioteca Ambrosiana in Milan. In its original form, put together in the late sixteenth century by the sculptor and bibliophile Pompeo Leoni, the Codex Atlanticus was a massive leather-bound volume over two feet tall. It contained 481 folios, some of them whole sheets of writing or drawing, but most a montage of smaller items, up to five or six on a page, sometimes glued down and sometimes mounted in windows so that both sides of the paper could be seen. The name of the codex has nothing to do with the ocean, but refers precisely to its large format – it is 'atlas-sized'. The name was coined by a librarian at the Ambrosiana, Baldassare Oltrocchi, who listed it in 1780 as a '*codice in forma atlantica*'. In the 1960s this sumptuous scrapbook was dismantled and reordered so that all its constituent pieces (over 1,100 of them) are now mounted separately.

There are two other major miscellanies, both now in England. One is the collection in the Royal Library at Windsor Castle, which includes the famous folios of anatomical drawings. This is another inheritance from Pompeo Leoni, indeed some of the smaller fragments at Windsor were demonstrably snipped by Leoni out of larger sheets now in the Codex Atlanticus. At some point it was brought to England and entered the collection of Charles I. It surfaced at Kensington Palace in the mid eighteenth century: according to a contemporary account, 'this great curiosity' had been deposited in a 'large and strong chest' during the Civil War, and there lay 'unobserved and forgotten for about 120 years till Mr Dalton fortunately discovered it at the bottom of the same chest in the beginning of the reign of his present Majesty [George III]'. The other major collection is the Codex Arundel in the British Library, a hotchpotch of 283 folios written over a span of nearly forty years. It was purchased in Spain by the Earl of Arundel in the 1630s.

To these collections of actual Leonardo manuscripts one should add another kind of miscellany – the Codex Urbinas in the Vatican, which is a compilation of Leonardo's writings about painting, put together after his death by Francesco Melzi. An abbreviated version was published in Paris in 1651; this digest is generally known as the *Trattato della pittura* ('Treatise on Painting'). At the end of the codex, Melzi lists eighteen Leonardo notebooks which he had used as source material: ten of these are now lost. Some of these lost works may yet surface – two leather-bound volumes of manuscripts were discovered by chance, in Madrid, as recently as 1967, and there have been tantalizing but unconfirmed sightings of the lost treatise on light and shade known to Melzi as 'Libro W'.

The collections are magnificent, but the true spirit of Leonardo is to be found in his notebooks. About twenty-five individual notebooks survive – the exact number depends on how you reckon them, as some of the smaller notebooks have been bound into composite volumes. For instance, the three Forster codices in the Victoria & Albert Museum – formerly owned by Dickens's friend and biographer, John Forster – actually contain five notebooks. The largest concentration of notebooks is in the Institut de France in Paris. They arrived in France en masse in the 1790s, Napoleonic booty expropriated from the Biblioteca Ambrosiana. Others are in Milan, Turin, London, Madrid and Seattle. The last is the home of the Codex Leicester, the furthest-flung of all Leonardo's notebooks, purchased by Bill Gates in 1994 for a reported $30 million.

There have been some pages lost here and there – a light-fingered bibliophile, Count Guglielmo Libri, stole several in the mid nineteenth century – but these notebooks are essentially as Leonardo left them. Some still have their original bindings: he favoured a kind of wrap-around cover of vellum or leather, fastened with a small wooden toggle passed through a loop of cord (an arrangement oddly suggestive of a duffel coat). In size the notebooks range from standard octavo format, which look like what we call exercise-books, down to little pocket-books not much bigger than a pack of playing cards. The latter, which Melzi called *libricini*, served as both notebooks and sketchbooks, and some show clear signs of having been on the road with Leonardo. An eyewitness account of him in Milan mentions 'a little book he had always hanging at his belt'.

The keynote of Leonardo's manuscripts is their diversity, their multiple miscellaneity: there is so much going on. The great lesson of them is that everything is to be questioned, investigated, peered into, worried away at. He sets himself tasks both large and small. Here is a list of things-to-do from a Milanese notebook of *c.* 1508: 'Describe how the clouds are formed and how they dissolve, and what causes vapour to rise from the waters of the earth into the air, and the causes of mists and of the air becoming thickened, and why it appears more or less blue at different times.' And here is another, from one of the anatomical folios: 'Describe what sneezing is, what yawning is, the falling sickness, spasm, paralysis, shivering with cold, sweating, fatigue, hunger, sleep, thirst, lust.' And another: 'Describe the tongue of the woodpecker.'

★

One of the pleasures of Leonardo's manuscripts is their populousness. They are filled with people, or at any rate with names – friends, contacts, creditors, patrons, apprentices, lovers – and sometimes with fragments of other handwritings which testify to a moment of shared physical presence.

On a folio in the Codex Atlanticus is a list of artworks, compiled by Leonardo in about 1482 as he prepared to leave Florence for Milan. It is often transcribed, for its biographical and arthistorical value, but what is not usually mentioned is that the first two lines were written by someone else, after the rest of the list, and upside down to it. On another Atlanticus folio is a whole sonnet written in the same hand; it is almost entirely obscured with an ink blot, but the opening lines are partly legible –

> *Lionardo mio non avete d* [. . .]
> *Lionardo perche tanto penato*
> ['My Leonardo you don't have any [. . .]
> Leonardo, why so troubled?']

The writer of these words was a popular poet of the day, Antonio Cammelli. He was a native of the Tuscan town of Pistoia, where Leonardo's aunt lived, and where Leonardo himself was probably holed up in 1477, in the aftermath of a run-in with the Florentine vice-squad the previous year. Cammelli is a great character and a good writer – he is one of those slangy, satirical poets known collectively as the 'Burchielleschi', after an early exponent of the genre, a Florentine barber nicknamed 'Il Burchiello'. The name derives from the phrase *alla burchia*, meaning 'in haste' or 'higgledy-piggledy' – they are 'poets in a hurry', dashing off rough and often ribald sonnets with a feel of improvisation. They were the jazz-poets or rap-artists of the Quattrocento, very different from refined neo-Petrarchan poets like Poliziano and Landucci. Some of Cammelli's satirical poems are just a catalogue of ingenious insults – the railing which he calls *'dire pepe'*, 'talking pepper' – but he has also a likeable, down-at-heel nonchalance. The elegant Cardinal Bibbiena summed up Cammelli's abrasive style well enough: *'le facezie, il sale, il miele'* – 'jokes, salt and honey'.

I was glad to become acquainted with Cammelli through his presence in Leonardo's manuscripts, and with the even more scurrilous Tuscan satirist Bernardo Bellincioni, with whom Leonardo later collaborated in a Milanese theatrical extravaganza called *Il Paradiso*. They are not perhaps the kind of people one would associate with the great 'Renaissance Man' of legend, but they were flesh-and-blood companions of the real Leonardo in Florence in the late 1470s. Leonardo's skills as a player of the *lira da braccio* (not a harp-shaped lyre, but an early kind of violin) would be connected with these rimesters.

Another man whose handwriting is found in these pages is the engaging Tommaso di Giovanni Masini, generally known under the imposing alias of 'Zoroastro', though also answering to other nicknames such as 'Indovino' ('Fortune-teller') and 'Gallozzolo' ('Gall-nut'). A humble gardener's son from Peretola, near Florence, Tommaso gained a picturesque reputation as an alchemist and magician; he was also a vegetarian (as

Leonardo was reputed to be) – 'he would not kill a flea for any reason whatever; he preferred to dress in linen so as not to wear something dead.' He flits through Leonardo's story, over many decades – he probably joined Leonardo's workshop in Florence as a teenager in the late 1470s, and is later mentioned (as 'Geroastro') as part of Leonardo's entourage in Milan. In 1505, back in Florence, he is documented 'grinding colours' for the *Battle of Anghiari* fresco in the Palazzo Vecchio. Despite his picturesque reputation, he appears in eminently practical roles in Leonardo's notebooks. A list of studio activities in 1493 mentions him making candlesticks; a contemporary described him as a 'blacksmith'. In 1493 Leonardo was involved in casting the gigantic equestrian bronze known as the Sforza Horse, and doubtless Masini was involved in that too, and in many other projects: military, architectural and indeed aviational. Given his alchemical skills, I cannot resist attributing to him a recipe written out by Leonardo, probably in the late 1480s. Headed 'Deadly smoke' ('*Fumo mortale*'), and appearing on a sheet related to naval warfare, its constituents are:

Arsenic mixed with sulphur and realgar
Medicinal rosewater
Venom of toad – that is, land-toad
Slaver of mad dog
Decoction of dogwood berries
Tarantula from Taranto

Tommaso died in Rome in 1520, the year after Leonardo. A Latin epitaph inscribed on his tomb in Sant'Agata dei Goti commemorated him as 'Zoroastro Masino, a man outstanding for his probity, his innocence and his liberality, and a true Philosopher who looked into the darkness of Nature to the admirable benefit of Nature herself'. Leonardo would not have minded this for his own epitaph: '*ad naturae obscuritatem spectat . . .*'

It was Tommaso Masini who compiled a list of Leonardo's household expenses on two sheets now in the Codex Arundel – a list all the more pungent because it belongs to the summer of 1504, and therefore offers a kind of domestic glimpse behind the scenes of the *Mona Lisa*, on which Leonardo was then at work. 'On the morning of St Zanobio's Day, 25 May 1504, I had from Lionardo Vinci 15 gold ducats and began to spend them,' Tommaso writes. His shopping is itemized as follows: clothes, eggs, velvet, wine, bread, meat, mulberries, mushrooms, salad, fruit, candles, a partridge, flour. Another shopping list, in Leonardo's hand, belongs to around the same time. In this he records buying a rather spicier fare of peppered bread (*'pane inpepato'*), eels and apricots, as well as two dozen laces, a sword and a knife, and a little cross purchased from a man called Paolo. There is a visit to the barber, for he kept himself well groomed, and then a curious item which has attracted some note: *'per dire la ventura . . . 6 soldi'*. That a man so axiomatically unimpressed by superstition spent good money for 'having his fortune told' is surprising – what is it that he wishes to know about his destiny? Further accountings of 1504 are on a page of the Codex Atlanticus – 'On the morning of Friday 19 July I have 7 florins left and 22 in the cashbox,' etc. – and on the same page, poignantly mingled among the day-to-day disbursements, Leonardo records the death of his father: 'On Wednesday at the 7th hour Ser Piero da Vinci died, on 9 July 1504.'

The name most frequently found in Leonardo's notebooks is that of 'Salai', which is the nickname (roughly meaning 'Little Devil') of his wayward young apprentice Giacomo Caprotti. He joined Leonardo's Milanese studio in 1490, at the age of ten, and remained with him for nearly thirty years: his companion and confidant, and (on the well-informed testimony of the Milanese painter Giovanni Paolo Lomazzo) his lover. The narration of Giacomo's escapades during his first year of apprenticeship is certainly the longest continuous account of another person's activities to be found in all Leonardo's writings. Its intention is precisely an account, since it itemizes the expenses arising from the boy's misdeeds. It seems to have been written at a single sitting: the ink colour is a uniform dark brown. It was no doubt intended for Giacomo's father, who was to foot the bill, but it acquires *in extenso* a curiously personal coloration, a tone of exasperated fondness, so that what is intended as a rather crotchety list of complaints achieves a quality almost of reverie:

> On the second day [23 July 1490] I had 2 shirts cut for him, a pair of stockings and a jerkin, and when I put aside the money to pay for these things he stole the money out of my purse, and I could never make him confess, though I was quite certain of it. *4 lire.*

> The day after this I went to supper with Giacomo Andrea, and the aforesaid Giacomo ate for 2, and did mischief for 4, inasfar as he broke three oil-flasks, and knocked over the wine, and after this he came to supper where I . . . [sentence unfinished]

> *Item.* On 7 September he stole a pen worth 22 soldi from Marco [d'Oggiono], who was living with me. It was a silverpoint pen, and he took it from Marco's studio, and after Marco had searched all over for it, he found it hidden in the said Giacomo's chest. *1 lira.*

> *Item.* On the 26th January following, I was at the house of Messer Galeazzo da Sanseverino, arranging the pageant for his joust, and certain footmen had undressed to try on costumes for the wild men in the pageant. One of them left his purse lying on a bed, among some clothes, and Giacomo got at it and took all the money he could find in it. *2 lire, 4 soldi.*

> *Item.* At that same house Maestro Agostino da Pavia gave me a Turkish hide to have a pair of short boots made, and within a month this Giacomo had stolen it from me, and sold it to a

shoemaker for 20 soldi, and with the money, as he himself confessed to me, he bought aniseed sweets. *2 lire*.

Item. Again, on the 2ⁿᵈ April, Giovan Antonio [Boltraffio], having left a silverpoint on top of one of his drawings, this Giacomo
stole it. And this was of the value of 24 soldi. *1 lira, 4 soldi*.

In the margin, summing it all up, Leonardo writes four words:
'*ladro bugiardo ostinato ghiotto*' – 'thief, liar, stubborn, greedy'. The
account finishes with a list of clothing expenses, from which it
appears that Salai had been furnished with one cloak, six shirts,
three jerkins, four pairs of stockings, one lined doublet, twenty-
four pairs of shoes, a cap and some laces, at a total cost of
thirty-two lire.

Here again one finds the notebooks full of physical presence,
and of things – the aniseed gobstoppers, the Turkish leather, the
purse on the bed, the little flasks of oil broken on the floor.

★

Perhaps the most surprising feature of the Leonardo notebooks
is their scattering of levity. One of my favourite moments of
light relief is a passage in a notebook of *c*. 1508, which has the
dense and rebarbative look of one of his scientific 'demonstra-
tions', but which is actually entitled 'Why dogs willingly sniff
one another's bottoms' (I like that 'willingly'), and which solemnly discusses the issues of canine sociology involved.

Leonardo liked jokes, and he wrote a number of them down.
This is a conventional activity to which no special significance
should be attached – the *zibaldoni*, or commonplace books, of the
day are full of them – but it seems that humour was a part of
his life. The jokes are of variable quality: I suppose the written-
down joke must be considered a pale reflection of the told
joke – one must imagine the magisterially deadpan delivery.
Some of them turn on terrible puns, and some seem to have lost

whatever point they had down a lexical cul-de-sac. Some are satirical, particularly anti-clerical, and some are mildly dirty, in what we would think of as a robust Chaucerian vein. Both the satire and the bawdy have antecedents in the *novelle* of Boccaccio and his imitators, and more immediately in the Renaissance collections of *facezie* – 'pleasantries' – pre-eminently those of Poggio Bracciolini, some of which are quite salty. Here are a couple of Leonardian rib-ticklers written down in the early 1490s:

> A man was trying to prove on the authority of Pythagoras that he had lived in this world before, and another man would not accept his argument. So the first man said, 'As a sign that I have been here before, I remember that you were a miller.' And the other, thinking this was said to mock him, replied, 'You are right, for now I remember you were the ass which carried the flour for me.'

> A woman was washing clothes, and her feet were very red with cold. A priest who was passing by was amazed by this, and asked her where the redness came from, to which the woman replied that it was caused by a fire underneath her. Then the priest took in hand that part of him which made him more priest than nun, and drawing near to her, asked her very politely if she would be kind enough to light up his candle.

And here is a literary joke: 'If Petrarch was so madly in love with bay leaves, it's because they taste so good with sausage and thrush,' punning on *lauro*, the bay tree, and Laura, to whom Petrarch's love-poems are addressed. To our ears these jokes are not very funny, but they carry a far-off sound of laughter which we might otherwise forget to listen for.

13

The Secrets of St Proculus

A Reattribution

[1999]

In the former *fabbriceria*, or works department, of the Basilica di San Petronio in Bologna stands a white marble statue. It represents the Christian martyr St Proculus, who was beheaded in Bologna in AD 19 and is one of the city's favourite saints. According to the conventional wisdom it was sculpted in the late 1520s, precisely here in the *fabbriceria*, by a jobbing sculptor named Alfonso Lombardi.

If you crouch down below the saint and peer up between his legs – a procedure that is best managed alone, for fear of offending local sensibilities – you can see a horizontal line, where the tasselled hem of his tunic overhangs his smooth muscular thighs. The question is: is this line a mere indentation, or is it a join of two separate pieces of marble? The art historian and archaeologist Mario Pincherle says it is the latter – he claims to have slid the blade of a knife into it, one day in the 1970s. I am unable to repeat this experiment and so remain uncertain. According to Pincherle only the bottom half of the sculpture is by Lombardi. The top half, he believes, is the work of the young Michelangelo.

It is documented that Michelangelo visited Bologna in late 1494, at the age of nineteen, and stayed there several months. He sculpted at least two of the figures on the reliquary ark in the church of San Domenico, for which he was paid twelve scudi. But these are small works, around two feet tall. If Pincherle is right about the St Proculus statue, it would be the earliest life-size sculpture by Michelangelo in existence.

I knew nothing of this when I first met Pincherle last year, in a cheerful restaurant called La Baita, set among the chestnut woods of Monte Serra in northern Tuscany, and known for its down-home dishes of hare and wild boar. He is a short, magisterial figure with a shock of white curls, born into a Bolognese Jewish family of scientists and mathematicians, but now living in Tuscany. He will be eighty this year, and if his schedule goes according to plan he will publish his hundredth book. Art history is only one of his interests. His publications include various learned excursions into early biblical history, ancient languages, palaeotechnology and Egyptology. His best-known book is *Il quinto Vangelo* ('The Fifth Gospel'), a translation of a Coptic manuscript attributed to the apostle St Thomas. He has also translated texts from Akkadian, the language of Mesopotamia, compared to which, he says, 'Sanskrit is a recent invention.'

When he learned I was researching a book about Renaissance artists, he asked: 'But have you seen the Michelangelos in Bologna?' I confessed I hadn't even heard of them. I was invited to visit him so we could discuss it further.

He lives on the top floor of a modern apartment block in Bientina, with his companion, Giuliana; his wife died some years ago. The main room is predictably filled with books and papers and paintings, but also with microscopes, precision drills and chemical vessels. A man of many sidelines, he makes jewellery out of 'granulated gold', which he prepares according to a technique 'practised in Mesopotamia five millennia ago'. In this process, he explains, the object consists of fused 'microspheres' of gold rather than gold lamina. He sits there like some old alchemist amid the clutter of his arcana. He demonstrates ancient hieroglyphs with a squeaky felt-tip pen. The conversation darts around. I learn he was for some years a practising exorcist.

I steered him back onto the 'unknown' Michelangelos of Bologna. He outlined his theories, and gave me a copy of his book on the subject, *Il sigillo sull'unghia* ('The Sign on the Fingernail'), published in 1980 but now out of print. The title refers to a form of passport used in Renaissance Italy: Michelangelo would have had his thumbnail stamped on entering the city. I asked him if his theories had been accepted by other Michelangelo experts. He made a circling, dismissive gesture with his hands. 'Fifty-fifty,' he said.

So it was that I came to be in Bologna on a chilly January morning, squinting up the white marble skirts of St Proculus, looking for evidence of the supposed join between the Michelangelo torso of *c.* 1494 and the Lombardi legs of *c.* 1528. I noted the various stylistic points which might be compared to known works of Michelangelo: the chisel-cuts used to give an apparent nap to the saint's cloak; the fringing of the tunic; the moulding of the biceps; the disposition of the curling hair. The marble itself, stippled faintly by inclusions of magnetite, is of a type the maestro liked to use.

From the basilica I walked northwards, through the rust and ochre streets of the old city, and up to the hilltop church of San Michele in Bosco, where the city is spread hazily below you and the brick-built basilica in the centre looks like some huge medieval warehouse. In the church is another Lombardi marble, a rather fine Madonna and Child, dated 1533. This, too, is canvassed by Pincherle as an 'unknown' Michelangelo. I taxed a church official with this possibility. He smiled mournfully and stated the obvious counter-argument: the sculptures look something like Michelangelo's because Lombardi was, inevitably, influenced by him.

It was all rather inconclusive, but it had been a pleasant ambulatory day, and I had looked attentively at some statues I might otherwise have ignored. These are the delights of the great Italian pastime of reattribution. I found myself warming defensively towards Alfonso Lombardi – aka Alfonso Citadella,

Alfonso da Lucca or simply, in the Bolognese archives, 'Alfonso the sculptor' – whom Pincherle paints as a talentless and under-hand hack.

A few days later, eager to discuss all this, I paid another visit to Mario in Bientina. I found him in excitable mood. He did not want to talk about Michelangelo; he was no longer interested in such '*robaccia*', or rubbish. He wanted to talk about his forth-coming book, *Il vangelo di Gesù bambino* ('The Gospel of the Baby Jesus'), another foray down the byways of the biblical Apoc-rypha. After that will come his study – or 'solution' – of the mysteries of the Etruscan language. And then a controversial memoir concerning another Bolognese, the famous inventor of the radio, Guglielmo Marconi.

According to Pincherle, Marconi stole his ideas from an obscure inventor from Ancona, one Temistocle Calzecchi Onesti. He was a spiritualist, and got the idea for this 'spiritual telephone' during a séance. He constructed a prototype and brought it to the University of Bologna, where it was tested by Professor Augusto Righi. Marconi, whose best friend was the son of Righi's labora-tory assistant, stole the designs and had them patented at the London Patent Office, where his Irish uncle worked. Thus Pincherle, who says he was told all this, as a child, by Professor Righi's widow; a more sober account of Onesti's contribution says only that in the 1880s he developed a prototype for the *coesore*, or coherer, which was a key part of early radio technology.

It was dark and I was getting ready to leave, but first he wanted me to listen to some music. He put a tape on – a strange lilting dirge, played on some kind of wind instrument, or perhaps an organ. It was, in fact, Beethoven's Moonlight Sonata played back-wards. 'And if you repeat the procedure with the opening of the Ninth Symphony, it is also very interesting . . .' I saw the gleam in his eye. If Beethoven had a secret, it is soon to be revealed.

14

A Renaissance Life of Riley

Ippolito d'Este and Lorenzo de' Medici
[2004 and 2005]

Maintaining the magnificence of the Italian Renaissance was a full-time job – not just for the grandees whose status depended on ostentatious display, but for the army of retainers and servants who worked away in the background to keep the show going. In sixteenth-century Ferrara more than 2,000 men and women worked inside the duke's castle – perhaps 10 per cent of the city's population. Mary Hollingsworth's meticulous account of life in one noble Ferrarese household in the 1530s* is rather like one of those behind-the-scenes documentaries which show the complex workings of some grand hotel or luxury liner.

Her subject is Ippolito d'Este, second son of Alfonso, Duke of Ferrara, and her raw material the cache of Ippolito's personal papers – some 2,000 letters and 200 account books – which she found stacked in a basement storeroom of the Estense archives in Modena.

The d'Este dynasty was one of the oldest in Italy. Their fiefdom included Ferrara, Modena, Ancona and Reggio. There was also a German branch of the family, founded in the late eleventh century, from which are descended the Houses of Brunswick and Hanover, and thence the British royal family. Ippolito's aunt was the formidable Isabella d'Este, Marchioness of Mantua, a voracious collector who typified the epoch's devotion to style and money. His mother was the even more formidable

* Mary Hollingsworth, *The Cardinal's Hat* (Profile, 2004).

Lucrezia Borgia, the illegitimate daughter of Pope Alexander VI. She arrived in Ferrara in 1502 trailing a lurid if largely unsubstantiated reputation for murder, incest and general depravity, but proved to be a popular and dutiful duchess. A supposed portrait by Bartolomeo Veneto shows a disarmingly pretty young woman with blonde ringlets, a posy of daisies, and one small, adolescent-looking breast provocatively displayed. She died giving birth to her ninth child in 1519, when Ippolito was eight years old.

Ippolito had a vaguely illustrious career of the silver-spoon sort. As a second son he was destined for a career in the Church, and it was helpful to inherit the Archbishopric of Milan from his uncle when he was nine years old. He became a leading cardinal, and was tipped as a candidate for the papacy. His jockeying in pursuit of the cardinal's hat, which he finally received from Pope Paul III in 1539, is one of the narratives which Hollingsworth patiently draws out of the ledgers. He later built the magnificent Villa d'Este at Tivoli, and was a patron of the musician Palestrina.

But in the years covered by this book Ippolito is hardly remarkable – a minor Italian princeling in his mid twenties, a B-list Renaissance celebrity, pursuing a life of pleasure, entertainment and light diplomacy. On the death of his father in 1534, he inherited a fine town-house, the Palazzo San Francesco, and a bequest of 13,000 scudi (a skilled craftsman earned about fifty scudi a year), together with various Church benefices and agricultural estates, and perks such as a tax on all live animals entering the city. He hunted, gambled, partied and progressed, with his entourage of footmen liveried in orange and white, and his valets in black velvet, and his hunting-dogs in silver-encrusted collars.

Ippolito comes across as a man of charm and discernment, and we hear of many small acts of charity which relieve the egotistic careerism of his playboy-prelate lifestyle. But the great achievement of Hollingsworth's book is its resurrection of the supporting cast of his stewards, valets, secretaries, estate managers, cooks, larderers, launderers, blacksmiths, saddlers, kennel masters, falconers, et al. Her spotlight briefly illuminates the careers of his horse-trainer Pierantonio, his sommelier Zebelino, his French tailor Antoine, and many others, though his mistress Violante, by whom he had a daughter, remains a shadowy figure. She received a Christmas gift of a barrel of malmsey and four capons at Christmas 1536, and is probably the '*persona segreta*' to whom he sent eight jars of carnation petals the following summer. There seems to be no surviving portrait of Ippolito, though there is a moody Titian portrait of his master of the wardrobe, Tommaso Mosto.

The Titian reminds us of the sophisticated visual standards of the time. Ippolito's lifestyle was elegant and exquisite rather than naff: he had the dandy's finesse. In winter he rode out in an overcoat of scarlet wool lined with sable and fox fur. His tailor Antoine earned forty-eight scudi a year, twice as much as his cook Andrea, though much of these retainers' income was in the more erratic form of *mancie*, or tips. An inventory of his wardrobe lists over 400 items – damasks and velvets and taffetas, quilted jackets lined with lynx fur, hats decorated with peacock feathers, his fancy-dress costumes for carnival (including three peasant's outfits, a pair of sailor's breeches and two fleece wigs) and his leather tennis shoes. He was a keen tennis player; the d'Este had one of the earliest purpose-built tennis courts in Italy. The game had been imported from France – in those days the ball was literally 'served', by a servant, who set each point going before retiring off-court through a side-door.

The sugar-sculptures of the goddess Venus which adorned his banqueting tables may after all be a little naff, but the dishes served up there seem to avoid the alarming candied-meat tendency in Renaissance cooking. You might go for the fresh egg pasta stuffed with pine nuts, followed by the grilled bream with parsley and chives, and for dessert a ricotta cheesecake filled with pears, quinces or medlars. Cinquecento diners shared our fondness for expensive reworkings of rustic fare, among them a 'thin English soup' made of scraped parsley roots and ginger, thickened with egg yolk and poured over toast. All these are recipes from Ippolito's catering manager Cristofero di Messis-bugo, whose cookery book *Banchetti* ('Banquets') was published in Ferrara in 1549.

Behind the veil of sumptuousness the Renaissance courtier lived a life of hard travel, political danger and primitive sanitation, yet the life expectancy of those who survived the hazards of early childhood was higher than one might think. Of the hundred or so people mentioned in Ippolito's letters, the average age of death was fifty-six, and excluding those assassinated or executed the figure goes up to sixty. Ippolito himself died in his early sixties, of complications arising from gout. He had lived a Renaissance Life of Riley – how fine to have a biography which includes such sentences as 'Ippolito spent much of the winter of 1537–8 playing cards' – and Hollingsworth has vividly recovered the daily mechanics of his lifestyle.

*

Another book that takes us behind the scenes of the Renaissance highlife is a brisk analysis of the business dealings of the Medici by Tim Parks.* According to the conventional view, the Medici were the premier family of Renaissance Florence, whose enlightened rule set the scene for the city's great achievements in art, architecture, philosophy and (to a lesser extent) literature.

* Tim Parks, *Medici Money: Banking, Metaphysics and Art in Fifteenth-century Florence* (Profile, 2005).

But there are other, less flattering views of them, in which words like 'corrupt' and 'despotic' feature prominently, and their role as art-patrons is seen as mercenary and propagandist. Parks tends strongly towards this more sceptical view, as he picks over the relationship between art, religion and big business – an uneasy triangle – in Medici Florence. He is in many ways the perfect man for the job, applying to the Quattrocento that mordant eye which he deploys in his anatomies of contemporary Italy, such as *Italian Neighbours* and *A Season with Verona*.

He is not, of course, treading virgin ground. The Florentine historian Francesco Guicciardini has some bitter comments on the Medici in his *Storia d'Italia*, written in the late 1530s. Among modern scholars the most notable for 'resisting the myth' (as Parks puts it) is Lauro Martines. His magisterial study of the Italian city-states, *Power and Imagination*, indicts the family as the ruin of Florentine republicanism, and in his latest book, *April Blood*, he argues that Florence would have been well served if the Pazzi conspiracy of 1478 had achieved its aim of assassinating Lorenzo de' Medici.

The panache of the Medici is not in doubt, but their chief flair was undoubtedly for making money. In the first two decades of the fifteenth century, under the guiding hand of Giovanni di Bicci de' Medici (great-grandfather of Lorenzo), the Medici bank made profits of around 150,000 florins, of which Giovanni pocketed three quarters. Over the next thirty years, under Giovanni's son Cosimo, the profits were about 477,000 florins, netting the family and its partners average earnings of 15,000 florins per annum. 'Keep firmly in mind', Parks adds, 'that a respectable palazzo would cost only a thousand to build, and that the vast majority of the populace were too poor to pay so much as a single florin in tax.'

Moneylending at interest was condemned by the Church and

outlawed by legislation. The Medici bank's chief form of profit was a type of currency dealing, whereby 'bills of exchange', which enabled merchants to trade internationally, always ensured a healthy rake-off for the bank. The Medici were themselves traders as well as bankers. They imported a huge range of luxury goods – tapestries, sculptures, illuminated manuscripts, silverware, gemstones – to feed the upmarket tastes of bourgeois Florence. Less glamorously they cornered the market in alum, a gritty white sulphate used in cloth-dyeing. All this was above board, but the accumulation of such wealth remained morally ambiguous, and it is no doubt true that they commissioned scores of devotional works partly to salve their consciences – lavish altarpieces atoning for sinful profit margins.

Parks is informative on the mechanics of Medici banking, and trenchant on the family's ability to consolidate power within a republican ethos apparently dedicated to avoiding the oppressive hereditary systems which were the norm elsewhere in Italy. 'Stay out of the public eye,' advised Giovanni on his deathbed in 1429, but it was advice his successors chose not to heed, and when his son Cosimo died in 1464 he was accorded the title Pater Patriae, the 'father of the homeland', acknowledging the family as a kind of presidential dynasty – dukes in all but name.

By the time of Lorenzo, 'Il Magnifico', the family business was in a parlous state, and the note of despotism was more pronounced. The city was 'completely in his will, as if he were a prince waving a baton', wrote Guicciardini. The republic's committees and assemblies were stacked with Medici cronies, and with cynical time-servers who, in the words of Marco Parenti, 'denounce the Medici over dinner' in the privacy of their villas, and 'then vote as they're told when they are back in Florence'. By historical luck as much as judgement, these contradictions were masked with a heady cultural imagery of optimism and achievement: that 'feel-good factor' which the artists and

pageant-poets of the day did much to fuel, and which is still
seen as the keynote of Lorenzo's Florence. 'What was still possible', as Parks elegantly puts it, 'was the grand gesture, the
legitimacy of individual virtuosity, a cocktail of education,
glamour and charisma. In the new world that was coming, the
cult of the leader might perhaps replace the legal right of the
king.'

Lorenzo remains a figure of tremendous charm, with his ugly
yet compelling features, and his irrepressible energy, and his salacious carnival poetry, but the currencies of historical opinion
continue to fluctuate and the 'magnificence' for which he is a
byword can no longer protect him from questioning.

15

Screaming in the Castle

The Case of Beatrice Cenci
[1998]

Beatrice Cenci was – to take a sample of sound-bites over the centuries – a 'goddess of beauty', a 'fallen angel', a 'most pure damsel'. She was also a convicted murderer. This is a charismatic combination, not least here in Italy, and her name has lived on, especially in Rome, where she was born and where she was executed in 1599.

The story as it comes down to us has the compactness of legend. It tells of a beautiful teenage girl who kills her brutish father to protect her virtue from his incestuous advances; who resists interrogation and torture with unswerving courage; and who goes to her execution unrepentant, and borne along on a wave of popular sympathy. There have been many literary treatments of the story, the most famous of which is Shelley's verse-drama *The Cenci*, written in 1819. Other writers drawn to the subject include Stendhal, Dickens, Antonin Artaud and Alberto Moravia. The appeal of the story is partly lurid – a pungent mix of Renaissance sex and violence; a sense of dark deeds behind the closed doors of a prominent Roman family. It affords a glimpse, in Shelley's words, of 'the most dark and secret caverns of the human heart'. There is also the ethical conundrum it poses, its puzzle of legal guilt versus moral innocence. At the end of Moravia's play *Beatrice Cenci* (1958) she tells her prosecutors:

Accuse me if you wish, but I am innocent . . . According to *your* justice you will certainly be able to prove that I am guilty of my

father's death. But you will never be able to prove that I am not
at the same time innocent according to another justice – a justice
which you can neither know nor even less administer.

The beautiful murderess, the innocent sinner: La Cenci has cast
her spell on the imagination – especially on a certain kind of
male imagination – and it is with some difficulty that one digs
back through the silt of literary sentiment to the event itself,
which took place 400 years ago this week, in the precipitous
little village of La Petrella Salto, in the foothills of the Abruzzi
Mountains about sixty miles north-east of Rome.

*

Sometime after seven o'clock on the morning of 9 September
1598, a woman called Plautilla Calvetti was combing flax in her
house at La Petrella. She heard a confused clamour outside –
'shouted words that I could not understand'. She hurried out
into the street. Someone she knew called to her: 'Plautilla, Plautilla, they are screaming in the castle!'

The castle, known as La Rocca, stood on a steep crag above
the village (see Plate 8). Now ruined and overgrown, it was
then the kind of rough hewn, strategically placed fortress-
cum-country-house that a very wealthy and rather dodgy
Roman nobleman might choose to hole up in when things got a
bit hot for him down in the city. This was broadly the case with
the current tenants of the building: Count Francesco Cenci, a
52-year-old Roman around whom accusations of corruption
and violence clustered like summer flies; his second wife,
Lucrezia, *née* Petroni; and his youngest daughter, Beatrice. The
two women were essentially prisoners in the castle, slaves to
the count's brutality, paranoia and – if the rumours were to be
believed – sexual abuse.

Plautilla knew the castle, and its secrets, better than most in the village. Her husband, Olimpio, was the *castellano*, or castle manager, and she herself worked there as a housekeeper. This was why the villagers were here at their house, shouting that something was wrong – even wronger than usual – up at La Rocca. Olimpio was absent, however. Plautilla ran straight away up the steep winding track to the castle, 'with one slipper on and one slipper off'. She saw Beatrice Cenci looking down at her from one of the windows. She called up to her, 'Signora, what is the matter?' Beatrice did not answer. She was clearly distraught but 'strangely silent', unlike her stepmother, Lucrezia, who could be heard crying hysterically inside the castle.

Some villagers came hurrying down the track. As they passed Plautilla they told her: '*Signor Francesco è morto.*' The infamous Count Cenci was dead.

His body was lying in a dense patch of scrub below the castle rock which was used as a rubbish tip. It appeared he had fallen from the wooden balcony on the upper storey of the castle, a drop later estimated as six *canne* (about forty feet). Part of the balcony had collapsed: one could see splintered wood, though the gap looked small for the bulky count to have fallen through. Ladders were fetched, and some men climbed down the 'wilderness wall' to retrieve the body. They confirmed that Cenci was dead, despite his fall having been broken by the branches of an elder tree. Indeed, the body was already cold to the touch, suggesting death had occurred some hours before. The corpse was hauled up with difficulty, roped to one of the ladders, and on this improvised stretcher carried down to the castle pool, below the outer gate of the castle. A crowd of people had gathered, among them three priests. They stared at the mortal remains of the great Count Cenci. His head was matted with blood, and his costly camel-hair *casacca*, or gown, was smeared with detritus: a 'miserable rag'.

It was there at the castle pool, during the washing of the body, that questions started to be raised. As they rinsed the blood off his face they found three wounds. Two were on the right temple, the bigger of them 'a finger long', but the deepest and ugliest was near the right eye. A woman called Dorotea made irreverent comments about the dead man, and thrust her forefinger into the wound with grisly relish. 'It turned my stomach,' one of the priests, Don Scossa, later recalled. Another onlooker, Porzia Catalano, said: 'I turned my eyes aside so I didn't have to look, because it frightened me.'

But it was not the ghoulish jesting of Dorotea that struck the priests: it was the nature of the wounds. How much their statements were shaped by later knowledge we do not know, but the priests who witnessed the washing of the body all claimed to have recognized instantly that the damage to Cenci's head had been caused not by a fall from the balcony but by a violent blow with a sharp instrument. They thought it might have been a 'cutting tool like a hatchet', or a 'pointed iron', or possibly a stiletto. One of them, Don Tomassini, also noted a deep bruise on the count's arm, above the left wrist.

Thus, even before the dead man's eyes had been closed (or, rather, as Don Scossa pedantically noted, 'the left eye closed, for the right eye was completely destroyed'), and even before the body, clad in a fresh shirt and laid on sheets and cushions from the castle linen chest, had been carried down the lane to the village church of Santa Maria which was to be its resting-place, it was already suspected that Count Cenci's death was not an accident but a case of murder.

Standing at the site of the castle pool four centuries later, and assisted by the conventions of the Hammer horror-movie which this story often resembles, one envisages that moment of dawning recognition, when the assembled villagers fall silent, and their eyes slowly turn back up to the forbidding silhouette of La Rocca, to the 'strangely silent' figure of Beatrice at the window.

★

This brief account, based on witness statements, catches something of the reality of the Cenci murder. It is a local event, as all historical events are to begin with: a sudden noisy intrusion into the routines of a late summer morning in La Petrella. This is the event before the dust has settled. Thereafter it becomes progressively distorted by various kinds of partisanship – the police investigation, the extraction of confessions, the hectorings of the trial, the cruelties of the verdict – and then by the obscuring draperies of legend.

The investigation by the Neapolitan authorities (who then controlled the province of Abruzzo Ulteriore) was thorough, and even the ardent defenders of Beatrice do not dispute its findings. Count Cenci had indeed been murdered, horribly. While he slept, drugged by a sleeping draught prepared by Lucrezia, two men had entered his bedroom. Despite the drug it seems he awoke. One of the men held him down – the bruise on the wrist which Don Tomassini spotted – while the other placed an iron spike against his head and drove it in with a hammer. The two slighter wounds on the count's head were probably botched blows before the *coup de grâce* smashed home. They then dressed the body, humped it to the edge of the balcony and threw it down into the rubbish-tip. Leaving a half-hearted hole in the balcony floor to make it look like an accident, and a mass of 'scene of crime' evidence to show that it wasn't, they rode off into the night.

One of these men was Olimpio Calvetti – the trusted *castellano* of La Rocca, the husband of Plautilla and very probably, as it later transpired, the lover of Beatrice. The other was a hired

accomplice, Marzio Catalano, aka Marzio da Fiorani. These were
the murderers of Count Cenci, but they were really only hit-
men. The true architects of the crime were the count's immediate
family – Lucrezia and Beatrice, his long-suffering wife and
daughter; and Giacomo, his eldest surviving son. Giacomo was
actually in Rome when it happened, but his extensive confessions provided the bulk of the case against them. Beatrice was
said to have been the most implacable of the conspirators, the
one who urged the assassins on when they baulked at the last
moment. She refused to confess, however, even under torture.

The judicial process lasted exactly a year, during which time
both of the assassins died – Olimpio Calvetti, on the run in the
Abruzzi Hills, had his head sliced off with a hatchet by a bounty-
hunter, and Marzio Catalano died under torture in the Tor di
Nona Prison in Rome. On 11 September 1599 Giacomo, Beatrice and Lucrezia were executed outside the Castel Sant'Angelo
on the banks of the Tiber. Giacomo's death was protracted – he
was drawn through the streets on a cart, his flesh mutilated with
heated pincers, his head smashed with a sledgehammer, his body
quartered – but the two women walked to their death 'unbound
and in mourning garments' and were 'cleanly' beheaded. A not
entirely trustworthy account of the execution adds that Lucrezia had difficulty settling at the block because of the largeness
of her breasts. A fourth Cenci, Bernardo, too young to be
actively involved, was forced to watch the killing of his kin, and
was dispatched to the galleys thereafter.

The affair was a cause célèbre. It echoes briefly through the
newsletters of the day: 'The death of the young girl, who
was of very beautiful presence and of most beautiful life, has
moved all Rome to compassion' . . . 'She was seventeen and
very beautiful' . . . 'She was very valorous' at her death, unlike
her stepmother, who was a 'rag'.

★

These are the bald facts of the case. They do not go very far in explaining the passionate interest it has aroused. It is not so much the actual murder of Count Cenci which arouses this interest: on that, posterity's verdict has been a simple 'good riddance'. It is rather the particular quality – real or imagined – of the person who has become the star of the story: Beatrice Cenci. Though there was undoubtedly a continuous knowledge of the case from the late sixteenth century onwards, the legend of Beatrice Cenci is essentially a Romantic construct. Its origin can be traced to a long and highly coloured account of the story in Ludovico Antonio Muratori's *Annali d'Italia*, published in the 1740s. This popular book brought the case to a new generation of Italian readers, and when Shelley arrived in Rome in 1819 he found that 'the story of the Cenci was a subject not to be mentioned in Italian society without awakening a deep and breathless interest.' For Beatrice herself, he added, 'the company never failed to incline to a romantic pity' and a 'passionate exculpation' for the crime she had committed.

Shelley almost certainly knew Muratori's version, and may also have known an early dramatization of the story by the prolific Florentine playwright Vincenzo Pieracci. But the only source he chooses to mention in the preface to his play is an old manuscript 'copied from the archives of the Cenci Palace at Rome' (though not, it seems, copied by him: in a later note on the play Mary Shelley says it was 'communicated' to him by a friend). What exactly this manuscript was, and how much Shelley's historical errors or reworkings were taken from it, is unclear. Shelley's version of the murder itself, for instance, is oddly sanitized: the count is strangled by Olimpio, 'that there might be no blood'. This accords rather better with his idealization of Beatrice than the savage reality of the murder.

Shelley's poetic heroine, agonizing at length between the impossible alternatives of incest and parricide in tones that sometimes recall Shakespeare's Isabella in *Measure for Measure*, is the exemplar of the Romantic Beatrice, and ushers in a parade of doomed angels in prose works by Stendhal (*Les Cenci*, 1837), Giovanni Battista Niccolini (*Beatrice Cenci*, 1844) and Francesco Guerrazzi (*Beatrice Cenci*, 1854) – this last a very treacly confection – together with shorter essays or treatments by the elder Dumas and Swinburne. In the twentieth century the legend has persisted: a film (*Beatrice Cenci*, 1909) directed by the Italian expressionist director Mario Caserini; a 'Theatre of Cruelty' version, *Les Cenci*, by Antonin Artaud, first performed in Paris in 1935 with Artaud in the role of the wicked count; and Alberto Moravia's wordy play, *Beatrice Cenci* (1958).

Interwoven with these is a more demotic oral tradition. A typical synopsis of the story runs: 'her father dishonoured her, and for revenge she killed him by stabbing a silver pin into his ear' (Carlo Merkel, *Due leggende intorno a Beatrice Cenci*, 1893). Another, recorded in La Petrella in the 1920s by Corrado Ricci, describes her torture: 'they hung her up by her yellow hair, which reached to her knees.' This finds its way into Artaud's play: 'From the stage's ceiling a wheel is revolving on its invisible axis. Beatrice, attached to the wheel by her hair, is urged on by a guard who is gripping her wrists behind her back.'

These literary or anecdotal aspects of the legend are closely connected with a visual aspect – the supposed portrait of Beatrice by Guido Reni (see Plate 9). It shows a beautiful young girl with brown hair and wide, lustrous eyes. According to tradition, scrupulously nurtured by all the nineteenth-century writers on the subject, the portrait was done from the life during Beatrice's imprisonment, i.e. in late 1598 or 1599. An alternative version, taking into account the improbability of the unknown Guido being able to visit her in the Corte Savella Prison, says it was based on a glimpse of her in the street as she walked to her execution. Shelley saw the painting in 1818, in the Palazzo Colonna in Rome, and described the face as 'one of the loveliest specimens of the workmanship of Nature':

> There is a fixed and pale composure upon the features: she seems sad and stricken down in spirit, yet the despair thus expressed is lightened by the patience of gentleness . . . Her eyes, which we are told were remarkable for their vivacity, are swollen with weeping and lustreless, but beautifully tender and serene. In the whole mien there is a simplicity and dignity which, united with her exquisite loveliness and deep sorrow, are inexpressibly pathetic.

This portrait was, in Mary Shelley's view, the spark which ignited the poet's interest – Beatrice's 'beauty cast the reflection of its own grace over her appalling story. Shelley's imagination became strongly excited . . .'

A few years later the expatriate French novelist and *flâneur* Marie-Henri Beyle, better known as Stendhal, was similarly moved, seeing in the portrait 'a poor girl of sixteen who has only just surrendered to despair. The face is sweet and beautiful, the expression very gentle, the eyes extremely large; they have the astonished air of a person who has just been surprised at the very moment of shedding scalding tears.' Dickens found it 'a picture almost impossible to be forgotten', full of 'transcendent sweetness' and 'beautiful sorrow'. In her face 'there is a something shining out, that haunts me. I see it now, as I see this paper, or my pen' (*Pictures from Italy*, 1846). Nathaniel Hawthorne, meanwhile, found the picture 'the very saddest ever painted or conceived: it involves an unfathomable depth of sorrow'. It is 'infinitely heartbreaking to meet her glance . . . She is a fallen angel – fallen and yet sinless' (*Transformation, or the Romance of Monte Beni*, 1860).

Despite these heavyweight endorsements, there is little reason to think this face has anything to do with Beatrice Cenci. It could not have been painted from the life, for though there is some debate about when Reni moved from his native Bologna to Rome, it was certainly not before 1601, two years after her death. From its imagery – particularly the turban-like drapery – the picture is more likely to be a representation of one of the prophetic Sibyls. (There is a turbanned Cumaean Sibyl by Reni in the Uffizi.) The girl's extreme youth suggests she is the Samian Sibyl, often referred to in Classical sources as a *puella*.

The earliest connection of the portrait with Beatrice appears to be in a catalogue of paintings owned by the Colonna family in 1783 – 'Item 847. Picture of a head. Portrait believed to be of the Cenci girl. Artist unknown.' This identification – in itself tentative – belongs to the late eighteenth century, to the time of this upsurge of interest in Cenci arising from the account in Muratori's *Annali*. Probably her name was appended to the picture to give it a spurious interest. This seems to have been the result, for when Shelley showed a copy of it to his Roman servant, he 'instantly recognized it as the portrait of La Cenci'.

The painting now hangs in the gloomy corridors of the Palazzo Barberini. The label below it has a question mark after both the artist and the subject, and adds an apologetic note that the painting is of 'poor quality' and is only famous because of its supposed connection with Beatrice. Some scholars believe it is a mid-seventeenth-century work by Reni's assistant, Giovanni Andrea Sirani, or by Sirani's talented daughter Elisabetta. A couple of rooms away hangs the gallery's masterwork: Caravaggio's *Judith Cutting off the Head of Holofernes*. In the expression of Judith, resolute but disgusted by the sheer messiness of the operation; in the fountains of blood spurting over the bed-sheets; in the scarcely veiled eroticism – her hardened nipple is visible beneath the white gown – one might see an entirely different reading of Beatrice Cenci: not sweet and mournful like the young Sibyl, but steeled to a necessary, or perhaps merely expedient, act of butchery. There is no provable connection between Caravaggio's Judith and Beatrice, but it is not implausible. Caravaggio was working in Rome at the time of the trial and execution, and the painting is broadly dateable to this time. It is not a portrait of her – one discerns the familiar features of Fillide Melandroni, Caravaggio's favourite model – but it may well contain a vein of comment on the Cenci case. It is rather more likely to do so than the dubious Reni portrait, which caused such a flutter beneath the frock-coats of the literati.

*

In the later nineteenth century the case began to attract more serious historical investigation. Some findings contradicted the received pseudo-facts of the legend, though they did little to displace it or diminish its popularity. Even sober scholars found it hard to resist Beatrice's peculiar allure. When a Victorian antiquarian, Edward Cheney, discovered an autograph letter of Beatrice's in a Roman archive, he duly published the text in a learned periodical (*Philobiblon*, Vol. 6, 1861). Halfway through his transcription he signals an omission, with a note that states: 'Here the manuscript is illegible from tears having blotted it.' I have seen a photograph of the original document. There is some deterioration of the paper, but no sign whatever that this was caused by La Cenci's teardrops. The bibliophile has suffered that characteristic rush of blood to the head which Beatrice excites in all the historians, particularly male ones.

The most challenging documentary discoveries were made by a tenacious archival ferret, Dr Antonio Bertolotti. In 1879 he published his findings in a slim and refreshingly dry volume, *Francesco Cenci e la sua famiglia*. His first discovery was a manuscript volume in the Vittorio Emmanuele library in Rome, headed '*Memorie dei Cenci*'. In it he found, in the surprisingly elegant hand of Count Cenci, a precise register of the births and

deaths of his many children. Among these Bertolotti was surprised to find the following:

> *Beatrice Cenci mia figlia. Naque alla 6 di febbraio 1577 di giorno di*
> *mercoledi alla ore 23, et e nata nella nostra casa.*

So we learn that the beautiful teenage girl of legend, invariably
described as sixteen or seventeen, was actually twenty-two years
and seven months old when she died. Her birthplace – 'our
house' – was the rambling Palazzo Cenci, on the edge of Rome's
Jewish ghetto. It is still standing, though split into apartments
and offices: one may imagine her passing under its dark archways, lingering by the small fountain in the courtyard, walking
up the pock-marked marble stairs. From the top floors she could
see the broad sweep of the Tiber, and on the far bank the drum-
like shape of the Castel Sant'Angelo, where she would meet her
death. The topography suggests the narrowly circumscribed
circuit of her life.

Bertolotti also made a remarkable discovery in his examination of Beatrice's will, or rather – crucially – wills. (The fact
that she was allowed to write a will at all puts a question mark
over the popular view that Pope Clement VIII hounded the
Cenci to death in order to swell his coffers with confiscated revenues.) In her first will, notarized on 27 August 1599, Beatrice
left a great deal of money – about 20,000 scudi in all – to charit-
able and religious causes. She made particular provision, in the
form of trusts, for the dowries of 'poor girls in marriage'. She
also made a number of smaller bequests, typically a hundred
scudi, to individual relatives and retainers. What caught Bertolotti's eye, however, was the following clause, and the rather
more secretive trust fund it alluded to:

> *Item.* I bequeath to Madonna Catarina de Santis, widow, 300
> scudi in money, to be placed at interest, and the interest to be
> given in alms according to the instructions I have given her. If

the said Madonna Catarina should die, this legacy is to be transferred to others, on condition that they use it for the same
purpose, according to my intention, as long as the person to
whom these alms are to be given remains alive.

Beatrice's friend Catarina de Santis is obscurely traceable: a
respectable widow with three unmarried daughters (also
remembered in Beatrice's will). But who is the unnamed person
who is to be the beneficiary of the legacy, according to the
'instructions' given to Catarina verbally but not revealed in the
will? The probable answer was discovered by Bertolotti in a previously unknown codicil, added by Beatrice on 7 September
1599, witnessed by her brother Giacomo, and lodged with a
different notary. In this codicil, written four days before her
execution, she increases the sum allotted to Catarina to a thousand scudi, and specifies the purpose of the bequest as being 'the
support of a certain poor boy [*povero fanciullo*], according to
the instructions I have verbally given her'. She also adds that
if the boy attains the age of twenty, he should be granted 'free
possession' of the capital.

Bertolotti's compelling interpretation of these phrasings is
that the 'poor boy' for whom she made such generous and secret
provision was her son. If so, it is likely that the father of the boy
was Olimpio Calvetti, whose intimacy with Beatrice is noted by
many witnesses. The hushing-up of a pregnancy may be one of
the reasons for her 'imprisonment' at La Rocca.

From these documents a different Beatrice emerges. The
angelic Beatrice of legend, the sweet and mournful girl of
the Reni portrait, the spotless damsel (or sublimated Lolita) of the
nineteenth-century romancers, proves to have been a tough
young woman in her twenties, probably the mother of an
illegitimate child, probably the lover of her father's murderer.
This does not, of course, lessen the awfulness of her situation or
the tyranny of her father. Nor does it lessen the evils of the

sexual abuse she suffered, even if her vaunted chastity is no longer part of that equation.

But how much of this is fact? Did her father really violate her, or attempt to do so?

Throughout her interrogation Beatrice maintained her complete innocence of the murder. Her defence was simply that she had no motive for killing her father. It was only at the end, and especially during the long summing-up by her lawyer, Prospero Farinacci, that the question of incest arose as a powerful mitigation of her crime. Corrado Ricci notes sternly: 'in all the trial records from November 1598 until August of the following year – in more than fifty examinations – there is not the slightest hint of any such deed.' There is plenty of evidence of her father's violent temper – on one occasion he attacked her with a whip – but there is no mention of incest. Then, in her last examination, on 19 August 1599, comes the first hint, when Beatrice states that her stepmother Lucrezia had urged her to kill her father with these words: 'he will abuse you and rob you of your honour.' This suggests a threat of sexual violence, though the phrasing does not prove that anything had yet taken place.

Ten days later, a former servant at La Petrella, Calidonia Lorenzini, appeared before the prosecutor, at the request of certain friends of Beatrice. She deposed that a few days before Christmas 1597, she was in bed at 'the third hour of the night', when Lucrezia came in, saying she had been sent out of the bedroom by the count. A few minutes later, Calidonia relates,

> I heard a voice, which seemed to me that of Beatrice, saying: 'I do not want to be burned!' I heard nothing else afterwards. The following morning I asked Signora Beatrice what had ailed her when she said those words . . . She said that her father had come into her bed, and she had told him she did not wish him to sleep there.

In terms of witness statements this is as near as we get to first-hand evidence of incest. The prosecutor was not impressed: he was particularly sceptical that the chattery Calidonia could have kept all this secret from her fellow maid Girolama, who knew nothing of it.

Girolama herself gives a vivid glimpse of the brutishness of domestic life in the Cenci household. It was the count's custom, she says, to have his skin 'scratched and scraped' with a damp cloth – he suffered from a form of mange – and this duty often fell to Beatrice. 'She told me, that sometimes she scratched her father's testicles, and she said also she used to dream that I too was scratching them, and I said to her: That will I never do!' Another reminiscence of Girolama's is this:

> Signor Francesco used to go about the house in just a shirt and doublet and a pair of drawers, and when he urinated it was necessary to hold the urinal for him under his shirt, and sometimes she [Beatrice] was obliged to hold it; and it was also necessary sometimes to hold the close-stool . . .

These testimonies tell us much about life inside La Rocca, but they do not constitute proof that Cenci had raped his daughter. The truth, as with many cases of sexual abuse in the family today, will never be known. There are too many untrustworthy sources – suborned and frightened witnesses; statements made under torture; documents that may not after all mean what we think they mean – and then there is that infusion of folklore and fantasy and poetic wish-fulfilment which has soaked its way too deep into the story to be separated back out. Francesco Cenci was an arrogant, greedy, lecherous and violent man. There are many reasons why he might have had his head smashed in on a dark night in the Abruzzi. Lust for his daughter, credible but unproven, may have been one of them. At least five people were involved in the killing. Each had a motive of some sort, but only one (the hit-man Marcio, who was in it for money) had a motive that can be defined with any precision.

The ethereal legend of Beatrice is at least a kind of memory device, a retaining of her story in the collective memory. It loses the complexities of the case, the untidiness of events, but serves to remind us of the intense repressions and vulnerabilities suffered by a well-born young woman in late Renaissance Italy. In this sense, as an individual woman who speaks for countless others, Beatrice is a kind of heroine. But to the other questions we want to ask – What was she really like? What really happened and why? – she gives no answer. There was 'screaming in the castle'; there were 'shouted words'. They were audible for a moment above the white noise of history but can no longer be deciphered.

16

Man in a Fur Hat

A New Byron Portrait?
[1999]

The man in the portrait is handsome, the costume curious, the mood elusive. He looks quite young but he is deathly pale and his hair is flecked with grey. What strikes me most are his eyes: they are large and grey and unmistakably brimming with tears. It is certainly a very striking picture (see Plate 10), but is it – as its discoverer claims – a hitherto unknown portrait of Lord Byron?

The story of the portrait's discovery is picturesque in itself. It turned up in 1981, with some other paintings, in an old trunk in the attic of a country house in Herefordshire. It was found there by an aristocratic Hungarian émigré, Imre Kish, Count of Uray, an architect, art collector and amateur historian. Now sixty-eight, Kish has lived in England since the Communist takeover of Hungary in the mid fifties. This cache of paintings in the attic, all of which Kish bought, included a definite portrait of Byron – a later copy of a well-known original and not of intrinsic historical interest – and a pair of Italian paintings of the early seventeenth century which have possible associations with his years in Italy.

And there was the portrait in question, dirty and dilapidated, but bearing on the back of its worm-eaten frame an intriguing label which read: 'Manfred by Hurlstone, spoken of by B'.

Manfred was one of Byron's doomed Romantic heroes, the protagonist of his verse-drama *Manfred*, published in 1817. Like all Byron's works the piece was popular; it was performed at

Covent Garden in 1834 with John Denvil in the title role, and it
inspired musical settings by Schumann and Tchaikovsky. It is set
in the high Alps, which explains the curious fur hat worn by the
sitter in the portrait. The costume, Kish says, is the traditional
garb of the Alpine chamois-hunter. The tearful eyes of the portrait also relate to the Manfred story, which is about a young
man's contemplation of suicide.

The Hurlstone referred to on the label is Frederick Yeates
Hurlstone, a minor but fairly successful English artist, who was
born in 1800 and was therefore a younger contemporary of
Byron (who died in 1824). The National Portrait Gallery, which
saw the painting soon after Kish bought it, cautiously accepts it
as the work of Hurlstone. The label thus suggests, at the least,
that this is a representation of Byron's Manfred painted by Hurlstone. It also seems to suggest that the painting was 'spoken of'
by Byron, and was therefore painted during his lifetime. After
some considerable sleuthing – 'five years hard labour', as he puts
it – Kish has taken this to what might be called its logical conclusion. He believes that it is an actual portrait of Byron, in the
guise of Manfred, painted by Hurlstone in Italy in about 1823.

*

I was first shown a photograph of the painting last year, together
with copies of some related documents and letters of Kish's. I
was initially sceptical: it did not look to me like Byron, nor did
it look the right age for Byron at that date – he was thirty-five
in 1823, and the years of dissipation had left their mark. But I
was intrigued enough by the story to do some further research,
and was surprised to find myself becoming more convinced that
Kish's story had something in it. I recently met the redoubtable
count, and saw the original portrait hanging in his dining room
in Great Malvern, and listened to his intricate – some might say
obsessive – theories on the subject.

The provenance of the portrait is fascinating, and is where Kish has done his most valuable work. The trail does not quite take us back to Byron himself, but very nearly. The attic where Kish found the paintings was at Langstone Court, near Llangarron, on the Herefordshire–Monmouthshire border, which is described by Pevsner as the 'finest country house of its period in the county'. The paintings had formerly belonged to a Miss Parnell Jones (the great-aunt of the person who was selling them). She in turn had inherited them from her elder sister, Constance Jones, who died in 1935. Constance Jones had been Mistress of Girton College, Cambridge, and president of the University of Wales at Aberystwyth – she was what Byron would have called a 'blue', i.e. blue-stocking.

A generation further back in the Jones family and we have a major link to Byron, for Constance's father, John Jones, was a country doctor, and among his patients in the 1850s was the famous literary adventurer Edward John Trelawny. Trelawny had been Byron's close friend during the last years of Byron's life and was an assiduous contributor to the Byron legend for many decades thereafter. He lived at Usk, in Monmouthshire, for eleven years (1847–58). Constance Jones (born 1848) used to sit on his knee, we are told. Trelawny had a large collection of paintings, and when he came to leave the area a number of them were sold at auction, together with some furniture and about a thousand books. This auction was held at the Three Salmons Inn in Usk on 4 June 1858. At it, Kish contends, Dr Jones purchased the collection of Byronic paintings which was later owned by his daughters, and which wound up in the attic of Langstone Court.

This is certainly a plausible provenance, but it leaves us one degree of separation from Byron himself. The Manfred portrait may well have arrived in Herefordshire via Trelawny, but this still does not prove that it is actually a portrait of Byron.

*

Does it look like Byron? To answer this, one has to ask another
question: what *did* Byron look like?

One's image of him is mostly compounded of two famous
portraits, both in the National Portrait Gallery: Thomas Phil-
lips's stirring depiction of him in Albanian tribal costume; and
the red-lipped dreamer in profile, with chin resting on hand, by
Richard Westall. Both were painted in England in 1813: they
show Byron at age twenty-five. But in fact Byron's appearance
changed all the time – because different artists saw him differ-
ently, and because he was a great believer in diets and regimes,
and his weight fluctuated by as much as four stone. Various
portraits show round Byrons and thin Byrons, Byron with
moustache, with mutton-chop whiskers, in costume, in uniform, in Greek helmet, in his dressing gown, and so on.

Among the images of Byron in the NPG archive, I found
three lesser-known portraits of him which seem to me to look
very like the face in the Manfred painting. Two of the three are
dated: they belong to the years 1822–3. Both are profiles, so
their likeness to the full-face Manfred is a matter of interpretation (though could be tested scientifically). One is part of a
well-known series of sketches drawn from the life by Count
Alfred D'Orsay, who was a guest of Byron's in Genoa in mid
1823. It shows Byron in a large military-style cap. The other is
rather mysterious. It is visually very close to the D'Orsay sketch,
but if the date on it is correct – 'Pisa, July 22nd 1822' – it cannot
be by D'Orsay, who was then still in France. There is no artist's
signature on it, but there is instead the signature of Byron himself, which seems to imply that both the portrait and the date
are genuine. Could this possibly be another Byron portrait by
Frederick Hurlstone?

The third portrait which seems comparable to the Manfred
picture is full-face, but with a small moustache. It is listed as

'spurious' in the NPG, though an Italian source describes it as 'signed by d'Aurea' and says it was given by Byron to his Venetian lover, Teresa Guiccioli.

Some verbal descriptions of Byron's appearance in 1822–3 also bear a resemblance to the figure in the Manfred portrait. In 1822 Thomas Medwin wrote:

> He had a paleness in his complexion, almost to wanness. His hair, thin and fine, had almost become grey . . . His face was fine and the lower part symmetrically moulded, for the lips and chin had that curved and definite outline that distinguishes Grecian beauty . . . His eyes were placed rather too near his nose and one was rather smaller than the other; they were of a greyish brown, but of a peculiar clearness.

And Lady Blessington recorded her impressions in early 1823:

> His eyes are grey and full of expression, but one is visibly larger than the other . . . His mouth is the most remarkable feature in his face, the upper lip of Grecian shortness and the corners descending, the lips full and finely cut . . . His chin is large and well-shaped, and finishes well the oval of his face . . . He is extremely thin, indeed so much so that his figure has an almost boyish air. His face is peculiarly pale, but not the paleness of ill-health, as its character is that of fairness, the fairness of a dark-haired person – and his hair (which is getting rapidly grey) is of a very dark brown.

The extreme thinness she remarks on was due to his dieting: in 1823 his frame was, he said, almost as 'transparent' as it had been ten years before. Lady Blessington thought him too 'attenuated' for his proposed campaign in Greece.

One also notes Byron's particular horror at his own rapid ageing. He complained that a bust by Lorenzo Bartolini (1822) made him look like a 'superannuated Jesuit'. And in response to the

thinning hair of one of D'Orsay's sketches, Byron said he wished
the count would 'condescend to add a cap to the gentleman in
the jacket – it would complete his costume and smooth his
brow, which is a somewhat too inveterate likeness of the original, God help me!' (letter to Lady Blessington, 6 May 1823).
The D'Orsay sketch discussed above seems to be a response to
this request. The Manfred portrait would certainly have
appealed to Byron's vanity, capturing that 'boyish' look which
charmed Lady Blessington, and concealing the receding hairline
beneath the fur hat.

If we were to date the painting to 1822–3, it would be linked
in time to those Italian sketches which resemble it, and to
Byron's first acquaintance with Trelawny, who may have later
owned it. We would also find some reasons for this tearful, sui-
cidal picture – the death of his five-year-old daughter Allegra
in April 1822, and the drowning of his friend Shelley in July.
Frederick Hurlstone was still a young man at this time, though
already active as a painter – he won a gold medal at the Royal
Academy in 1823. This may not in the end be a very good representation of Byron, but it may nonetheless be an authentic one.
It should not, anyway, be dismissed according to a narrow
definition of the 'Byronic' look.

Kish's case is by no means proved, and perhaps never can be.
There are some historical problems to be addressed – I have
found no evidence that Hurlstone was in Italy at this time;
nor any record of Byron having 'spoken of' the painting, as
the label seems to claim. It is also a great pity that Kish had the
portrait restored and reframed when he acquired it, and that
the original label exists only in a photograph taken before the
restoration.

His claim for the portrait has been supported by Sir Hugh
Casson, former president of the Royal Academy (and, one must
add, an old friend of Kish). Others are less convinced. Kish is

particularly at loggerheads with the Byron Society – though having nearly been hanged and quartered by the Marlowe Society for certain theories I advanced about Christopher Marlowe, I know how rabid these literary societies can be. We are not short of portraits of Byron – the NPG archive records over forty different images – but the sad-looking man in a fur hat deserves further investigation.

17

'My Infelice'

In Search of Sarah Walker

[2001]

In early September 1878, an old woman named Sarah Tomkins lay dying at her lodgings on Penton Place, an undistinguished terrace in the South London district of Newington. The street was poor but clung to respectability: one might call it 'shabby genteel'. It had once led down to the popular Surrey Gardens, but now the gardens were closed and a tide of Victorian rush-housing was spreading across the area. No. 65 was a typical three-storey house of sooty London brick, with a yard or garden out back, and beyond that a railway line carrying the busy London–Dover service. There was a pub round the corner called the Giraffe, named after a popular attraction at the Surrey Gardens Zoo. Here Sarah Tomkins lived her last days, with the trains rattling her window and the smell of the sperm-oil works blowing over from Newington Butts. She was seventy-seven years old, a relic of the days of mad King George. She had outlived both her husband and her son. It was her daughter-in-law, Caroline, who was with her when she died.

There were no obituaries. It was a small event in a small corner of the metropolis, a drop in the great grey ocean of Victorian rooftops. Obscurity clouds most of Sarah's long life, and perhaps that was how she liked it. She had had her moment of fame or, as most would have called it, infamy. Even at her death, so long after the event, there were few in the literary world who would not have recognized her by her former name. For Sarah Tomkins had once been Sarah or Sally Walker; and she (they would doubtless tell you) was that scheming little 'lodging-house hussy' with whom the great William Hazlitt had fallen so hopelessly in love, for whom he had divorced his wife, and about whom he wrote, with alarming frankness, in his *Liber Amoris*. It had happened nearly sixty years ago – they first met in 1820; the *Liber Amoris* was published in 1823 – but memories had been jogged more recently. *Memoirs of William Hazlitt*, the two-volume biography by his grandson W. C. Hazlitt, had appeared in 1867. The reminiscences of old friends like Bryan Waller Procter and P. G. Patmore had been published. Hazlitt was in vogue again: new editions were being prepared, new judgements being framed. How much Sarah knew of all this, how much it touched her, is debatable.

Admirers of Hazlitt tend to wince when the name Sarah Walker comes up. She is his Achilles heel, his dreadful gaffe. The finest essayist and journalist of the Romantic era, the tough-talking champion of political liberties, is here discovered down on his knees, abasing himself before a common coquette less than half his age, and then – to compound the blunder – actually publishing his outpourings of sentiment in an anonymous *mémoire à clef* whose lock was so easy to pick he might as well have used real names. For his enemies in the combative world of the political magazines, the *Liber Amoris* was a godsend. The *Literary Register* called it 'Silly Billy's Tomfoolery' and dismissed it as 'indecent trash'. *John Bull* commented loftily that 'the dirty abominations of the raffs of literature are far below notice', then proceeded to devote three issues to reviews, spoofs and comments on the book. They even got hold of one of his love-letters to her, and published it (thus doing a service to Hazlitt scholars, as this is the only source for the whole letter). It was a total humiliation for Hazlitt, and presumably for Sarah, too, who found herself trailed through the press as a 'pert, cunning, coming, good-for-nothing chit', a 'dowdy trollop', a 'poor half-harlot', a 'callous jilt', and much else in a similar vein.

Hazlitt can, and did, look after himself. He was a spiky, awkward, self-absorbed man: total frankness was his forte — 'I say what think; I think what I feel.' Though he was, in the opinion of his friends, 'substantially insane' during the course of his three-year infatuation with Sarah, he picked himself up off the floor, got married for the second time to a well-off widow, wrote *The Spirit of the Age* and the *Life of Napoleon*, toured France and Italy, and died in Soho in 1830 reputedly with the words, 'Well, I've had a happy life!'

But what of Sarah Walker? She moves for ever — alternately prim and sensuous, banal and bewitching — across the lurid little stage of the *Liber Amoris*, but what do we really know about her? What were her feelings about the affair? And what happened to her after she cast off this unwilling role of Romantic dreamboat, and returned to the obscure reality of her lower-middle-class life in nineteenth-century London?

Hazlitt has attracted scores of biographers, but — with a single exception — none has had much interest in these questions. The *Liber Amoris* has its champions, Hazlitt has been forgiven his lapse, but Sarah continues to live this two-dimensional life, hardly real at all except as a figment of one man's *amour fou*. The honourable exception is the Hazlitt scholar Stanley Jones. In the late 1960s he succeeded in tracing a direct descendant of Sarah's younger brother, Micaiah Walker. He pursued certain trails opened up by this, and published new material about her and her family in his biography *William Hazlitt: A Life* (1989). To these I can now add some findings of my own, which put a little more flesh on the skeletal documentation of her life.

*

Sarah Walker was born on Great Smith Street, in Westminster, shortly before midnight on 11 November 1800. She was the second of five children of Micaiah Walker, tailor, and his wife

Martha, *née* Hilditch. The family was of Dorset origin: Anthony Walker, Sarah's grandfather, was born in Lyme Regis. In religion they were Nonconformists. In 1816 they moved into a large, rambling and probably rather scruffy house, No. 9 Southampton Buildings, between Chancery Lane and Staple Inn, in London's legal district. Here Micaiah pursued his career as a tailor – among his customers was Hazlitt's friend John Payne Collier, later famous for his Shakespearean forgeries – and his wife ran a lodging-house, letting furnished rooms to professional men. In 1819 their eldest daughter, Martha, married a well-to-do young solicitor, Robert Roscoe, who had been one of their first lodgers. This was an excellent match from the Walkers' point of view, one they were no doubt keen to repeat for Sarah, now in her late teens, and the other children, Micaiah junior (or Cajah), Leonora Elizabeth (or Betsey) and baby John.

Here, in the summer of 1820, William Hazlitt entered their lives, and here Sarah steps into the limelight of the *Liber Amoris*. That book remains the primary source for what happened between them, but if it is Sarah's story one is trying to tell, one has in some way to turn the pages inside out, to dispense with the egomanic confessional element, and see what documentary traces remain. The book has two main constituents. The first part is a series of 'conversations', or dialogues, between 'H' and 'S', charting the course of their curious, stalled romance. The rest of it consists of letters written by Hazlitt – three to Sarah; several to 'P—', who is his confidant Peter George Patmore; and then three to 'J. S. K—', or James Sheridan Knowles, recounting the final, farcical agonies of the affair. But the printed *Liber* is not the only source. There is a manuscript copy of Part One with additions and corrections in Hazlitt's hand. There are the uncensored originals of some of his letters to Patmore. There is the full text of that letter to Sarah acquired by the cheque-book journalists of *John Bull*. And, strangest of all, there is the small

leather-bound 'journal book' for March 1823 in which Hazlitt
records, unedited and *in extremis*, the 'trial' of Sarah's virtue by
his emissary, a certain 'Mr F—', who took rooms at the Walkers'
lodging-house for this purpose. This steamy logbook was not
published in its entirety until the late 1950s. To these may be
added some passages in other published writings by Hazlitt, and
some comments by well-informed bystanders, not least the out-
going Mrs Hazlitt, whose journal briskly records their divorce
proceedings in Scotland. From these overlapping sources one
can reconstruct a rather more detailed, if less poetic, picture of
events chez Walker.

Hazlitt took up his new lodgings on 13 August 1820. There is
a faint prior connection, for he probably knew Robert Roscoe,
the Walkers' new son-in-law; he certainly knew Roscoe's father,
who had been an early patron of his in Liverpool. But the
connection is not really needed. This was Hazlitt's stamping
ground, among the legal eagles and literary gents whose new
blue suits Micaiah Walker sewed. He had formerly had rooms
down the street at No. 34; he was an habitué of the Southampton Coffee-house round the corner, which features in his essay
'On Coffee-house Politicians'. He is a man in his milieu, an
intense, thin-lipped, dishevelled scribbler of medium height,
moving into rented accommodation not much different from
the last or the next.

He had a 'set', or pair, of upstairs rooms — bedroom and
sitting-room — at the back of the house. The rent was fourteen
shillings a week. Among his fellow lodgers were a Welsh apothecary named Griffiths, who had the garret-room on the floor
above him; a married couple, the Folletts; and a certain 'well-
made' young man, a solicitor's clerk, who is referred to in the
Liber as 'Mr C—', but whose real name is given in the manuscripts as Tomkins. Downstairs there was a front parlour, at
whose window Sarah sometimes sat; a back parlour where

Hazlitt stored a hamper of books, and where Griffiths hung up his grey-drab overcoat; and the kitchen, where the Walkers themselves congregated to gossip. Elsewhere – the topography fails us here – were the family's bedrooms. Sarah shared a bedroom with her sister Betsey, as she primly told Hazlitt when he suggested an assignation there.

Nothing remains of the house today. It seems to be commemorated by Hazlitt House, a vaguely neo-Classical office-block in red brick, dating perhaps from the 1930s. This building was recently the premises of Hasletine, Lake & Co. ('Patents, Trademarks and Designs': a reminiscence of the Great Seal Patent Office which stood near by). It is now, in its turn, slated for demolition. Whether it correctly marks the site of No. 9 I do not know.

Three days after he moved in – the hiatus is not explained – Hazlitt first saw the 'apparition' of Sarah Walker. She was a small, petite, 'delicate-looking' girl. The engraving on the title page of the *Liber* gives an idea of her face, though it is not quite a portrait: it is from a drawing by Hazlitt based on an Italian miniature which he (but not Sarah) thought 'like' her. She was dark in colouring but pallid in complexion. Hazlitt rhapsodizes on her skin as marble or alabaster, though he later told De Quincey that he had not really liked her 'look of being somewhat jaded, as if she were unwell, or the freshness of the animal sensibilities gone by'. She is variously glimpsed in a 'print dress', a 'mob-cap', a 'loose morning-gown'; he buys her a length of 'plaid silk' to make a summer dress; she goes out of an evening 'shawled and bonneted' and 'drest all in her best ruff'. One thing everyone noticed was her strange, gliding walk, which Hazlitt found entrancing but others thought sinister. And then there were her eyes, very dark, which she fixed on you with an intense gaze – 'one of her set looks' – into which much could be read or misread. Hazlitt fell victim to them instantly: 'The first time I ever saw you . . . you fixed your eyes full upon me as much as to say: Is he caught?' Again he recanted this – her eyes, he later decided, 'had a poor, slimy, watery look'. Her manner was prim and modest yet somehow disconcerting. She spoke 'in a pretty, mincing, emphatic way'. Her phrasing, as recorded in the *Liber*, is wooden and full of clichés. She is 'little Yes & No'. Hazlitt's emissary 'Mr F—' said, 'he thought at first she would not talk, but now he was convinced she could not.' But she was certainly not uneducated: she owned books and liked going to the theatre. She had read Byron's *Cain*, but not *Don Juan* because 'her sister said it was impious.' Stanley Jones surmises that her meaningful stares and melting sighs were in part an affectation picked up from romantic novelettes. Her handwriting is a neat, sloping, schoolroom script, rather cramped and buttoned up.

Few who passed judgement on her had actually met her. Mrs Hazlitt had, and thought, 'she was as thin and bony as the scrag-end of a neck of mutton,' but she was hardly impartial. Another who knew her was Hazlitt's genial friend Bryan Procter, who wrote under the pen-name Barry Cornwall. Some lines in his play *Mirandola*, performed at Covent Garden in 1821, were modelled on her (or so Hazlitt believed) – 'With what a waving air she goes / Along the corridor! How like a fawn / Yet statelier.' Many years later, Procter published a more prosaic reminiscence:

> I used to see this girl, Sarah Walker, at his lodgings, and could not account for the extravagant passion of her admirer . . . Her face was round and small, and her eyes were motionless, glassy, and without any speculation (apparently) in them. Her movements in walking were very remarkable, for I never observed her to make a step. She went onwards in a sort of wavy, sinuous manner, like the movements of a snake. She was silent, or uttered monosyllables only, and was very demure. Her steady, unmoving gaze upon the person whom she was addressing, was

exceedingly unpleasant. The Germans would have extracted a romance from her, enduing her perhaps with some diabolical attribute. To this girl he gave all his valuable time, all his wealth of thought, and all the loving frenzy of his heart. For a time I think that on this point he was substantially insane – certainly beyond self-control. To him she was a being full of witching, full of grace, with all the capacity of tenderness. The retiring coquetry, which had also brought others to her, invested her in his sight with the attractions of a divinity.

Despite his bluff disclaimer he, too, finds in her something disturbing. She is snake-like, a Melusine, potentially 'diabolical'. She would do for a German 'romance', or perhaps more particularly a Grimm fairy tale (first published in English in 1823). She is also an intentional entrapper, he thinks. Her 'coquetry' had already 'brought others to her'.

The affair began immediately: 'that very week you sat upon my knee, twined your arms around me, caressed me with every mark of tenderness.' It drifted on in a kind of idealized, erotic stalemate through the autumn and winter of 1820. The printed text speaks of kisses and caresses, of her sitting on his lap for hours on end, of the 'liberties' he took and the 'endearments' she whispered. The manuscript material, particularly the unprinted portions of the letters to Patmore, puts it more harshly: 'whenever I poked her up she liked me best' . . . 'she has an itch to be slabbered and felt' . . . 'she has been rubbing against me, hard at it an hour together', and so on. These frissons in a fusty room are as far as it ever went, physically. The affair was never consummated, which haunted him worse than anything – 'The gates of paradise were once open to me, & I blushed to enter but with the golden keys of love'; or more bluntly, in manuscript, 'I was only wrong in not pulling up her petticoats.'

Much of this, on Sarah's part, is the standard coquetry of the situation. Later revelations in the *Liber* make this clear. She is a teenage girl in a middle-market lodging-house. She flirts with the gentlemen upstairs, teases them with sexual possibilities that are never realized. It is a bit of a game, and it is good for business. This is what Hazlitt means when he calls her the 'decoy' of the house. Her behaviour is encouraged not by her 'strict' and mostly absent father, but by her mother, whom Hazlitt describes as a 'hag' and a 'bawd'. It is easy, but unfair, to deduce from all this that Sarah was a coldly calculating girl. One of the grating assumptions of the *Liber Amoris*, unthinkingly adopted by many biographers, is that Hazlitt was the exploited (a 'poor, tortured worm') and Sarah the exploiter. It is often construed that she had led Hazlitt to believe she really loved him, and then cruelly rejected him. But even the *Liber* makes this doubtful. His romantic protestations are always undercut by Miss's pursed-mouth answers. The love-affair is all in his head – 'La, Sir! You're always fancying things.' One of the book's recent champions, Michael Neve, finds it a 'subtle meditation on the philosophical ludicrousness of love', a 'picture of driven desire that, with Freudian exactness, ends up without even an obscure object'.

*

All the while Hazlitt continued his punishing schedule of literary work. In January 1821 he wrote an essay called 'On Great and Little Things', later published in the *New Monthly Magazine*. This marks Sarah's first appearance in his writing. He calls her his 'Infelice', his sad girl – 'Shouldst thou ever, my Infelice, grace my home with thy loved presence, as thou hast cheered my hopes with thy smile, thou wilt conquer all hearts with thy prevailing gentleness' (and much more in the same vein). It is to this that Mrs Hazlitt refers in her journal: 'I told him he had done a most injudicious thing in publishing what he did in the *Magazine* about Sarah Walker . . . and that everybody in London thought it a most improper thing.' He mumbled something in reply about the magazine having got hold of it without his consent, and then added: 'it had hurt the girl too, and done her an injury.' If this innocuous publicity had 'hurt' Sarah, how much worse, and more deliberate, was the pain inflicted on her by the *Liber Amoris*? His motives for publishing the *Liber* are generally given as catharsis and profit – he reputedly received £100 for the copyright – but one must also consider that old-fashioned balm for broken hearts, revenge.

About a year after their first meeting the relationship entered a stormy phase, as described in the dialogue entitled 'The Quarrel'. The cause of the quarrel, we learn, was a conversation in the kitchen which Hazlitt overheard and was shocked by. Readers of the book were spared the details, but a precise record of it is found in a letter to Patmore:

Betsey. 'Oh! If those trowsers were to come down, what a sight there would be!'

Mother. 'Yes! He's a proper one: Mr Follett is nothing to him.'

Mr Cajah. (aged 17) 'Then I suppose he must be seven inches.'

Mother W. 'He's quite a monster. He nearly tumbled over Mr Hazlitt one night . . .'

Cajah. (Laughing) 'Sarah says –'

Sarah. 'I say Mr Follett wears straps.'

To the sentimental lover lurking outside the kitchen door, this bawdy talk is a revelation of the true nature of his supposed 'angel'. Another accusation about her behaviour occurs in the same dialogue: 'Or what am I to think of this story of the footman?' In the printed text this is rendered unintelligible by a series of asterisks. 'It is false, Sir, I never did anything of the sort,' Sarah replies, but what is she supposed to have done? The missing words can be found in the manuscript, from which it appears that her mother had deliberately 'pulled up her [Sarah's] petticoats' in front of a visiting footman, this being a 'sport' they often indulged in.

From now on Hazlitt is in a fit of Othello-style jealousy, liberally seasoned with fears about his own sexual adequacy. He suspected just about everyone in the house – the apothecary Griffiths, whose dimensions were the subject of the kitchen talk; Mr Follett, whose intimate sartorial arrangements she appeared to know. And then there was Tomkins, or 'Mr C—', tall and 'well-made', a 'strapping lad' (those straps again?): 'The instant Tomkins came, she made a dead set at him, ran breathless upstairs before him, blushed when his foot was heard.' She denied it, of course: 'Mr C— was nothing to her, but merely a lodger' . . . 'she didn't think Mr C— was so particularly handsome' . . . 'she hated Mr C—'s red slippers', and so on. Hazlitt did not learn the truth until much later.

In early 1822, torn between obsession and doubt, Hazlitt left for Scotland to obtain a divorce. (The divorce was by mutual consent; it was precipitated by the Sarah affair, but the marriage had effectively broken down at least a year before he met her.) En route he stopped off at the Renton Inn, near Berwick, and here drafted up the 'conversations' which form the first part of *Liber Amoris*. He also corresponded with Sarah. Her letters, he complained to Patmore, are 'cold & prudish'. One of them, dated 17 January 1822, gives the authentic sound of her:

Sir

Doctor Read sent the London Magazine with compliments and thanks, no Letters or Parcels except the one which I have sent with the Magazine, according to your directions. Mr Lamb sent for the things which you left in our care likewise a cravat which was not with them. – I send my thanks for your kind offer [of theatre tickets] but must decline

accepting it. – Baby [her niece Emma Roscoe] is quite well the first
floor is occupied at present, it is very uncertain when it will be
disengaged. My Family send their best Respects to You. I hope Sir
your little Son is quite well.

From yours Respectfully
S Walker

This letter is known only from a very faded Victorian facsimile.
Another in the same vein, dated 26 February, was copied out by
Hazlitt and sent on to Patmore with some disparaging comments added. Her name at the bottom has been completely
effaced with lines and scribbles (see Plate 11). A Scottish drunk-
ard called Bell, who was involved in the divorce proceedings, told
Mrs Hazlitt he had seen some of Sarah's letters, 'and they were
such low vulgar milliner's or servant wench's sentimentality,
that he wondered Mr Hazlitt could endure such stuff'. Either he
saw some very different letters or he was lying. In these exemplars there is not a dram of sentiment.

Up in Edinburgh – the unlikely Reno of the story – the black
comedy of the divorce unfolded. By coincidence the Edinburgh
prostitute with whom he went in order to be caught in flagrante
was called Mary Walker. (He later told people she was 'one-
eyed', but this was perhaps a humorous embroidery.) The divorce
went through in mid July 1822. When it was over he hurried
back down to Southampton Buildings, a free man. There were
scenes: tearful recriminations, shaky reconciliations – and then
the axe fell. On an evening in late July, on King Street, he saw
her walking arm in arm with young Mr Tomkins: 'the murder
was out.' 'We passed at the crossing of the street without
speaking . . . I turned and looked, they also turned and looked,
and as if by mutual consent, we both retrod our steps and passed
again.' She showed 'no more feeling than a common courtesan
shews, who bilks a customer and passes him, leering up at her
bully, the moment after'. Later, amicably enough, he challenged

Tomkins. They talked for four hours. He learned she had been playing the same game with Tomkins; their affair had begun in earnest the previous autumn; they were now 'on the most intimate footing'. The extent of her duplicity was revealed. Tomkins took his breakfast earlier than Hazlitt; she had moved from one lap to the next without either man knowing. Tomkins 'again and again expressed his astonishment'. It was, he said, 'too much'. Here the *Liber* ends, with a kind of deliverance: 'she will soon grow common to my imagination, as well as worthless in herself.' By the end of September, Hazlitt was in new lodgings near Curzon Street. 'You see by this I have moved. I have come away *alive*, which in all the circumstances is a great deal.'

But the ending was not so neat: there remains the tawdry, unpublished coda of the 'trial'. This had long been mooted in the letters to Patmore – 'Try her!' – but did not actually happen until early March 1823. He is still obsessed, still in need of proof: 'to know if she is a whore or an idiot is better than nothing'. And so he sends in 'Mr F—' to test the limits of her virtue. Suggested identifications of this person include an actor named William Farren and the critic Albany Fonblanque, though I have a sneaking but unprovable suspicion that the 'F' stands for 'fuck'.

Over two weeks Hazlitt skulkingly records the progress of his proxy seducer. He 'kissed her several times on the staircase' and 'laid his hand on her thigh' and 'paddled on her neck'. When she lit his way upstairs, 'they had a regular scamper for it, he all the way tickling her legs behind.' Yet, on the evidence of this rather grotesque 'trial', Sarah had her limits, or indeed her self-respect. On the evening of 15 March, as she put down the curtains, 'F—' came up and 'put his hand between her legs'. She said coldly, 'Let me go, Sir,' and left the room. She was 'altered in her manner', and did not return. The following evening, at dusk, 'F—' saw her walking alone by Lincoln's Inn Fields.

When he asked if he might 'accompany' her, she refused, 'and on his offering to take her arm, stood stock still, immoveable, inflexible – like herself'. This last vicarious rejection brings the curtain down on Hazlitt's doomed courtship of Sarah Walker. The journal ends with a semi-legible scrawl up the margin: 'Let her lie to hell with her tongue – She is true as heaven wished her heart & lips be – My own fair hell.'

He wished now only to 'burn her out of my thoughts'. If he hoped to do so by publishing the *Liber Amoris*, he does not seem to have succeeded. It arrived on the bookstalls in early May, but four months later the painter Haydon reports: 'He came to town for a night or two, and passed nearly the whole of each in watching Sally's door.' But Haydon is not always a reliable witness, and this last vigil may be gossip rather than fact.

★

Whether 'Sally' was still to be seen at the door of No. 9 is uncertain. The scandal would have made her life there difficult, and there is another, more pressing reason for her absence. Perhaps as early as July 1823, and certainly before the spring of 1824, she became pregnant, and when the baby was born it was not at Southampton Buildings, or even near by, but in the distinctly poorer neighbourhood of St Pancras. She had family connections there. Her maternal grandmother, Sarah Plasted, had lived in the area, in the warren of lowly streets called Somers Town: we hear of Sarah's visits there in the *Liber*. Though her grandmother had recently died – she was buried at St Pancras Churchyard in February 1823 – this seems a cogent reason for the pregnant Sarah to be there. Under the circumstances, it is where we might expect to find her.

The father of the child was indeed John Tomkins, the rival suitor of the *Liber*, the tall, 'gentlemanly' young man whose red slippers she had once made fun of. He was now about twenty-five years old – two years older than Sarah – and was completing his articles of apprenticeship as a solicitor. He was a young man with prospects. Hazlitt thought she was attracted to Tomkins because of what she 'conjectured of his circumstances' – 'her sister had married a counsellor [i.e. solicitor] and so would she' – and perhaps he was right.

A son was born and christened Frederick, a popular name with royal associations. I have narrowed down his birth-date – between 31 March and 5 October 1824 – but cannot specify it. He is not to be found in the baptismal records of St Pancras parish church; it is more than likely he was baptized at one of the many chapels in the area, for which no registers remain. 'Miss is religious,' Hazlitt had said, a touch sourly, and perhaps she held to the Nonconformist principles of her family. It is remains possible that the child was illegitimate. No record of a wedding, shotgun or otherwise, has yet been found, and the family records unearthed by Jones are ambiguous on the subject. She took Tomkins's name, at any rate, whether officially or in 'common law'. More precious even than prospects, he offered her anonymity. In a documentary sense, Sarah Walker now ceases to exist.

In 1825, the year after the birth of Frederick, John Tomkins first appears on the *Law List* as a practising solicitor. Thereafter the trail cools. Sarah may have heard of the death of Hazlitt, from stomach cancer, in 1830. We can guess her presence at the family home after her mother's death in 1835. By this time her younger brother, Micaiah junior, was an up-and-coming solicitor and a father, while little Betsey, the impish child of the *Liber Amoris*, was now the rather posh Mrs Nott, with a father-in-law who had been knighted for colonial services in the East Indies. In the early summer of 1841, when the first national census was taken, John and Sarah Tomkins were living together at No. 31 Gloucester Street (now Old Gloucester St), a tall, narrow, shady

street just the other side of Holborn from Southampton Buildings. Their son, Frederick, now about seventeen, was not there.
This may be a casual absence – the census is only a snapshot – or
he may already be living and working elsewhere.

A few years later there comes a crisis in the career of John
Tomkins. In 1848, having appeared continuously for more than
twenty years, his name is dropped from the annual *Law List*. It
does not reappear, and ten years later his occupation is merely
'lawyer's clerk'. It seems possible that he and Sarah split up
around this time. He was not apparently present at their son's
wedding in the summer of 1849, and he is not found at the same
address as Sarah in the census of 1851.

Frederick Tomkins was now a solicitor's clerk in his mid
twenties, as his father had been when he courted Sarah; and per-
haps he, too, had 'prospects' when he married. His bride was
Caroline Jane Scarborough, twenty-two years old, born in
Whitechapel. Her father's occupation is given as 'messenger'.
The following year they were living at No. 25 Jewin Crescent,
in the downmarket London area of Cripplegate. Here, on 20
December 1850, their son was born. He was christened Freder-
ick William. It was thirty years since Sarah Walker had snared
Hazlitt with her girlish charms, and now she was a grandmother.

Sarah was probably present at the birth. Three months later,
at any rate, the census records her presence there on Jewin Crescent, as part of the household of which Frederick was the head.
She is 'Sarah J Tomkins, mother, aged 50'. Also living at No. 25
were a young Frenchman, Louis Francois Bavent, 'importer of
foreign goods'; and the Woodmans, William and Elizabeth,
with two young daughters. He was a clerk at a 'foreign newspaper office'. The Woodmans could afford a house servant; the
Tomkins, it seems, could not.

Tragedy lies round the corner. The next we hear of Frederick
Tomkins is the following year, up in Highgate. The address

sounds pleasant enough – No. 6 Prospect Terrace, on leafy
North Hill – but if he was there for reasons of health it was to
no avail. He died there on 6 October 1852, at the age of twenty-
eight, his head horribly swollen by cerebral dropsy, or 'water on
the brain'. The informant entered on the death certificate is one
of his in-laws, Mary Scarborough. This does not necessarily
mean that Sarah was missing at her son's death, only that it was
Mrs Scarborough who attended to the formalities thereafter.
The whereabouts of John Tomkins at this point are unknown.
He died five years later, at King's College Hospital, aged sixty.
The causes of death were paralysis and erysipelas. The latter,
popularly called 'the rose', is a febrile disease characterized by a
vivid red inflammation of the skin. According to the Victorian
medical text *Archives of Surgery*, it was associated with 'the too
liberal use of alcoholic beverages'.

   The next definite sighting of Sarah Tomkins is in early 1861:
she has migrated south of the Thames, to Newington – the fur-
thest move, as far as we know, in her circumscribed London life.
We can reconstruct a little of her progress there. Her daughter-
in-law, Caroline, now a widow at twenty-four, had soon
attracted a suitor, one Henry Horatio Neville Eastwood. He was
a 'merchant's clerk' a year older than her. He, too, had been
widowed, and had an infant son about the same age as Frederick
junior. They were married at Holy Trinity, Islington, in July
1855. A couple of years later they had a son. By 1858 they had
moved to Newington, where two more children arrived in
quick succession, and here I find them in the 1861 census, at No.
14 Newington Crescent, and with them Sarah Tomkins, 'mother
in law', now sixty years old.

   And Sarah has an occupation – in the poorly formed hand of
the census clerk I thought it was 'annuitant' (in other words,
that she was living off a legacy of some sort), but it is not: it is
'assistant'. We can trace her various addresses, and the family

events which touched her, but this is the only clue we have as to the kind of person she became in the long blank years after the Hazlitt affair. One wishes it said more. Whom did she assist and how? One thinks of the rather fastidious handwriting in the preserved letter to Hazlitt: was she perhaps a secretary of some sort, a businessman's or shopkeeper's assistant, a tidy keeper of lists and ledgers? Or maybe the term is more precise, and she is an assistant in the classroom (see *OED*, s.v. 'assistantship', citing an 1870s advertisement for such a post by a 'non-Certificated teacher'). Either way, unless the term disguises some more menial reality, we seem to find her, at the age of sixty, with a pen in her hand and a pair of small round spectacles on her nose.

Sometime after 1871 Sarah moved into her last lodgings, at No. 65 Penton Place, just around the corner from Newington Crescent. Perhaps there was no longer room with the expanding Eastwood family: they now had seven children. Her grandson Frederick continued to live with the family. He was now in his early twenties and had work as a 'clerk mercantile'. The word 'clerk' echoes dully through the story of Sarah's life: the literate drudges of Victorian law and commerce, the low-paid office-workers among whom she lived. How much she kept up with her own family is uncertain. Her brother Micaiah had prospered, and founded a successful law firm, Walker, Son & Field; he would live to the age of ninety-six. In 1882, four years after Sarah's death, he drew up the document entitled 'Particulars of my Family' which Jones later found. As well as some valuable facts, it contains a glaring untruth: he states that Sarah died unmarried and childless. A lingering sense of ignominy, rather than ignorance, must surely be the reason for this. She was not quite blotted out of the family, however. Micaiah's grandson, Reginald, knew of her as Sarah Tomkins, and knew she had a son; he was born in 1864, and may have met her as a child.

The house on Penton Place has gone – one finds instead

Lynford French House, a low-rise council-block on the edge of the Newington Estate – but it can be inferred from the extant houses opposite, with their sash windows and chimney pots and grey brick. The Giraffe pub is still in business, though I do not fancy Sarah as much of a tippler. Her landlady was Sarah Dods, a native of Burton-on-Trent; among other lodgers recorded in the house are an elderly nurse, a hackney-carriage driver and a print-worker. Here Sarah Tomkins *née* Walker died, on 7 September 1878. The death certificate gives the cause of death as 'old age', which seems perfunctory but which probably means she died peacefully. Perhaps she remembered those distant days of her youth, and that strange, hectic man who loved her so passionately, and wanted to marry her, and ended up marking her life and her name with a taint of scandal that would never quite go away. He had told her as much: 'My Infelice! You will live by that name, you rogue, fifty years after you are dead.' And she had replied in her pert way, 'I have no such ambition, Sir,' not then knowing the truth of what he said.

18

Bet Rimbo

Arthur Rimbaud's African House

[2000]

Little has changed in the old city of Harar, secluded in the hills of south-eastern Ethiopia. The rusting military hardware still sits beside the road from Dire Dawa, as it did when I last passed by six years ago. The waiters still move like somnambulists through the drowsy lobby of the Ras Hotel. The spider's web of twisting cobbled streets; the tall boys playing table football in a corner of the main square; the recumbent figures browsing on sprigs of *khat*; the beautiful eyes that flash suddenly out of shadowy interiors – it is all much as I remember it. So, too, is the smell, a gamut of aromas, from that quintessential Ethiopian fragrance of frankincense and roasting coffee, to the whiff of sewerage in a city beset by an almost continuous shortage of water.

For searchers of the picturesque – a quality which Harar has in spades – this continuity is reassuring. The place has not yet been 'spoilt'. It remains pungently itself. For the average Harari this may be less of a good thing: a sense of stagnation and lassitude are the reverse of this coin. It is a fairly general rule that the picturesque is based on someone else's inconvenience.

Harar is a walled city, very self-contained. Though you are no longer required to leave your spear at the city gates you are still very much an outsider here. Only two Europeans have made any impact, in the sense that their names are known and recognized. One is the English explorer Richard Burton, who arrived in 1855 and was probably the first European to enter this Muslim stronghold. The other is the nomadic French poet

Arthur Rimbaud, who worked here as a trader in the 1880s, and who made the place – more than anywhere in his brief restless life – his home.

It was Rimbaud who first brought me here, when I was researching a book about his years in Africa, and it is Rimbaud who brings me back, for the grand opening of the restored Maison Rimbaud, a handsome three-storey building of Indian workmanship which is 'said to have been' his house, and which is known locally as 'Bet Rimbo' (see Plate 12). This is the one bit of Harar that has visibly changed. Six years ago I picked my way across a rubbish-strewn courtyard, peered in disregarded corners, leant on rickety balconies, and was fed coffee and *gulban* (Easter bread) by an Amharic woman called Sunait who was living in a corner of the house. Now it has been thoroughly refitted. Its wooden façade gleams with varnish, its walls are stencilled with floating lines of exotic Rimbaldian imagery, its tall rooms are filled with photographs of old Harar, including some of Rimbaud's own.

A part of me regrets this transformation, but it is the selfish, picturesque-hunting part. (Another rule: the picturesque is enjoyable in inverse proportion to the number of people enjoying it.) In fact the 700,000 birr (£50,000) restoration, co-ordinated by the Centre Français des Études Éthiopiennes, has been sensitively done, has saved the building from imminent physical collapse, and is welcomed by the locals. A computerized record centre, for 'documentation and research on Harar and its region', is also being set up here.

All this has happened despite there being no firm evidence that Rimbaud ever lived here. According to one sceptical theory, the beams used in the house are surplus railway sleepers – this would date the construction to sometime after 1897, when work began on the Djibouti–Dire Dawa railway, and when Rimbaud himself had been dead for six years. This has not deterred tourguides and sightseers, for whom a palpably existent house is more important than a precise location. The writer John Ryle tells me of a novel spin on the subject. He was shown around the house by a guide who maintained adamantly that it had once been the home of Rembrandt.

On the day of the inauguration Harar was abuzz with dignitaries, and a concomitantly heavy presence of police and soldiers. At six o'clock in the evening, inside that once-dilapidated courtyard, were seated two French ambassadors, one British ambassador, one Italian first secretary, the Ethiopian commissioner for tourism, the vice-minister of culture and information, the president of the National Regional State Council for Harar, the venerable French novelist Jean-François Deniau, the equally venerable British historian of Ethiopia Dr Richard Pankhurst, the mayor of Charleville-Mézières (Rimbaud's hometown), and a clutch of visiting authors, academics, curators and journalists, among them the saturnine Rimbaud scholar Claude Jeancolas, editor of impeccably fine-tuned texts, and the discoverer of the only known photograph of Rimbaud after he left Europe, other than the three self-portraits taken in Harar in 1883.

Rimbaud was not a man to be impressed by this sort of gathering, and when the electricity cut out and the microphones died I thought he was about to wreak revenge. I remembered a precedent – the inauguration of the Place Rimbaud in Djibouti in 1938, an occasion whose descent into chaos is amusingly narrated by the French adventurer Henry de Monfreid, who was present. 'Who can say', concludes Monfreid, 'that this wasn't the ghost of Rimbaud, whistling like a wind of misrule among these official puppets who serve the mountebanks of international politics?' (*Le Radeau de la Méduse*, 1958).

On this occasion his ghost seems content with the arrangements. And why not? It is a fine house, far finer than the ones he actually lived in, and the insistence that it should be his is mainly a matter of hospitality, a virtue which the Harari prize highly and practise expertly.

The louche smuggler and scribbler Monfreid also lived here for a while. His house stands in rolling brown hills about an hour out of Harar (half the journey in a 4 × 4, and half on the bony chestnut nag which seemed a rather safer bet than the makeshift little buggies which the French contingent refers to as *cabriolets*). It is an undistinguished, single-storey, dirt-floor house with the remains of a fruit orchard outside. The women of the family sit patiently on the bed while the assembled experts peer through the gloom.

*

Rimbaud's house is historically dubious and Monfreid's shack frankly disappointing – the unexpected high point in terms of historical house-hunting was provided by the British ambassador, Gordon Wetherell. A tall, genial man in his early fifties, Mr Ambassador had already upstaged his Gallic counterpart by giving the first part of his speech at the Maison Rimbaud in fluent Amharic. He was actually born in Ethiopia. His father still lives and works in Addis Ababa – a coffee-trader like Rimbaud – but it was his maternal grandparents, one Yugoslavian, the other Greek, who first came here, in the 1920s. On the morning before our return to Addis, I went off with him and his wife Rosie in search of his grandfather's farm in a village near Harar, which he remembered from his childhood, and with the help of a villager whose father had worked there, we found it.

Though nominally the offices of the local Peasants' Association, the house is deserted and crumbling – precisely in that state of suspended animation which is so suggestive to memory and imagination, and which is swept clean away when a place becomes a museum. The remembered verandah is no longer there but you can see just where it was; those gnarled frangipani trees must have been planted when the house was built; those unusual rock formations are surely the ones in that little painting they have somewhere at home – and suddenly something flickers amid the broken masonry, that vestige which dead people leave, cunningly hidden, in the houses where they lived.

Back in Addis, luxuriously billeted in the ambassador's residence, I found myself once more in a house with stories to tell. In 1896, in the newly founded capital of Addis Ababa ('New Flower'), Emperor Menelik II granted a *gasha* of land to each of the superpowers – Britain, France, Italy and Russia – camped on his doorstep. A *gasha* is about forty hectares, or a hundred acres. The Russian patch has long since been split up, and the Italians had some of theirs taken away after their occupation of the country, but the British and French embassies still sit amid this huge swathe of land – indeed the Addis embassy is the biggest British diplomatic patch in the world. With its slope of shimmering lawns and rustling woodlands, its ancient shade-bearing trees and rare Himalayan cypress-pines, its paddock, golf course and tennis courts, it has the air of an extremely exclusive country club. Addis is a distant rumour beyond the security gates, a smudge of monoxide in the high mountain air.

The original building was a huddle of thatched Ethiopian *tukuls* (still standing) and a reception tent. A visiting Brit described the place as 'luxuriously furnished', with newspapers and periodicals, and 'files of Reuters telegrams, which were forwarded by camel post from Zeila to Harar, and thence by telephone' (P. H. G. Powell-Cotton, *A Sporting Trip through Abyssinia*, 1902). An early ambassador (or minister, as it was then a legation rather than an embassy) was Wilfred Thesiger. His son and namesake, born here in 1910, was the famous explorer and travel-writer. As a child he recalls seeing the infant son of Haile Selassie carried up the steps of the residence in a basket suspended from his tutor's neck.

The residence is a large, low, bougainvillea-clad house of local stone and cedar. Built in 1910, it radiates Edwardian optimism and opulence. A document in the embassy's excellent library informs me that the building costs came to £21,208, a fair whack in 1910. Old photograph albums show tea parties and gymkhanas and many district commissioners. Empress Zauditu pauses beneath a parasol, *c.* 1920, the daughter of Emperor Menelik and the owner of the city's only motor-car.

★

From Addis I travelled north on a brief trip into the old Christian heartlands of Abyssinia. Unfortunately I had no time to get to the ancient Tigrayan capital of Axum – flights there have been suspended owing to its proximity to the battlefront with Eritrea. I began my tour at Bahir Dar instead. We were ordered to shutter the windows as we came into land so we wouldn't see the Ethiopian fighter-planes lined up near the runway; at Dire Dawa a few days earlier I had seen a dozen MiGs camouflaged with branches of thorn-scrub.

Near Bahir Dar are the Blue Nile Falls, discovered – leaving aside the generations of locals who knew about them all along – by the Scotsman James Bruce. The embassy has a handsome first edition of Bruce's book *Travels to Discover the Source of the Nile* (6 vols., Edinburgh, 1790), though not even this quite prepared me for the scale and verdancy of the scene. In Gondar there are ghostly palaces, and the sumptuous interior of Debre Selassie Church, decorated in the late seventeenth century with vivid Ethiopian versions of the life of Christ. (The guidebooks sometimes refer to these as frescoes, but in fact they were not painted *a fresco* – on wet plaster – but on sized cloth later stuck to the walls.) At Lalibela I scrambled among the strange labyrinthine rock-churches, hewn out about 800 years ago by workmen still unknown.

On the night before my return to Addis, and thence to Europe, I sat in a house in the dirt-poor village of Lalibela. It belonged to the family of my guide for the day, a cheerful, intelligent, devoutly Christian young man in his early twenties called Yeheno. His room was as long as his rather short bed, and about the same across; the door gave straight on to the street, where children played in the dust. There was a vintage poster of Al Pacino as Serpico on the wall. Yeheno's younger sister was preparing coffee – a bed of pepper-tree leaves, a scraping of frankincense in the burner, the sharp tonic of the first infusion (etiquette demands you take three, the last being quite mild) – and Yeheno was filling me in on the family finances. His father, an ex-policeman, receives a state pension of 80 birr per month; his older sister, whose husband was killed in the civil war in 1991, receives a war-widow's pension, also 80 birr per month. The family's regular monthly income was therefore 160 birr: a little over £12. The fact that 160 birr was almost exactly the sum I was paying him for one day's services as my guide added a further twist. These figures allow precious little margin for the fluctuating food prices caused by the region's droughts and wars. Today they have food, he says, but tomorrow who knows?

This is by no means the lowest economic rung in Ethiopia – the second poorest country in the world, by some reckonings – but it was the rung I was sitting on at the moment. And so Yeheno's house in Lalibela, like those other more historic houses in Harar and Addis, had a story to tell. It is an old African story which one knows in outline – war, poverty, fingertip survival – but does not often hear *viva voce*.

19

Joe the Ripper

A New Suspect?
[2008]

They found Mary Jane Kelly lying on her bed, in the dingy room she rented in Miller's Court, off Dorset Street in Spital-fields. She was about twenty-five years old, a colleen from County Limerick, 'possessed of considerable attractions'. Wid-owed young, she had turned, like thousands of others in late Victorian London, to prostitution. One of her clients had taken her for a spree to Paris, and she had started to call herself Marie Jeanette. She was also nicknamed Ginger. She lay with her head 'turned on the left cheek'. One arm was across her stomach, the other turned outwards '& rested on the mattress'. She was naked and 'the legs were wide apart, the left thigh at right angles to the trunk'. These are the words of the police doctor summoned to the scene, Dr Thomas Bond. It was the morning of Friday, 9 November 1888, and Kelly had just become – at a conservative estimate – the fifth and final victim of the serial killer known as Jack the Ripper.

The positioning of the victim's body is consistent with the other murders, the splayed legs an immediately readable porno-graphic cliché: the prostitute in a pose of erotic availability. It is one of the Ripper's 'signatures'. It introduces a theme of retribution – this was her crime, and this is her punishment. Dr Bond does not venture these opinions, of course. His job was to observe, and to record as succinctly and scientifically as possible what he saw. His report continues: 'The whole of the surface of the abdomen & thighs was removed & the abdominal cavity emptied of its viscera. The breasts were cut off, the arms mutilated by several jagged wounds, & the face hacked beyond recognition of the features.' The eviscerated body parts were scattered – or, worse, arranged – about her body, 'viz. the uterus and kidneys with one breast under the head, the other breast by the right foot, the liver between the feet, the intestines by the right side', and so on. The heart was missing, however – 'the pericardium was open below & the heart absent.' It may have been burnt in the fireplace, which bore evidence of a 'fire so large as to melt the spout off the kettle'. More probably it was taken away by the killer. This is another of Jack's signatures: what is known in the lexicons of Ripperology as the 'harvesting' of body parts.

This murder scene is the most gruesome even by the Ripper's standards. Kelly was the only one of the five certain (or 'canonical') victims to have been murdered indoors. He had time to do what he wanted to her. The scene will echo on through innumerable retellings of the Ripper legend, in that rather capacious subsection of popular mythology reserved for serial killers and their atrocities, but is somehow more chilling in the clipped, forensic, almost laconic tones of the police doctor. These are unadorned, scene-of-crime observations – no fog licking at the windowpane; no mention of the blood, which must have been everywhere; no description of the smell in the room. The bare facts are enough to convey the shock of being there, of having this glimpse, as Charles van Onselen puts it, into 'the Angel of Death's laboratory'.

Van Onselen's long, disturbing and magnificently dogged book* takes us through a grim terrain spread across three continents, a world of squalor and violence, of prostitutes and pimps,

---

* Charles van Onselen, *The Fox and the Flies* (Jonathan Cape, 2007).

of tenements and penitentiaries – the world of the 'white slave trade' – but it is to here that the trail keeps winding back: to London's East End in 1888, to the scene in that bedroom in Miller's Court, and to the unanswered question which is at least part of the Ripper's enduring fascination – who was he?

*

An eminent South African historian, van Onselen has pursued this trail for nearly thirty years, though it was a good while before he realized where it was leading. He first caught a glimpse of his prey, as it were out of the corner of his eye, on a day in the late 1970s at Johannesburg Public Library, where he was researching a history of the city's immigrant underworld. He was leafing through an old newspaper, the *Standard & Digger News* of 1898, when he came upon a news item about the American Club. A dodgy establishment on Johannesburg's Sauer Street, the club's chief business was procurement and prostitution, both locally and internationally – a 'trade union' of pimps in 'coded telegraphic communication' as far afield as Russia, Argentina and the United States. There was nothing extraordinary about this, in a gold-mining boomtown awash with money and commercial sex. What caught the researcher's eye was a little anomaly – the president of the club's casual claim or boast that he had previously worked as a 'special agent' with the Society for the Prevention of Crime in New York City. Van Onselen was then 'more interested in processes than personalities', but was sufficiently intrigued to jot down the name of this racketeer-cum-detective – Joseph Silver.

A few weeks later – the serendipity of the archives – the name jumped out at him again. In 1903 Silver was in a court in Bloemfontein giving evidence about a break-in at a jewellery store. Certain details of the story suggested once more his ambiguous connections with the police. Still not knowing quite what he was looking for, van Onselen began to search more purpose-fully for Silver. He was difficult to follow because of his numerous aliases, of which Joseph Silver, first used in about 1891, was his most habitual. His real name was Joseph Lis. He was born in Kielce, Poland, in 1868, one of eight children of a Jewish tailor and petty criminal, Ansel Lis. The name Lis means 'fox', and gives van Onselen half of his title, and many over-tones of pursuit, cunning and predation. The Silver alias was a reference to his mother, whose maiden name was Kweksylber ('quicksilver'). He was at various times Joe Liss, Joe Eligmann, James Smith, Joseph Schmidt, Charlie Silver, Charles Grun-baum, Abraham Ramer, and many other ghost-names.

Silver had indeed been in New York City in the early 1890s, a low-grade thief, thug, jailbird and police informer. Convicted of stealing a couple of dollars and a silk shawl on the Lower East Side, he did two years in the notorious prison at Ossining in upstate New York, better known as Sing Sing. The receiving clerk described him as 5′ 8½″ tall, 140 pounds in weight, with grey eyes, brown hair and a sallow complexion. (However, in a passport application in 1914 he is an inch shorter, and his eyes are blue.) His face was 'full of pimples' and 'pitted' with small scars – the facial lesions associated with secondary syphilis, according to van Onselen, who perhaps makes too much of this conjectural infection and of the behavioural abnormalities of 'neurosyphilis' which it might have entailed.

After New York he is documented in London, *c.* 1895–8, where he ran a brothel near Waterloo Station, was acquitted of a rape charge on a technicality, and served time for petty larceny in both Pentonville and Wormwood Scrubs. Thereafter his operations expanded, mainly but not exclusively in the sex-trade, first into Southern Africa, and then to France, the Low Countries, Scandinavia, and across to Rio de Janeiro, Buenos Aires and Santiago (where he was known as José Silva or

J. Cosman). He 'cruised the Atlantic searching out micro-
climates capable of sustaining his frightening physical and
psychological needs'. The subtitle of the book summarizes him
as a 'racketeer and psychopath', but a more extensive curriculum
vitae assembled by van Onselen lists the following accomplishments: 'arsonist, bankrobber, barber, bigamist, brothel-owner,
burglar, confidence trickster, detective's agent, gangster, horse-
trader, hotelier, informer, jewel thief, merchant, pickpocket,
pimp, policeman, rapist, restaurateur, safe-cracker, smuggler,
sodomist, special agent, spy, storekeeper, trader, thief, widower, wigmaker and white slave trafficker'.

The late nineteenth-century 'white slave trade' – an over-
worked phrase vaguely suggestive of English roses in Middle
Eastern harems – is here given a grisly reality: abductions, rapes,
intimidations, transportations. Silver epitomized the burgeon-
ing internationalism of commercial sex at this time. Those
transatlantic steamers and long-distance trains hymned by the
early Modernist poets were also the vehicles that carried thousands of desperate and duped young women – many of them,
like Silver himself, Jews from Eastern Europe – to their distant
points of sale.

Four surviving photographs chart the racketeer's progress. In
the earliest, undated, perhaps around the age of twenty, he has a
jaunty, almost dandyish look, with a flower in his buttonhole.
Two mugshots from police records show him in criminal mode,
a cold-eyed hoodlum with bad skin and a faint smirk: one is
from Paris in 1909 (see Plate 13) and the other from Santiago.
The last of the portraits was taken in New York in about 1914,
when he was forty-six. It is rather stiffly posed (it is a passport
photograph, but it shows him nearly down to the knees). There
is the simulacrum of substance and success, or anyway a certain
dowdy formality – the waxed moustache, the rounded collar,

the tie-pin, the waistcoat – but the glassy stare and the parted lips give him a sinister, zombie-like look.

Increasingly van Onselen caught the acrid personal scent of the man – his 'pathological misogyny', his need to 'exploit and humiliate'. He 'routinely assaulted' the women who worked for him. There are traces of at least three wives, all of whom worked for him as prostitutes: his 'whore wives', held in physical and psychological thrall. Two of them – Hannah Opticer, whom he married in London, and Hannah Vygenbaum alias Annie Alford – disappear from the record. A third, Rachel Laskin, born in Poland in about 1880, was raped and subjugated by Silver in London, and brought with him by ship to South Africa. She died there in 1945, having spent the last forty years of her life in mental hospitals, known only by the name he had given her, Lizzie Silver.

Silver's violence was the pimp's coercive thuggery laced with psychopathic tendencies. On one occasion he plotted with others to punish a prostitute by chloroforming her and inserting 'blue vitriol' (hydrated copper sulphate) into her vagina. But the episode van Onselen finds most resonant was in Johannesburg in 1899, when Silver threatened another prostitute, Lillie Bloom, who was going to give evidence against him. There were policemen there, but Silver managed to get her aside, and hiss a word of warning. He spoke in Yiddish. He told her that if she betrayed him to the court he would 'open up her belly'.

*

So we come to the book's central assertion – that Joseph Lis or Silver was himself that notorious opener-up of women's bellies, Jack the Ripper. It has to be said that the evidence is often tenuous, and the links speculative, but perhaps tenuous and speculative are as good as we are going to get in a 120-year-old cold-case which from the outset generated so many conflicting accounts and theories.

The first problem is that while there is good documentation of Lis-Silver in London in the later 1890s, after his first spell in New York, very little is known of his movements back in 1888, when the murders occurred. What we do know, thanks to van Onselen's tireless ferreting, is that on 14 August 1884, in Kielce, the sixteen-year-old Lis obtained a passport to travel to England. The typical route for emigrants from Northern Europe was by ship from Hamburg to Hull, thence either by train across to Liverpool for a passage to America, or south to London to disappear into the ghettoes of the East End, which in the 1880s housed an estimated 30,000–40,000 Russo-Polish Jews. By this route, van Onselen believes, Lis arrived in London in about 1884 or 1885.

There is no documentary record of a Joseph Lis in London at this time – which may not be surprising given his fondness for aliases – but there is another Lis there. Sometime after 1881, Lewis Lis set up business as a 'general dealer' in Plumber's Row, just south of the Whitechapel Road, and close to the zone of the Ripper murders. It is an unusual name, and he may be a relative. He was still in business there in early 1888, when his daughter married his clerk, Moses Gourvitch. Around the same time, one Haskel Brietstein alias Adolph Goldberg, a 'chronically unsuccessful actor and burglar', was involved in a break-in at a warehouse directly opposite the Lis family's store on Plumber's Row. This Goldberg was later a close associate of Joseph Lis in New York, and is the only actual source – a not very trustworthy one – for Lis's presence in London at this time. He stated in a New York courtroom that he had known Lis in London in the early months of 1889.

These shreds of evidence make it possible, even plausible, that Joseph Lis was in the Whitechapel area in 1888, though none of them proves it. They are enough, at least, to make the pursuit of other links between Lis and the Ripper worth while. Lis's subsequent career – the career of Joseph Silver, with its catalogue of misogynist violence and cruelty – is one such link: a retrospective psychological profile. Another is Lis's Jewishness. It was widely believed at the time that the Ripper was a Jew, which can certainly be seen as anti-Semitic scapegoating, but which may nonetheless be true. Van Onselen spends a lot of rather rhetorical energy showing how ancient Jewish notions of sexual pollution might conceivably get warped into the ritual butchery of prostitutes practised by the Ripper. The savage precepts of the Book of Ezekiel are seen as a particular blueprint – the 'filthiness' of a woman who has 'committed whoredoms', and the vengeance to be visited on her: 'They shall deal furiously with thee. They shall take away thy nose and thine ears; and thy remnant shall fall by the sword . . . Thus will I make thy lewdness to cease from thee.' Sir Robert Anderson, who was in charge of the investigation in its early stages, later wrote in his memoir that his chief suspect was a 'Polish Jew'. But this man, whom he does not name, was almost certainly Aaron Kosminski, who was incarcerated in an asylum though never charged with the murders. Other Jewish suspects were John Pizer, a shoemaker known as 'Leather Apron'; Severin Klosowski alias George Chapman; Michael Ostrog, described by a police investigator as 'a mad Russian doctor and convict, and unquestionably a homicidal maniac'; and Joseph Isaacs.

A few brief sightings of the Ripper, of varying reliability, concur in certain aspects – a man of middling height with dark hair and a moustache. One of the witnesses said he 'looked like a foreigner', another that he was of 'Jewish appearance'. His physique was 'broad-shouldered' or 'stout', and his style 'shabby genteel'. Lis could fit well enough with this, though not with the general estimate of the suspect's age, which was a decade or

so older than Lis's twenty years. The most detailed description
was given by a labourer, George Hutchinson, an acquaintance
and possibly a client of Mary Jane Kelly. He saw a man go into
Miller's Court with her shortly after 2 a.m. on the night she was
murdered. He infers from their demeanour that the man was
already known to her. He wore a long dark coat with the collar
and cuffs 'trimmed astracan', and a dark felt hat, and his moustache was 'curled at the ends'. Though of 'respectable appearance'
he was 'very surly looking'. He 'walked very sharp'. This
description is tantalizing but problematic. Hutchinson's long
account has more visual and dramatic detail than could reasonably be expected in the circumstances, and is often dismissed as
a fabrication – indeed out in the further reaches of Ripperology
it is mooted that Hutchinson was himself the Ripper, and his
statement a decoy.

It is around the murder of Kelly that the ghost of Joseph Lis
seems almost palpable. One of her neighbours, a German charwoman named Julia Venturney, told police that Kelly had
spoken to her about a 'man named Joe', who she was 'very fond
of'. He sometimes gave her money, but had 'often ill-used her'.
Over in Paternoster Row, meanwhile, a woman came forward
to say that a lodger in her house had acted suspiciously around
the time of the murder, upstairs pacing around in his room all
night, and had disappeared immediately after it. This man was
also called Joe. He was Joseph Isaacs, who was shortly afterwards arrested: according to newspaper reports, he precisely
matched the description given by George Hutchinson, even
down to the astrakhan coat. Nothing much is known about
Isaacs, except that he had previously been imprisoned as a petty
thief. Like all the suspects brought in for questioning, he was
never charged.

Van Onselen believes that the Joe whom Mary Jane Kelly
knew was indeed the agitated lodger Joseph Isaacs; that Isaacs

was none other than Joseph Lis, employing one of his many aliases; and that all these Joes, when properly arranged, lead us to Jack.

And then there are the curious claims of Jabez Spencer Balfour — disgraced Liberal MP, convicted fraudster and journalist — which are mere unattributed third-hand rumours, but arrive at an eerie exactitude. In an article published in 1906, Balfour claimed that the Whitechapel murderer was 'living still' in a 'remote British colony' in Southern Africa, and that his identity was known to some people there. A man Balfour knew said he had conversed with the murderer 'on the night train between the Transvaal and the Orange River Colony in about 1903'. Van Onselen shows how these statements correspond precisely with Silver's known movements in South Africa at this time.

*

'It all fits!' is the axiomatic cry of the conspiracy-theorist, but of course it only does so after a stringent process of selection, in which convenient pieces of the evidential jigsaw are accounted significant, and many others less convenient are discarded. Inevitably van Onselen's argument proceeds in this way, but it feels cogent and compelling even when there is little more than self-belief holding it up.

This is certainly a more meaningful kind of inquiry than the more fashionable subgenre of the celebrity suspect. Over the years these have included Queen Victoria's grandson, the Duke of Clarence; a celebrated doctor, Sir William Gull; a Liverpool merchant, William Maybrick, supposed author of the manuscript known as the Ripper's 'Diary'; and the artist Walter Sickert. Sickert's candidacy has been energetically championed by the thriller-writer Patricia Cornwell, though she did not originate the theory. Sickert had a louche interest in the London underworld, and the Ripper in particular, and he did a series of paintings, the 'Camden Town Nudes', loosely inspired by the murder of a prostitute in 1905. But Cornwell seems to have missed an early and major fork in the biographical highway, where one road leads off to the painting of pictures on disturbing sexual themes, and the other to the actual perpetration of sex-crimes. That one might be seen as actual evidence of the other is implausible both psychologically (do we suspect the author of *Titus Andronicus* of cooking up children in a pie?) and logistically (being rather a give-away after he had concealed his identity so well at the time). Cornwell's book, *Portrait of a Killer* (2002), is now mainly memorable for its enormous research bill – she reportedly spent $30 million acquiring Sickert works and memorabilia – and for her alleged *folie de grandeur* of destroying a painting in the hope of finding traces of the artist's DNA, to match with traces on one of the letters purportedly (but almost certainly not) written by Jack.

Van Onselen hopes that he has shown 'beyond reasonable doubt' that Joseph Lis-Silver was the Ripper; most readers will probably conclude that he has not, or at least not yet. What he has done is to probe deeply and incisively, and in a sense courageously, into that underworld of late nineteenth-century sex and violence. If not the Ripper himself, one sees in that last, sinister photograph of Silver a true denizen of the Ripper's world. And if one shivers a little – those vacant eyes, those lips parted below the moustache, those powerful, spatulate, thick-fingered hands resting on the thigh – that is undoubtedly a compliment to the author of this engrossing book.

20

'The wind comes up out of nowhere'

Arthur Cravan in Mexico

[2006]

In the annals of French literature Arthur Cravan is more often a colourful footnote than a sober paragraph. He is usually referred to as 'the poet and boxer Arthur Cravan', and this odd-seeming conjunction is often fleshed out with more disreputable terms such as 'con-man' or 'adventurer'. He is also described as Oscar Wilde's nephew, which is true up to a point – he was actually the nephew of Wilde's wife, Constance. As a writer Cravan had a brief and stormy career, in Paris, in the years around the outbreak of the First World War. His chief influences were Rimbaud, Alfred Jarry and the Italian Futurists; he preceded by a few years the Dadaists and Surrealists, who acclaimed him a pioneering figure. He was, said André Breton, a 'barometer' of the avant-garde. As a heavyweight boxer his career peaked in 1916, when he fought the formidable Jack Johnson in Barcelona. He lasted nearly six rounds. These two strands of Cravan's career are not as diverse as one might think. His stance as a writer was extremely combative: confrontation and 'anti-art' polemic were his métier. As the poet Mina Loy, who was briefly his wife, put it: 'The instinct of "knock-out" dominated his critique.' One of my favourite Cravan pronouncements is the contemptuous dismissal *'Toute la littérature, c'est: ta, ta, ta, ta, ta, ta.'* One might translate *'ta ta'* as 'blah blah', but the sentence is also very physical, the repeated monosyllables delivered like a series of jabs to the chin of literature.

At its best Cravan's writing has a wayward brilliance, but

probably his greatest creation was himself, or at least the deeply dodgy persona which he presented to the public. Before a fight he would unnerve opponents with a bellowed recital of his accomplishments — not his successes in the ring, which were in the end not much to boast about, but a dubious curriculum vitae including 'hotel-rat' (i.e. thief), muleteer, snake-charmer, chauffeur, 'ailurophile' (cat-lover), gold-prospector, nephew of Oscar Wilde and 'poet with the shortest hair in the world'. These pre-fight performances are comic, and he is often very funny on the page, but his eccentricities hover on the edge of a more menacing kind of craziness. He stood about 6′4″ tall; for the Johnson fight he weighed in at 105 kilos (16½ stone) but was heavier when out of condition. In civvies he was insouciant, dandified, caddish-looking: a fur collar, a *chapeau melon*, his huge shoulders draped in an expensive-looking coat probably bought on credit (see Plate 14). Fair-haired and square-jawed, in certain photographs he is very handsome, and he was known as a voracious womanizer. Mina Loy's first impression when they met in New York was that he combined 'the air of a Viking with the repartee of a Victorian charwoman'.

His name is not much known this side of the Channel, where there is as yet neither a biography nor a full translation of his writings. (A long-awaited biography is in preparation by the leading Anglophone Cravaniste, Roger Lloyd Conover, and a selection of his work, translated by Terry Hale and others, appears in *Four Dada Suicides*, 2005.) This lacuna is curious, because although Cravan was Swiss by birth, and wrote exclusively in French, he was actually a mix of Irish and English by blood.

I have long been fascinated by this hyperbolic but ultimately enigmatic figure, and not the least enigmatic thing about him is the matter of his death. In early 1917 he left Europe for the United States, on the run from the draft — '*On ne me fait pas marcher, moi!*' There he continued to sow scandal, notably when arrested for indecent exposure at the opening of an exhibition by the 'Independents' (Francis Picabia, Marcel Duchamp, et al.) at New York's Grand Central Gallery. The entry of the United States into the war made him liable once more to conscription, and in the last days of 1917 he crossed the border into Mexico. He was last seen in about October 1918, but whether this is correctly the date of his death remains open to question. If it is, he died at the age of thirty-one. It is generally said he drowned off the Mexican coast, but among the many legends that surround him are alleged later sightings, and there are some picturesque theories concerning his survival. On a recent visit to Mexico, I attempted some sifting of the facts and fantasies of his disappearance – if not to answer, then at least to pose more clearly, the questions that hang over his last months.

*

It comes as no great surprise to learn that Arthur Cravan was not really Arthur Cravan. He first used the name in 1910, when he was in his early twenties. It is a *nom de plume*, but the nature of the man tempts one to call it an alias. It is generally said (though never, as far as I can find, by Cravan himself) that the forename is a tribute to Arthur Rimbaud, whose poetry and lifestyle were undoubtedly a major influence; and that the surname is taken from a small village in Burgundy (now Cravant) where his first wife, Renée Bouchet, came from.

He was born Fabian Avenarius Lloyd, in a residential suburb of Lausanne, on 22 May 1887, the second son of a well-to-do Anglo-Irish gentleman, Otho Holland Lloyd, and a former governess, Clara 'Nellie' Hutchinson, whose origins are obscure but who was certainly born illegitimate. They were married in 1884, just a month after Otho's sister, Constance, had married Oscar Wilde. (Cravan's claim to be 'the grandson of the Queen's Chancellor' – one of his pre-fight brags – was grounded in truth:

his grandfather Horace Lloyd was a distinguished jurist and privy councillor. Many of Cravan's statements put one in mind of Theodor Adorno's psychoanalytical maxim 'Only the exaggerations are true.') Though Cravan never met him, his notorious uncle Oscar was a profound influence – more so than his father, who deserted the family shortly after Cravan's birth. He was thirteen when Wilde died in Paris, but the name had never been mentioned in his bourgeois family. It was a later meeting with his cousin Vyvyan Holland – Wilde's second son – which kindled his interest. One of his first truly Cravanesque pieces, self-published in 1912, is a strange séance-like 'interview' with the long-dead Wilde, whom he also calls Sebastian after Wilde's Parisian alias, Sebastian Melmoth. The piece veers between adulation and insult; Cravan is seduced by the possibility that he was Wilde's illegitimate son. The ending is rather fine:

> Out on the pavement he squeezed my hand and, embracing me, he murmured once more: 'You are a terrible boy.' [These words in English in the original] I watched him going off into the night, and just at that moment something tempted me to laugh, and from afar I stuck my tongue out at him, and made a gesture of giving him a great big kick. It was not raining but the air was chill. I remembered that Wilde had no overcoat, and I thought how poor he must be. A wave of sentiment rolled through my heart: I was sad and filled with love. In search of consolation I looked up – the moon was so lovely it only swelled my grief. I was thinking that Wilde had perhaps misunderstood my words; that he did not realize I could never be serious; that I had caused him pain. And I began to run after him like a madman. At every crossroads I strained my eyes for him, and shouted 'Sebastian! Sebastian!' I careered up and down the boulevards until I was certain I had lost him. Wandering the streets I slowly made my way home, my eyes forever fixed on that useless idiot, the moon.

This is typical of Cravan's style, the overwroughtness expressed in a style of controlled lucidity. As early as 1905 he wrote in a letter to his mother that he preferred a 'down-to-earth style' ('*le style terre-à-terre*') and apart from some flowery juvenilia he mostly stuck to that maxim, however bizarre the content. The Wilde 'interview' was convincing enough to inspire a po-faced report in the *New York Times* of 9 December 1913. Its headline, 'No one Found Who Saw Wilde Dead', is an amusing vindication of Cravan as prankster, but has also a rather chilling note of prophecy concerning Cravan's own demise five years later.

The Wilde piece appeared, like most of Cravan's extant work, in the magazine *Maintenant*, which ran for five issues at irregular intervals between 1912 and 1915. (A sixth issue was advertised but seems never to have appeared.) A complete flush of *Maintenant*s recently sold at auction for 15,000 euros. A confection of poetry, essay, polemic and scandal, *Maintenant* was entirely written and published by Cravan – the other contributors (Robert Miradique, W. Cooper, E. Lajeunesse, Marie Lowitska, etc.) are all pseudonyms. Even the advertisements bear his skewed imprint – the restaurant Chez Jourdain entices customers with the words 'Where can you see Van Dongen [the Flemish painter Kees van Dongen] put food in his mouth, chew, digest, smoke?'; and a glue has the slogan 'You can't break everything, but with Seccotine you can glue everything together again.' The most extensive of Cravan's subsidiary identities, it seems, is that of 'Edouard Archinard', who not only contributed to *Maintenant*, but actually had a small exhibition of paintings in Paris in 1914. He is still mentioned briefly in French art reference-books ('Little is known about . . .'), but Roger Conover argues convincingly that he was yet another of Cravan's disguises, even down to the discovery that Archinard was the name of a headmaster at the college in Lausanne which Cravan attended. In 1992 four small Archinard canvases were exhibited at Paris's

Gallerie 1900–2000, whose owner, Marcel Fleiss, is a noted Cravaniste. Cravan's ventriloquy seems almost obsessive: 'my fatal plurality', he calls it; 'my character, heart of my inconsistencies'; 'my detestable nature, which . . . makes me sometimes honest and sometimes sly; vain and modest, coarse and distinguished' (*Maintenant* 3). He presented, said Loy, 'an unreality of himself to the world, to occupy himself with while he made his spiritual getaway'.

Cravan sold his magazine in the streets of Paris, out of a wheelbarrow, typically stationed outside some grand cultural event comprehensively trashed in the issue he was selling. He was the '*critique brutale*', the prize-fighter amok among the aesthetes. A particular target was André Gide. In *Maintenant* 2 (July 1913) Cravan announced, 'I have to go and visit Gide, he's a millionaire: no kidding, I'm going to fleece that old scribbler.' The next issue duly featured an interview full of taunts and abuse. Part of the reason was Gide's equivocal comments about Wilde, and the two are compared throughout: Wilde, said Cravan approvingly, 'looked like an elephant', while Gide looks 'neither like an elephant, nor like an ordinary man: he looks like an artist' – the latter a term of execration. Another writer he tangled with was Guillaume Apollinaire, who challenged him to a duel further to some obscene comments about the painter Marie Laurencin. Other provocations were issued in a series of Cravan 'lectures' – anarchic improvisations somewhat akin to the 'happenings' of the sixties. A typical *annonce* reads: 'At Les Noctambules on Friday 6 March [1914], at 9 o'clock in the evening, Arthur Cravan will lecture, dance and box.' He gave these one-man shows in curious and often revealing attire – a sense of brute erotic prowess was one aspect of the provocation. During one of these 'pantomimic atrocities' (as Loy called them) he brandished a loaded shotgun and threatened to commit suicide on stage; at another he hurled a heavy attaché case full of papers into the audience. Of these performances Picabia said drily: 'Cravan never tried to shock others: he tried to shock himself, which is a much harder thing to do.' Among his friends were the artist Robert Delauney and the poet Blaise Cendrars. The latter recalls Cravan dancing the tango at the Bal Bullier nightclub, in a black shirt with the front cut away to reveal 'bleeding tattoos and obscene inscriptions on his skin'.

Among those he encountered in the Paris nightclubs was the former heavyweight champion Jack Johnson, who had fled prosecution in America under the Mann Act for his liaison with a teenage girl. Cravan said of him: 'After Poe, Whitman and Emerson he is the greatest glory of America.' There was a background of artistic interest in boxing at this time, but though Braque and Picasso made drawings of black boxers they never went as far as getting into the ring with them. Cravan fought Johnson amid much fanfare at the Plaza de Toros in Barcelona on 23 April 1916; some scratchy footage of the fight remains. It was a one-sided contest but Cravan lasted five three-minute rounds before being felled in the sixth. 'Johnson laughed,' he later recalled, 'and I think I laughed too. I knew I was going to get beaten.'

With his share of the 50,000-peseta purse Cravan bought a ticket on the steamship *Montserrat*, and in early January 1917 he embarked at Cádiz, destination New York. It was not the first time he had been to America. From his youth he had been a prodigious traveller – 'I have twenty countries in my memory, and I carry the colours of a hundred towns in my soul' – and while some of his more exotic itineraries are hard to verify it is fairly certain he had travelled in the States as a teenager, and perhaps also in the East and Australia. One of his best poems, '*Sifflet*' ('Whistle'), evokes the charisma of the docks, where 'the rhythm of the ocean cradles the liners' and 'the gaslights dance like spinning tops' and 'the heroic express-train whistles'. Among his fellow passengers on the *Montserrat* was Leon Trotsky, a rather different kind of exile (though also headed for a fatal rendezvous in Mexico). Trotsky noted in his journal that the ship was full of 'undesirable elements' – 'deserters, adventurers, speculators' – among them 'a boxer and part-time writer, a cousin [*sic*] of Oscar Wilde, who frankly declared that he would rather smash a Yankee's face in the noble art of boxing than be done in by a German'.

In New York Cravan met and fell in love with the English Modernist poet and painter Mina Loy. She was thirty-four years old, very beautiful, 'splendid and inaccessible'; alternatively (in the view of Cravan's mother) she was a neurotic Jewish divorcee with two young children parked in Italy. Their affair has the sparkle of obsession – 'tenderness awakened in him,' she later wrote, 'and tenderness in a strong man is always a deluge.' But soon the threat of conscription grew acute, and in the late summer of 1917 Cravan set out on an ill-fated and rather desolate tramp northwards with a writer, A. B. Frost, who contracted tuberculosis and subsequently died. The journey can be traced in Cravan's increasingly desperate letters to Mina: New York – New Haven – New London – Boston – Portland – Bangor – Meductic – Sydney, Novia Scotia – St John's, Newfoundland. There, it is said, he enlisted in the crew of a Danish fishing-boat. It was probably during this journey that Cravan's last extant literary text was written. A sheaf of what might be called 'automatic writings', it remained in Loy's possession and was first published in New York in 1942, in its original French, under the title 'Notes'. Introducing it, André Breton said: 'connoisseurs will breathe in these pages the pure climate of genius, of genius in the raw.' Sometimes unreadable, it occasionally blossoms into moments of beauty:

> It is snowing on the empty benches – the biggest monuments make the most dust – all these fruits promised by autumn – all that shines in springtime is promised by winter – the silvery sun

of winter – Canada, I know you are green – and to take a walk
in the woods . . .

In December Cravan wrote to Loy from the border-town of
Nuevo Laredo, announcing his imminent departure for Mexico,
and telling her to mail any letters to 'Arturo Cravan, General
Delivery, Mexico City'. He sends her a photograph 'taken for
my Mexican passport', apologizing for the 'piteous state' of his
clothes – 'just look at that torn *faux col*!' This is perhaps the
extant passport photo of Cravan, almost certainly our last image
of him, haunting in its sense of the dandy now somewhat battered by fortune's knocks. (Is he wearing a *faux col* – a detachable
collar – and if so is it torn? It is crumpled certainly.) The letter
includes the ominous comment '*Je suis l'homme des extrêmes et du
suicide*', but this refers to the apparent breakdown of his relationship with Loy (who consistently failed to answer his letters) and,
as the breakdown was only temporary, it need not fuel the
theory that Cravan later committed suicide. He crossed into
Mexico on 20 December 1917.

★

Cravan in Mexico – it is not quite a zone of silence, but it must
be reconstructed from difficult sources. There are only two eyewitness accounts. One is *Colossus*, Mina Loy's fragmentary
memoir of her relationship with Cravan, unpublished in her
lifetime, but it is not very informative, being mainly bound up
with emotional and poetic concerns. The other is a little-known
book by Bob Brown, a New York journalist who wrote about
the 'slackers' – as the dropouts and draft-dodgers of the day
were known – in a fictionalized memoir called *You Gotta Live*,
published in 1932. In this, Cravan appears as 'Rex Johns' and
Loy as 'Rita'. Brown writes of Rex's 'striking figure', his 'smooth
manners and grace of being', his charisma ('What Rex Johns
had, he had for women') and his hybrid exoticism: 'Educated in

Europe and England, talking French, German, Italian and Spanish as no native would, Rex's nationality was hard to place: he
seemed like a Scandinavian of the wealthy, aristocratic class.'
Brown certainly knew Cravan and Loy in Mexico, but his novel-
izing streak puts a question mark over what he says about them.
To these sources can be added some notices of Cravan in the
Mexican press, exclusively in a boxing connection; and a few
brief letters he wrote to his remarried mother, Nellie Grandjean, in Switzerland. (These letters have never been published in
full; they were in the possession of Cravan's elder brother, Otho
Lloyd, until his death in 1979; they are partly cited, in Spanish,
in Maria Lluïsa Borràs's *Arthur Cravan: Una biografía*, 1993.) At
the outer periphery of information there is a buzz of second-
and third-hand testimonies, plugged rather into the mythology
than the facts (a distinction, admittedly, which Cravan blurs
more radically than most). The following is a brief resumé of
what we know about 'Arturo Cravan' in Mexico.

In early 1918, in Mexico City, he worked as a boxing instructor
at the Escuela de Cultura Fisica Sandow, in a large town-house
on Calle Tacuba which is still standing, elegantly refurbished,
with tall french windows illuminating the former gym on the
first floor. During his first weeks in the city he lodged at Hotel
Juarez, a few blocks down on the same street. This may possibly
be the 'Slackers' Hotel' described by Bob Brown as an 'ancient
hidalgo mansion, grand, crazy and creaky with ghostly stair-
cases', but it is certainly not the glass and concrete building that
stands at the address today. Calle Tacuba lies behind the fashionable shopping streets of Cinco de Mayo and Francisco Madero:
quieter, more humdrum. It was thus when Graham Greene
passed through in the 1930s – it is the street 'where you can buy
your clothes cheaper if you don't care much for appearances'.

In mid January, Mina Loy arrived in Mexico City, and there
they were married on 25 January 1918. 'We left the town hall,

walking with great strides like conquering giants,' she wrote. They set up home, very poor, in a 'terrible' room with arum lilies on the patio and 'old sorceresses' squatting on the pavement outside. Brown pictures Mina cooking tortillas on a charcoal stove in their 'dark, earthen-floored cave . . . in the garbaged outskirts', but a letter of 30 April gives their address as Calle de Soto, which is just off the central boulevard of Paseo de la Reforma. In May, Cravan was sick, and there were fears for his life, but by July he had sufficiently recovered to resume training. On 9 August he fought a Mexican heavyweight, Honorato Castro, at the Teatro Principio in Mexico City; he went ten rounds and lost on points. His promoter was a man named Red Winchester, described by Brown (under the name 'Red Remington') as a 'flame-haired New York Jew', and one of the most energetic of the Slackers in Mexico. 'Red walked beside Rex like a keeper beside his elephant; he was only half Rex's height but his face seemed twice as beaming-wide.'

Cravan's last known letter, written to his mother from Mexico City, is dated 3 September 1918; in it he says he will be leaving Mexico in twelve days' time, and tells her to write to him at Poste Restante in Buenos Aires. His anticipated departure doubtless depended on the proceeds of his forthcoming fight with Jim 'Black Diamond' Smith, slated for 15 September. (Boxing archives list various Jim Smiths around this time: he may be the heavyweight from Westchester County, New York, who was fighting in the States between 1908 and 1917.) Two days before the fight, a glimpse of Cravan is granted us by the Mexican magazine *Arte y deportes*, whose reporter, signed only as 'Chaplin', caught up with him at a rooming-house on Calle Nuevo Méjico:

> Stairs lead up from a small entrance hall, to a dining room where they are making chocolate. I ask a little nervously for Señor Cravan, the boxer who will fight Jim Smith next Sunday . . . In

his room I meet the strong and muscular fighter, who grips my hand as if we were old friends, invites me to take a seat, and says: 'I am a native of Switzerland, my name is Arthur Cravan, 27 years old, married. I have been boxing for seven years in all parts of the world.' . . . He tells me that Mexico is an unforgettable experience, that the climate here is delightful, the landscapes enchanting. He says he is being prepared for the fight by Rosendo Arnaiz, the Mexican champion, and that he devotes three or four hours a day to training. 'I begin at five in the after-noon and finish at eight or nine. Much of the day I spend walking in Chapultepec. Most nights I am asleep by half past eight. My agent is Señor Winchester, here present: he accepts all kinds of bets on me.'

One does not quite trust the reporter's verbatims, which seem strained, but this is a more vivid glimpse of Cravan in Mexico City than either Loy or Brown gives us – the thick sweet smell of cacao, the walks in the woods of Chapultepec, the genial patter with its casual untruths (he was not twenty-seven but thirty-one). These are the last recorded words of Cravan: all bets are on!

The fight with Black Diamond Smith took place at the Plaza de Toros on Sunday, 15 September 1918, the last fixed date in Cravan's life-story. It resulted in a humiliating KO. The contest was 'laughable', reported *Arte y deportes*. Cravan did little except use his superior height to keep Smith at bay; Smith dispatched him early in the second round with a 'blow to the thorax' fol-lowed by '*un terrible swing*' to the jaw. According to Loy, Cravan's purse for the fight was about 2,000 pesos, which he shared with others who had earlier 'helped him when he starving and sick'. Cravan and Loy probably left Mexico City shortly after this. They had certainly left sometime before 18 October, when it was reported in the same magazine that Cravan 'is in Veracruz, and will probably return for a rematch against Smith'. On this

last point *Arte y deportes* was wrong, for the next we hear of them
they are in the highlands, in the airy town of Oaxaca. During
this journey, Loy says, they earned a few pesos by putting on
'little theatrical shows' in the plazas and villages they passed
through – a tantalizing revenance of the Parisian Cravan. Cravan also boxed in Oaxaca, and according to Brown scored some
notable victories, but Brown's 'Rex' wins fights more often than
Cravan really did. And, by this stage visibly, Mina was pregnant.

★

The scene of Cravan's disappearance lies on the Pacific coast of
Mexico, at the point below Acapulco where the coast curves
round to run almost due east towards the Guatemalan border. It
is hardly populous now, and was doubtless very wild nearly
ninety years ago, when Cravan and Loy arrived at the small sea-
port of Salina Cruz. They came in by train, on the narrow-gauge
line which still snakes through the outskirts of the town, though
now disused. This train-line tells a story of boom and bust. It
ran across the isthmus from Veracruz, linking the Caribbean and
Pacific coasts, and when it was completed in 1907 Salina Cruz
was transformed into an international port. But just seven years
later the Panama Canal was opened: the rail-link was instantly
obsolete, and Salina Cruz's glory years were over. Today the
station where Cravan alighted in 1918 is deserted: a boarded-up
ticket-office in fake red brick, a girdered terminus rampant with
shrubbery and patrolled by feral cats. Some of its high glass roof
is still intact, making it a giant hothouse. I think of Cravan's
'*Sifflet*' – the train 'whistles infinitely across the valleys, / Dreaming of the oasis: the station with a sky of glass'.

'Arrived at a new town,' wrote Loy,

> [Cravan] would give it a glance and assess its population, then
> tramp through every street, round its suburbs, along the har-
> bours, through the warehouses on the wharves, past the shunting

lines of railways . . . Wherever one went with him one was sure
to arrive sooner or later in some forbidden spot, so intuitively
did he separate himself from the accepted places. He was looking for something of his own among all this, that something the
poet always seems to have mislaid.

Salina Cruz today is a brash, friendly, upbeat place, buffeted
by a warm ocean wind that whips grit in your eyes and rolls
plastic bottles down the street. A measure of prosperity has
returned since the port was renovated as an oil terminal in the
1970s. The centre of town is a pleasant palm-shaded plaza where
the *urraca*, the glossy little crows of the region, descend in hordes
at twilight with a shrilling so intense it's like an electric current.
Around here are some places that Cravan would have known. A
block away is the old Hotel Gambrinus, its arches now scrawled
with graffiti, its ground floor subdivided into murky boutiques.
The swanky place to stay was the Hotel Terminus (or Hotel
Salina Cruz), with its long colonnaded breezeway, and its spire
like a minor French chateau, but one must be content with an
old photograph. It was recently demolished – soon to be
replaced, I am told, by a Mormon temple. But these hotels
would not have housed our indigent poets; they stayed at a place
which Brown generically calls the 'Slackers' Hotel', of which
we learn only that it had green shutters and looked out at a
warehouse where molasses was stored. Another of Cravan's
haunts was a dive called Otto's Bar, but Brown's description – a
'shaky shack' with 'pink cotton mosquito netting at the doors
and windows'– does not encourage the idea of its survival.

The heart of the town was its docks and they are gone, or
rather transformed beyond recognition. The cantinas in the
dockside alleys have closed down, though their cheery promises
of food and drink 'and a little bit extra' remain painted on the
walls. Since its development Salina Cruz is an oil refinery with a
capacity of 300,000 barrels a day, a refrigerated terminal for

liquid petroleum gas, and the only dry-dock on the Pacific seaboard between San Diego and the Panama Canal. Around these facilities lies a rind of razor-wired walls and security gates. The old fishermen's wharf is somewhere inside it, but you cannot go there if you are not a fisherman; you are directed instead down an unpromising little trail that skirts the cordon. Across the ubiquitous train-tracks, past the wire-netting with scraps of black plastic caught like chars from a bonfire, and suddenly you are out on the wide Pacific seashore. It was perhaps here that Cravan worked fixing up an old boat, as described by Brown. 'Rex . . . found a stout sailing vessel that suited. Because of a hole stove in its hull he bought it cheap . . . He had the boat towed to a small private pier a mile from town, where he worked at refitting it.'

This boat plays a crucial role in the story of Cravan's disappearance. In Brown's version, when the boat was ready, 'Rex' sailed it out one evening, intending just to 'go out a little way to get the sails working' and then 'tack back', but never returned. The chapter ends with 'Rita' forlornly waiting on the seashore, 'staring out over the black water'. This is poetic licence: Mina was almost certainly not in Salina Cruz when Cravan sailed out. She had boarded a Japanese hospital-ship bound for Buenos Aires, where she had arrived by the beginning of November. Her own version of events is inscribed in a long, lucid letter to his mother, Nellie Grandjean, dated 7 March 1921. It is not first hand, but it is based on the eyewitness account of Owen Cattell, another member of the 'slacker' crew at Salina Cruz. According to this, Fabian – she uses Cravan's real name in this family letter – left Salina Cruz to sail up the coast to Puerto Angel, a journey of four days 'in his little boat'. (The distance is about 150 nautical miles across the Gulf of Tehuantepec.) There his plan was to buy or fix up a larger boat, big enough to take him and three others down the coast to Argentina – or anyway towards Argentina: actually to sail round the Horn to Buenos Aires, which she implies was their intention, would have been very ambitious. The three others she identifies as Red Winchester, Owen Cattell and an unnamed Swedish mariner who was Cattell's friend. Loy writes:

> They all pooled their money and gave it to Fabian so he could buy a boat. They waited for him at the hotel in Salina Cruz, so that they did not have to pay for the journey to Puerto Angel, as they had very little money left . . . There is not the slightest possibility of him disappearing on purpose. He left all his belongings with his friends who were waiting for him, despite them urging him to take them with him in case something happened. But he did not want to. He took Cattell's clothes (who was half his height) because his pack was easier to stow in the boat which he took to Puerto Angel: he wanted everything shipshape so he could slip away at night in the boat with as little luggage as possible.

The date of his departure from Salina Cruz would have been mid October 1918. It cannot be much earlier: he was still in Mexico City in mid September, and had since travelled many hundreds of miles, fought boxing-matches, and bought and repaired a boat. It cannot be much later, for by 3 November Loy was writing from Buenos Aires asking Nellie Grandjean if she had news of him: Cravan was by that point missing.

In the same narrative Loy states that 'Fabian bought a boat in Puerto Angel', but, as no one ever saw him after his departure from Salina Cruz, this seems to be a supposition. Did Cravan, in fact, ever make it to Puerto Angel? In the somewhat unlikely hope of an answer I set off for this picturesque little fishing-port, four days' sailing in Cravan's 'little boat', but nowadays reachable in a few hours by bus on an exhilarating coast road skirting the lower flanks of the Sierra Madre del Sur. An interview with the jovial harbourmaster, Captain Bartolomé López Ruiz, draws a predictable blank. There are no old ledgers in his neat office with its nautical charts and rule-books. All boats docking in Puerto Angel have to register here, he says, but after five years all the paperwork is sent up to the Coordinación General of the merchant navy (part of the Department of Communications and Transport) in Mexico City. The likelihood of documentation back to 1918? He seems to find the date amusingly distant. It is 'not impossible', he says, though I was later told that even thirty years ago registration was almost non-existent.

No building remains here from 1918: the coast was hit by a tsunami in 1928 which wiped out the entire waterfront. Juanito or John – a grizzled, pipe-smoking American of Finnish extraction, who has lived for years in Puerto Angel – filled me in on some local history. At the time of Cravan's visit the waterfront consisted of a single wharf and a couple of warehouses. The main trade was coffee, brought down from the Sierra by mule and loaded by launches on to ships in the bay; there were also mixed cargo vessels which carried passengers, and occasional visits from boats looking for pearls. There was no hotel or rooming-house here until the late thirties. Juanito mused on Cravan's requirements for the journey to Argentina. 'To make that journey in those days he would have probably been sailing a small schooner. The trading vessels working up and down the coast today are diesel-powered, but in the old days it would have been a schooner-rigged sailing boat. For four people the minimum size would be thirty feet. But I'm beginning to wonder why he came here to buy a boat, since there were no resident boats here to be purchased. Perhaps someone took him on a wild goose chase from which he never returned.' Juanito also mentioned the possibility of pirates. 'Pirates ruled this coast,' he said. 'Don't underestimate the objective dangers. This was a wild and primitive coast.' If Cravan was murdered, piracy is more probable than the other scenario sometimes floated, which is that he was killed in connection with a fight-fixing scam: this seems to trace back to an unconvincing episode in Brown's memoir, in which 'Rex' fixes a fight in Mexico City.

If Puerto Angel was indeed Cravan's last port of call, there remains no documentary trace of his visit, and no architectural trace of the place he visited. But what does remain is the ocean, and the intimate knowledge of those who live by it. As I outlined the Cravan case to Captain López he took on an air of professional resignation. He was sailing in October? This is a very dangerous time: the *época mala*. It is the time of the *nortes*, or northerlies – cold fronts in the Gulf of Mexico are displaced southwards, sending strong north winds gusting across the isthmus. They are particularly active in the Gulf of Tehuantepec, which Cravan had to cross – indeed the fishermen here call these winds *tehuantepecaños*. He hauled out an old handbook from the Mexican Meteorological Service. A table of tropical storms in the Gulf over a 24-year period (1950–73) shows that nearly half occurred in September or October. The strongest recorded wind, a north-westerly in 1957, was measured at 54 metres per second, or about 120 mph.

Juanito also had experience of the *nortes*: 'There's no visual indication, no clouds, just clear air, then the wind comes up out of nowhere, hurricane force, strong enough to pick up stones, strong enough to knock you flat and sink your boat.'

*

Local knowledge cannot re-create the event but has a coherence which the legend of Cravan's survival surely lacks. It tells us of the real and regularly occurring dangers faced by a man crossing the Gulf of Tehuantepac in October in a small and perhaps imperfectly repaired craft. On a thorny headland above Puerto Angel, watching a lone fishing boat head out into the pink-washed immensity of the Pacific at twilight, I know that the most plausible answer to Cravan's disappearance is that he was lost at sea.

But if anyone resists the notion of plausibility it is the great and implausible Cravan, and the case for his survival should not go unremarked. A couple of small oddities can be discarded fairly quickly. The first is an item in *Arte y desportes* on 1 November 1918, promising an 'interesting bout' in Mexico City between Black Diamond Smith and 'a worthy opponent just arrived from Merida'. This sounds like a reference to Cravan, whose rematch with Smith had been trailed two weeks earlier, but the report is too vague to be taken as evidence that he had surfaced in Mexico City. The second is a telegram received by Cravan's mother on 9 March 1919, purportedly written by Cravan himself in Buenos Aires. But this was probably sent by Mina as a desperate and rather heartless ploy to get information: so Mme Grandjean suspected, anyway. A third scenario refers to a report of two unidentified men shot dead by Mexican police on the Rio Grande: one of them is described as 'very tall' and 'dark blond'. This report is not documented, as far as I know, and so is just another rumour.

But there is a more persistent ghost than these — an elusive figure going under the name of 'Dorian Hope', who was active in New York and Paris in the early 1920s, offering fabricated Oscar Wilde manuscripts for sale. The forgeries were accomplished, and were initially accepted as genuine by Robert Sherard, Wilde's first biographer; some of them are now in the William Andrews Clark Library in Los Angeles. A book collector named Herbert Boyce Satcher met Hope in New York in 1919; he described him as 'a strange sort of vagrant poet', who wrote refined verses 'completely at variance with his character'. His appearance was 'rather derelict, with a velour hat down close over his eyes'. Satcher's last relic of Dorian Hope was a postcard from Southampton, dated 6 July 1920. A few months later, from Paris, begin a series of letters from Hope, now describing himself as André Gide's secretary, offering more counterfeit material to book-dealers in London and Dublin. He also used other aliases, such as 'Sebastian Hope', 'B. Holland' and 'James M. Hayes'. A book-dealer, William Figgis, met him in Paris in 1922, 'dressed like a Russian count with a magnificent fur-lined overcoat'. Many years later Wilde's son Vyvyan Holland said of Dorian Hope: 'I always understood that he was my first cousin Fabian Lloyd. The Dorian came from Dorian Gray and the Hope from Adrian Hope, who was one of the family trustees. He also called himself Arthur Cravan and edited a short-lived Dadaist magazine' (letter to William Figgis, 23 September 1955). However, Hope's presence in Paris in the early 1920s seems to argue against its being him: Cravan had been a well-known figure there a few years previously. It is one of the problems of these supposed sightings: the settings are unimaginative – a creaky ghost in predictable haunts. A glimpse of him in Tahiti or Tashkent would fit the bill rather better.

A theory recently aired is that A. Cravan reinvented himself as the no less mysterious author 'B. Traven', who wrote hard-bitten, Mexico-based novels, most famously *The Treasure of the Sierra Madre* (1927). This is proposed in Mike Richardson and Rick Geary's comic-strip biography, *Cravan* (2005). Other than orthographic neatness, and the fact that Traven lived in seclusion in southern Mexico, the theory has little to recommend it. Though Traven's true identity remains controversial, he was almost certainly of German origin, and photographs of him as an elderly man look nothing like Cravan.

It is tempting to think of Cravan slipping off into the Mexican sunset, making his 'spiritual getaway' to start a new life under a new name. It chimes in with a Modernist or Existentialist theme of rootlessness, of which he is an early example, though it would also be a sour reflection on his character, as his great escape would have involved leaving his pregnant wife virtually penniless in Argentina. Personally I am unconvinced by his afterlife. In terms of available evidence it is more probable he was drowned or murdered while crossing the Gulf of Tehuantepac in October 1918: a journey he is known to have made, at a time of year known be dangerous. All the other scenarios are rumours or inventions to fill the vacuum of uncertainty. Physically huge but strangely weightless, Fabian Lloyd lived a life of indefinition – aliases, disguises, blurrings of fact and fantasy. He was a kind of illusionist, his greatest feat the creation of 'Arthur Cravan', his last trick the classic one of vanishing.

Mina Loy gave birth to a daughter, back in the comforts of her mother's home in Surrey, on 5 April 1919. The child was named Fabienne in memory of the father she never knew. She was by all accounts a bright, charming, happy child; there is a photograph of her as a young girl by Man Ray. She later lived in Aspen, Colorado, with her architect husband, Frederic Benedict, and their four children; she died in 1997.

Cravan was declared legally dead in 1920, but his memory haunted Mina long after. In her poem 'The Widow's Jazz' (1931) she addresses him, the 'colossal absentee' –

> Husband
> how secretly you cuckold me with death
> while this cajoling jazz
> blows with its tropic breath
> among the echoes of the flesh.

She outlived him by nearly half a century. Her last years were spent in Aspen, close to Fabienne, and there she died in the late summer of 1966, aged eighty-three. She was once asked, in a foolish questionnaire sent by a literary magazine, what had been the happiest moment in her life. She replied: 'Every moment spent with Arthur Cravan.' And the unhappiest? 'The rest of the time.'

21

Lingering Fever

The Gold Prospectors of El Dorado
[1993]

'There's Laime,' says the boatman, and steers the *curiara* in towards the river bank. I see a stocky, stooped figure in a tattered red shirt. For a moment, it seems that he is expecting us, but he cannot be: I come unannounced, like all his visitors. As I climb out of the canoe, he turns away and starts fiddling with a fishing-line. He has already summed me up: another gringo in search of the picturesque, another visitor with questions to ask.

Alexander Laime (pronounced 'limey') was born in Latvia in about 1910, and came to Venezuela in 1939, a refugee from the war to come. For the past forty years he has lived alone in a tiny hut in a clearing near the Carrao River, an exile in a rugged landscape of forests and rivers and towering, sheer-sided table mountains. But even this far up the line, it's hard to be a hermit, and Laime has become a local legend.

His speech is slow, almost pedantic, and he looks up and away as he talks, like a professor outlining a tricky theorem. 'It is unusual', he says, 'to see an Englishman here, because it costs them a lot of money to come here, you see, and they don't like to spend money.'

He has rheumy eyes, and smells of river-water. He wears a baseball cap, and when he takes it off I see that his hair is still sandy: remarkable for a man in his eighties who subsists on a diet of rice, macaroni, sugar and lemon-grass tea. His life seems a feat of endurance, a triumph of eccentric individualism. His hut is five minutes' walk from the riverside. It is a simple affair:

wattle walls, a tin roof. An acre of gently sloping ground surrounds it, shaded with tall mango trees.

I ask if he planted the trees himself. 'Who else?' he replies.

*

Administratively, this wild corner of eastern Venezuela is
known as Bolívar State, geographically as the Guiana Highlands. It is a region rich in gold, which is what brought Laime
here. For centuries the area has been the haunt of prospectors;
indeed, it was once thought to contain that legendary city of
gold, that luckiest of lucky strikes, El Dorado itself. El Dorado
has had many locations – its site, having no existence outside the
minds of those who searched for it, shifted with each expedition – but by the end of the sixteenth century, the search was
concentrated in this *terra incognita* between the Orinoco and the
Amazon.

Sir Walter Ralegh was among the first European travellers
in the region, and in 1595 he led an expedition up the Orinoco
in search of 'that great and golden city'. With a hundred
men, packed into five shallow-draught rowing boats, he ventured through the mangrove swamps of the Orinoco delta.
'What with the victuals being mostly fish,' he later wrote, 'and
the wet clothes of so many men thrust together, and the heat
of the sun, I will undertake there was never any prison in
England that could be found more unsavoury and loathsome.'
Ralegh and his men survived Indian attacks and hungry alliga-
tors but in June 1595 they were halted by the impassable
Cachamay Rapids at the mouth of the Caroní River. The rains
set in, and, after some tentative forays overland, they hurried
back downriver.

But this is a land of tall stories, and even El Dorado turns
out to be true, almost. There was no 'golden city' lost in the
jungle, but there was real and abundant gold in the rocks and

river-gravels, and in the 1850s the first major strike was recorded at Tupuquen, north of the Yuruari River, near present-day El Callao. In 1857 Federico Sommer, a German prospector, found gold nuggets embedded in clay; one stupendous specimen weighed more than fifteen pounds. The site swiftly grew into a shanty-town of eighty houses, together with shops and hotels and ironsmiths and carpenters. It was christened Nueva Providencia. Other settlements followed, named with the same poignant optimism: villages whose names translate as Hope and Silence and Perseverance. There is even, inevitably, an El Dorado – a scruffy gold-trading town near the border with Guyana and the home of the prison which once held Henri Charrière, the criminal and jailbreaker known as Papillon.

By the early 1880s there were more than 8,000 settlers in the area, and El Callao was producing more than fifteen tonnes of gold a year (worth about $200 million at today's prices). Until the discovery of the Rand goldfields in South Africa in 1886, Venezuela was the largest producer of gold in the world; now it ranks seventeenth.

These settlements were in the foothills: the heart of the Guiana Highlands remained unbroached. Expeditions were mounted but it was the advent of light aircraft that finally opened up the land of El Dorado. And so one comes to the era of the jungle pilots, and to Jimmy Angel.

★

James Crawford Angel was born in 1899, in Springfield, Missouri. If he wasn't actually born with wings, he acquired them as soon as possible. The legend – largely self-generated – has it that Angel first flew in a home-made glider fashioned from his mother's window-blinds; that the famous Angel Ride at Coney Island was based on a machine he invented at the age of nine;

that he took his first real flight when thirteen years old, after meeting Weldon B. Cooke, a famous stunt pilot, at a fair in Eugene, Oregon; and that he once demonstrated his skill at low-level flying by slicing off, with his wing-tip, the top of a hard-boiled egg held by his brother.

These apocrypha shade into documented feats of aerobatic prowess. During the Great War – in which he served, under age, in the Royal Canadian Flying Corps – he set records for the highest flight (26,900 feet, in a Le Pierre fighter-plane); the highest landing (14,112 feet, on Pikes Peak, Colorado); and the most loops (310, in a Morane Parasol). These, together with various colourful jobs – running the mail through Mexico; training Sun Yat-sen's pilots in China; stunt-flying in *Hell's Angels*, the film directed by Howard Hughes – are the prelude to the Amazing True Story of his discovery of the torrent of water now known as Angel Falls.

The story begins in Panama City, in 1921. There, in the Metropole Café, Jimmy Angel met a certain J. R. McCracken, who beguiled him with prospector's talk about a 'river of gold' in the Guiana Highlands. The two men flew there in a Bristol fighter-plane, without instruments, McCracken giving directions with hand signals. East of the Caroní, somewhere near Auyán Tepuy (or 'Devil's Mountain'), they found the promised river. In just three days they panned out a huge quantity of pay-dirt (forty pounds of pure gold is the figure generally mentioned).

For years afterwards Angel flew around the area, trying to relocate that 'river of gold'. On one such trip, on 25 March 1935, he piloted his single-engined Cessna up a narrow canyon close to Auyán Tepuy, and there saw the waterfall that now bears his name. Up in Caracas, his account of this natural phenomenon was dismissed as exaggeration, but two years later he found the place again, and in 1949 an overland expedition established what Angel had claimed all along – that he had discovered the longest waterfall in the world, 3,212 feet from summit to foaming base. This was one of my reasons for seeking out Alexander Laime, for it was he who had guided this expedition.

Photographs of Angel show a thickset, jowly man in a battered pork-pie hat. Dr Carlos Freeman, a long-time friend of Angel, remembers him as a 'stocky, pock-marked man with a wheezing, bullfrog voice'. (The pock-marks were, in fact, burns, suffered in a plane crash in the Chilean Andes in the thirties.) According to Terry León, a journalist who spotted Angel having his shoes shined in the Plaza Bolívar and elicited an interview for *El Nacional*, a Caracas newspaper, 'He was a gold prospector, not a heroic type. He was fat. He smoked too much, drank too much whisky.' In his later years Angel could be found at the American Club in Caracas: 'he would', says Dr Freeman, 'surreptitiously pull out one of several nuggets from his pockets' and regale people with stories about the riches still hidden in the jungles of Bolívar State. He died in 1956, in a plane crash in Panama.

*

Inside Laime's hut (see Plate 15), the brilliant afternoon light squeezes through the chinks in the wooden walls, illuminates the charred firewood, the tins of Quaker Oats, the log-chairs, the grubby old hammock tethered like a moored boat at the back of the hut. There are shelves of yellowing books, some with the covers facing out from the shelves, as in a bookshop: he once had 3,000 books, he says, but gave most of them away. Sartre's *Situations* is in his library, and a couple of Arthur C. Clarkes, and Spanish pop-science books such as *El Cerebro y sus incógnitas* and *Nuevas fronteras de la genética*, but the book he pulls down is Steinbeck's *Log from the Sea of Cortez*. He praises its toughness and clarity. 'In Spanish they take so many words to say something, but this: each word, just right, just so.'

I want to talk about Jimmy Angel; about the arduous trails Laime carved to the base of the falls; about his discovery on the summit of Auyán Tepuy of a plane Angel had crashed in 1937 and left there with the words ALL OK displayed on the wings in strips of cloth torn from his wife Marie's skirt. I want dusty legends and tough-talking romance. But this is no longer on Laime's agenda: he has talked too much about 'all this nonsense'.

Whatever your reason for visiting Laime you will sooner or later have to listen to his 'theories'. They will be illustrated by arcane diagrams drawn in the dirt with a stick; by piles of jottings in his large careful script; by tatty cardboard models too small to convey the meanings he intends. As he warms to his theme, he seems a true adept of the esoteric tradition: an old medieval alchemist or numerologist, struggling to find the pattern, the system, the answer.

His theory concerns the significance of the *tepuys*, or table-mountains, in particular the beautiful, anvil-shaped mountain called Weik Tepuy. He believes that – taking into account the 'solar year' of 28,000 years, and the tilt of the earth's axis (6.5°) which has occurred in those years – its peculiar indentations are evidence of a prehistoric solar observatory.

'So do you believe that the *tepuys* were put here, like Stonehenge?'

'I cannot explain it in any other way.'

And then there are his 'creatures'. On one of his expeditions into the *tepuys* he saw a pair of them, sporting in a small pool near the summit like giant long-necked otters. They were, he says, about three metres long, and looked something like plesiosaurs (aquatic reptiles of the Jurassic Period, generally thought to have become extinct some 100 million years ago). He has a drawing, in crayon. There is some scientific grounding for his creatures: the *tepuys* are biological 'islands', sandstone pedestals separated from the surrounding terrain some two billion years ago. On their wild, boggy summits are found unique species of plants and mosses, and two unique subspecies of flycatcher. There is even a prehistoric reptile of sorts, *Oreophrynella quelchii*, a species of toad so rudimentary that it can neither hop nor swim. It is barely an inch long, however, and is not Laime's plesiosaur.

On the floor next to Laime's desk, in permanent readiness, sits his old canvas backpack, with ropes and sleeping-bag and boots. All is prepared for what he impassively calls his 'last expedition'. 'When the time comes I will go, up there.' He gestures out of the window, towards Auyán Tepuy. 'Then you won't see me any more. Laime will be gone. Yes, I will disappear.'

It will not be long, one fears. In a sense, he has already 'disappeared': an old man marooned in paradise, a mind tuned to inaudible signals.

*

Laime is a relic of a bygone era, like his chimerical plesiosaurs, and although there are still plenty of prospectors searching the hills of Bolívar State, their days, too, may be numbered. Most of these men have no title to the land they work and are, in the eyes of the government, illegal. Travelling on upriver, and across the Sierra de Lema, I came to El Pistón. It is a gold-miners' camp, typical of many in the region: a make-shift street built of tin and wood, tapering quickly off into the wilderness. Some of the shacks have a homely look: they have little kitchens, and washing-lines, and backyards shaded with papaya and guava trees. Others serve as bars, stores, workshops, stables. And here is the village flophouse, its walls painted blue, a dirt floor to dance on, and, out back, a row of 'short-time' cubicles for the prostitutes to ply their trade. The only thing missing is the people. The place is empty: a ghost village. In this, too, El Pistón is, increasingly, typical.

One day last September the Guardia Nacional came in helicopters. They gave the people of El Pistón twenty-four hours to clear out. 'There were 400 people living here,' says Victor, a handsome young man from Maracaibo, 500 miles away on the Caribbean coast, who once worked here and who, like many of his colleagues, prefers to leave his surname a mystery. 'There were families with children. The Guardia threw everything out into the street. There were fires burning. The people didn't want to go, but they had no choice.' El Pistón, and several thousand hectares around it, is now part of a concession leased by the Venezuelan government to a consortium from Japan. Although 11.7 tonnes of gold were extracted from Venezuela in 1992, the estimated annual national capacity is 250 tonnes; at a time when Venezuela's oil revenues are falling, corporations and modern industrial methods have an irresistible allure for the government. The demise of El Pistón is one example of a tough new policy aimed against the *mineros*, the independent gold-miners. The government describes the policy as a 'rationalization'. The miners call it *el desalojo*: 'the eviction'.

At nearby Chivao, there's a similar story. Two years ago, this rambling shanty-town housed 5,000 people; now there are about twenty families. Right next door is a new camp: radio antennae, aluminium speedboats, a neat grid of wooden huts. This is Camp Guayana 6: an 'exploration concession' along eight kilometres of the Chicanán River, operated as a joint venture between Goldfields of South Africa and the Cisneros Group, a powerful Venezuelan dynasty that owns television stations, supermarkets and the national franchise for Pepsi-Cola.

The chief engineer at Guayana 6 is Peter Brown, a bearded Briton from Hampshire. He is not sentimental. 'We do not forcibly remove the *mineros*,' he assures me, 'but gradually it

becomes very difficult for them to work in the same location.'
No one should romanticize the life of the *mineros*, he says, nor
minimize the damage they cause. Their camps are 'havens of
vice', where prostitutes sell themselves for a gramme of gold
dust (worth about ten dollars). Malaria is endemic, cholera and
AIDS growing (the latter largely blamed on immigrants from
Brazil). The indiscriminate use of mercury – used to 'fix' the
particles of gold in the alluvial gravels – poisons the rivers, and
indeed the people, for miles around.

Such practices are the dirty reality behind the dream. Modern
methods and disciplined workforces may, perhaps, alleviate
these failings; others, particularly ecological, will arise – profit,
not problem-solving, is the criterion. Profit, of course, always
was the lure, but in these ghost-towns, as in the old hermit's hut
by the Carrao, I have a sense that a long adventure is coming to
an end – that this is the last episode in that centuries-old soap
opera called El Dorado.

22

Heading for Z

The Legend of Colonel Fawcett
[2009]

It is more than eighty years since he disappeared, deep in the Mato Grosso of Brazil, but the name of Colonel Fawcett still resonates. He was the last of the old-style Amazonian explorers, on the cusp of a new age of light aircraft and two-way radio, time-saving and sometimes life-saving conveniences which he disdained. In the words of David Grann, whose compelling new book* tries to make sense of the man and his last mission, Fawcett 'ventured into blank spots on the map with little more than a machete, a compass and an almost divine sense of purpose'. He was an imposing figure, 6′ 1½″ tall, lean tending to cadaverous, with steely grey eyes and a fierce-looking beard. Photographs from his expeditions show him in jungle clearings, hollow-eyed with heat and hunger, wearing a stetson, jodphur-like trousers and tall leather boots. He looks like an Edwardian Indiana Jones, or some strange dystopian scoutmaster living half-wild in the woods.

Fellow explorers described him as having an 'indomitable will' and 'infinite resource', a man 'in hand-to-hand combat with the wilderness'. In Conan Doyle's South American fanta-sia, *The Lost World* (1912), the explorer Lord John Roxton is partly based on Fawcett, whose lectures in London Doyle had attended. He had 'something of Don Quixote,' Doyle wrote, 'and yet again something which was the essence of the English

* David Grann, *The Lost City of Z* (Simon & Schuster, 2009).

country gentleman'. In the more tight-lipped terms favoured by the Royal Geographical Society of the 1920s, Fawcett was a model of physical efficiency, who 'was prepared to travel lighter and fare harder than most people would consider either possible or proper'. That last word strikes a curious note – the idea that matters of propriety were involved in the business of jungle survival – but has a sociological point. Whatever their ostensible purpose, his arduous expeditions were also seen as a proving-ground for the strength, resolve and all-round superiority of the English gentleman. Colonel Fawcett was, as the American newspapers liked to put it, a 'ramrod Englishman'. His chief rival in Amazonia was a publicity-hungry American millionaire, Dr Alexander Hamilton Rice, whose state-of-the-art radio had an aerial the size of a hang-glider. When Rice turned back after a hostile encounter with the Yanonami, Fawcett reported with satisfaction that he had 'skedaddled' because he was 'too soft for the real game'.

But then there is the other side of the Fawcett story, which makes it something more than a *Boy's Own* tale of derring-do in deep jungle. His last expeditions were increasingly quests, with all of that word's obsessive and quasi-mystical overtones. For various reasons, some better than others, he believed that there lay concealed in the jungle the remains of a lost city, formerly inhabited by what he called a 'robust and fair people', a proto-Indian race which 'must have a civilized origin'. He argued that the 'ethnology of the continent has been based on a misconception' because it was founded on observations of assimilated Indians, degraded by colonization and much inferior to these 'fair' or 'copper-skinned' forerunners. In his notebooks, ever wary of the possibility of competitors, he referred to this lost city only as 'Z', and when he set off on his last expedition, in the spring of 1925, it was in the belief that he would finally locate this phantom metropolis.

In his historical studies of the Amazon, *Die If You Must* and *Tree of Rivers*, John Hemming dismisses Fawcett as a 'Nietzschean explorer' whose theories are nothing more than 'eugenic gibberish'. At the other end of the spectrum there are doubtless some who still think that Fawcett was a visionary, that he found the ancient capital he sought, and that mysterious forces at work there account for his disappearance. One heard this sort of view on the 'Gringo Trail' in the early 1970s, when it was still possible for a super-charged, centenarian Fawcett to be alive – those who held it tended also to believe that the Nasca Lines in Peru were UFO landing-strips, as posited by Erich von Däniken in his then-current *Chariots of the Gods?* Fawcett's own writings, unpublished till the 1950s, lead into this sort of terrain. Though originally he described Z in 'strictly scientific terms', Grann writes, 'by 1924 Fawcett had filled his papers with reams of delirious writings' about a 'mystical Atlantean kingdom which resembled the Garden of Eden', and which might also be one of the primal 'White Lodges' of which the spiritualist Madame Blavatsky spoke.

Thus Fawcett becomes annexed into that other-worldly side of South American exploration, as typified by the searchers after El Dorado, the fabled 'city of gold' of which Fawcett's Z is a notional suburb or satellite. He crosses that line where the dangerous realities of the jungle merge with the yet more dangerous chimeras of the imagination.

*

Lieutenant-Colonel Percy Harrison Fawcett was born in Torquay in 1867. His father was a blue-blooded spendthrift and crony of the Prince of Wales, who died young of alcohol and tuberculosis when Fawcett was seventeen, and is chiefly remembered as a brilliant batsman for Cambridge University and Sussex. Fawcett, too, was a fine cricketer, following his father in that, though diametrically opposed to him on matters of drink and loose living. His childhood, as he recalls in writings edited by his son Brian in *Exploration Fawcett* (1953), was 'devoid of parental affection' but full of 'grand times' with his brother and sisters. At the age of nineteen he was a commissioned officer in the Royal Artillery, handsome in a lanky, buttoned-up sort of way, and was stationed out in Trincomalee, in Ceylon, where he met a spirited and beautiful young widow, Nina Pritchard, who became his wife in 1901.

Fawcett made his first *entrada* into the South American wilderness in 1906, a qualified military surveyor working for the Bolivian Boundary Commission, and made dozens more over the next two decades. The Great War was a hiatus: he emerged from the jungle in 1914, after a year-long expedition, and promptly returned home to join the fight, it being 'the patriotic desire of all able-bodied men to squash the Teuton'. He spent three years in the hell of the trenches, including the Somme, and was awarded the DSO for valour. In early 1919 he returned to the family home in Devon, where he brooded on the traumas of war and became involved in spiritualism. The following year he returned to South America. When asked about the Amazonian practice of cannibalism, he would drily observe that it 'at least provided a reasonable motive for killing a man, which is more than you could say for civilized warfare'.

Now the practical purposes of his expeditions – cartographic, ethnographic, botanical – began to be supplanted by the glimmering obsession with lost cities. The first impetus was based on genuine observation. He saw archaeological remains – pottery, petrographs, the vestiges of ancient engineering – which made him question the received wisdom that Amazonia had always been a habitat too hostile to favour any advanced social development. He noted the admirable organizational skills of certain Indian groups: stockpilers, engineers, healers – the Echoja and the Guarayo, the 'brave and intelligent Maxubi', the Yuracare and Yanonami, though already there creeps in the jarring racial note, for some of these were the fairer-skinned tribes then called 'white Indians'.

Grann is even-handed in his assessment of Fawcett. He stresses that in ethnographic terms he was far in advance of his time – today there is growing evidence, pushing ever further back into the past, of advanced early cultures in the Amazon. This is in turn an aspect of Fawcett's empathy with the Indians. More orthodox minds at the Royal Geographical Society accused him of 'going native' on his expeditions. His habit of painting his face with bright colours from berries like an Indian warrior was particularly noted. There is 'no disgrace' in living like the Indians, he said. Rather, 'it shows a creditable regard for the real things of life at the expense of the artificial'. These were valuable attitudes in an era of exploration not noted for its tactful contact with indigenous people. Only later were they muddied by master-race theories and Blavatskian hocus-pocus. These eccentricities caused a cooling-off in support from the RGS, which contributed a modest £5,000 to Fawcett's 1925 expedition – less, as Grann notes, than the cost of one of Dr Rice's radios.

Grann gives a vivid insight into life on a Fawcett expedition. These forays into what he called the 'deep interior' were through dense, pathless regions where pack-animals could not survive. Everything had to be carried by the expeditioners and their local porters. Though he was praised for travelling light, this is decidedly relative. By his last expeditions Fawcett had refined his requirements down to a sixty-pound pack – four pounds heavier than a large sack of coal. One tries to imagine it, toiling forward with this great canvas beast dragging at your shoulders, adding its weight to the sapping onslaught of heat, mud, humidity, biting insects and parasitic infestations. One would also be constantly hungry, given the typical fare en route – breakfast at

6.30 a.m., 'one plate of porridge, two cups of tea, and one third cup of condensed milk', supper at 5.30 p.m., 'two cups of tea, two biscuits, *goiabada* or sardines, or one plate of *charque* and rice', and no mention of sustenance in the eleven hours between. Among the contents of Fawcett's pack were the usual impedimenta – guns, machetes, flares; a sextant and a precision chronometer for determining latitude and longitude; a small glycerine compass; an aneroid for measuring atmospheric pressure; a pan for sifting gold dust – and, rather less predictably, a ukulele. In one of the last descriptions of Fawcett before his disappearance, he is giving an impromptu recital on this instrument to a group of bemused Xingù Indians. 'Music', he told his wife, 'is a great comfort in the wilds, and might even save a solitary man from insanity.' He also carried handwritten copies of poems, including an extract from 'Solitude' by Ella Wheeler Wilcox –

> There is room in the halls of pleasure
> For a long and lordly train,
> But one by one we must all file on
> Through the narrow aisles of pain.

The lines seem appropriate in their mix of grit and sentimentality.

Sentimentality was not a word that would leap into the minds of those who travelled with him. Fawcett was an exacting leader – he had, he said, 'no mercy for incompetence' – and those under him were closely scrutinized for any tremulousness of the upper lip. James Murray, an eminent Scottish biologist who accompanied Fawcett's 1921 expedition along the upper Heath River, was tested particularly harshly, being an interloper from the more showily dramatic – and better-funded – world of polar exploration. Exhausted, disorientated, and devoured by a legion of insects and parasites, including some inch-long maggots nesting in his arm, Murray was castigated for slowing the party down. 'You have no right to be tired!' snapped the colonel, who had suspected him all along for a 'pink-eyed weakling'. Grann brings out the black comedy of these scenes, where amid harrowing tropical hardships Murray is scolded for having scoffed some communal caramels. Fawcett's preferred sidekick was Henry Costin, a trusty batman sort of figure who called him 'chief'. A former corporal and gym-instructor in the British Army, and a crack shot, he was summed up by his son as a 'tough bugger who hated bullshit'. Joining up for another Fawcett adventure, after months of recuperation from a near-fatal fever picked up on the previous one, Costin struck the right note of subaltern stoicism. 'It's hell all right,' he said, 'but one kind of likes it.'

★

On the doomed expedition of 1925 Fawcett was accompanied only by his son Jack, and Jack's best friend, Raleigh Rimell. Jack Fawcett was a handsome 21-year-old with a pencil moustache who had spent time in Hollywood and aspired to movie star-dom (another Fawcett cricketing fact: the bat seen in the film *Little Lord Fauntleroy* was lent by Jack to the film's star, Mary Pickford). Though untried in the rigours of Amazon explor-ation, or any exploration at all, the two young men were approvingly described by Fawcett as 'strong as horses and keen as mustard'. One discerns the defiant – or fatal – note of ama-teurism. This was the team that set out to find the mysterious city of Z – three toffs from the English shires, a few native por-ters, some mules (though only for the early stages) and a pair of dogs, Pastor and Chulim. Dogs were also among Fawcett's preferred travelling companions, invaluable as hunters and retrievers, and loyal to the end.

The journey led them up into the headwaters of the Xingù River, one of the great southern tributaries of the Amazon.

Fawcett had reconnoitred the first stages back in 1920, but the region they were heading for was completely unmapped. It was as he liked it – a place where even the rivers 'are guesswork'. We can trace the itinerary up to the expedition's vanishing-point. They arrived at the Brazilian frontier-town of Cuiabà, the capital of Mato Grosso, on about 3 March 1925, and began assembling porters, provisions and animals. This small circus moved out from Cuiabà on 20 April, arriving nearly four weeks later at the last white settlement on their route, a tiny upriver trading depot called Bakairí Post. Here they rested up – it had been a 'rather strenuous journey' – and sent dispatches home. Jack talks breezily about the thrill of seeing his first 'real savages', and retails news of his father – 'Daddy had gone on ahead at such a pace that we lost sight of him', 'Daddy is in first rate condition', and so on. His letters are full of public-school innocence and Wodehousian jollity – 'bugs galore!' Fawcett, meanwhile, confers with a local chief, who 'under the expanding influence of wine' corroborates the story of 'old cities' in the region. It seems his goal is at last in sight, and on 20 May, as they prepare to leave Bakairí, he writes to Nina that he expects 'to be in touch with the old civilization within a month', and to be at the 'main object' – in other words, Z – by August.

Fawcett's last dispatch, 29 May 1925, was carried back to Bakairí by the Indian porters, who were unwilling to venture further into another tribe's territories. It begins, in concise but ominous tones: 'Here we are at Dead Horse Camp, Lat. 11° 43′ S. and 54° 35′ W., the spot where my horse died in 1920. Only his white bones remain.' He briefly describes the conditions: 'The season is good. It is very <u>cold</u> at night, and fresh in the morning; but insects and heat come by mid-day.' He might be talking of the minor inconveniences of a camping-trip. And then the last sign-off, upbeat, almost headmasterly in tone: 'you need have no fear of any failure.'

The rest is silence, though, as Fawcett had warned they might be out of contact for up to two years, it did not at first seem a worrying silence. What happened to the three Englishmen after they left Dead Horse Camp has never been established with certainty, though some answers to the puzzle were provided by later expeditions in search of them. The first of these, still optimistic enough to be styled a 'rescue mission', was led by Commander George Dyott in 1928. He traced Fawcett's trail to a village of the Nahukwá tribe, where the chief's son had hanging round his neck a small brass plate marked 'W. S. Silver and Company' – a London firm which had supplied Fawcett with some airtight metal cases. From there, Dyott learnt, they had traversed across to the upper Kuluene River, the domain of Kalapalo Indians. This should have been a three-day journey, but they were going slowly because one of the younger men, probably Rimell, was lame and exhausted. After resting a few days they set off eastwards, into difficult and unknown country. The Kalapalo reported seeing smoke from their campfires for five days, and then nothing on the sixth day. They indicated to Dyott, in sign language, their belief that the party had been massacred. He considered it the most likely explanation, and it remains so. He thought the culprits were the Nahukwá, but they blamed a notoriously fierce group called the Saya.

The story ran and ran. 'Hardly a week passes in which some English newspaper does not make an apocryphal reference to the lost explorer,' wrote Peter Fleming (brother of Ian) in the early 1930s. 'Fresh rumours are always coming in, fresh expeditions are always on the point of starting.' Fleming was himself part of one, and wrote about it in *Brazilian Adventure* (1933). One of Grann's interviewees estimates that a hundred people have lost their lives in the search for Fawcett, or for clues about what happened to him. In 1951 Orlando Villas-Bôas, the famous champion of Indian rights, announced that he had found

Fawcett's remains in a shallow grave in Kalapalo territory. But the bones, examined by the Royal Anthropological Institute in London, were not Fawcett's: the jawbone did not match a spare denture he had left in England, and the shinbone suggested a man some six inches shorter than him. As late as 1979 Fawcett's gold signet-ring turned up in the backroom of a shop in Cuiabà. It is engraved with the family motto, one which Fawcett exemplified to the full – '*Nec aspera terrent*': 'Hardships hold no fear'. Despite the staring-eyed fantasies of his last years, he was in many ways an admirable Englishman, austere, laconic, honourable and incredibly tough, playing with a straight bat on some of the stickiest wickets the planet could provide. He called himself a 'lone wolf', determined to 'seek paths of my own rather than take the well-trodden ways'. The path led him, both physically and psychologically, into very wild country, and so to that point of no return where a few distant wisps of smoke above the canopy marked the end of the line.

23

The Capital of Memory

Alexandria Past and Present
[1996]

The glories of Alexandria are past and gone, but that has been the case for nearly two millennia now, and I doubt I'm the first visitor to feel a touch of disappointment on arriving. It is now a major metropolis: Egypt's second city. Coming in on the bus from Cairo – three hours up the Desert Highway, brain numbed by Egyptian soaps on the video – you see it sprawled like a long grubby mirage along a strip of land between the Mediterranean and the polluted marshes of Lake Mariout. The population is officially four million, but is almost certainly nearer five. It is not as crowded and traffic-ridden as Cairo, and the sea is always just a few blocks away, but if you are looking for tranquil reveries of ancient history you will look in vain in downtown Alexandria.

Though the glories are gone, much of the city's charm still remains. It is a curious, slightly seedy charm, not easy to discern at first, and not easy to define thereafter. The British novelist Lawrence Durrell, who lived here for years, speaks of 'glimpsing the phantom city' which lies somewhere behind the ramshackle modern façade.

I had a reservation at the Metropole Hotel. I was looking for 'character', and the Metropole, I was assured, had bags of it. A dowdy neo-Classical building with thin balconies and tall shutters, it once housed the semi-legendary Office of the Third Circle of Irrigation, where the eccentric Alexandrian poet Constantine Cavafy earned his living for more than thirty years.

Among his acquaintances was another literary visitor, E. M. Forster, who wrote: 'You turn and see a Greek gentleman in a straw hat, standing absolutely motionless at a slight angle to the universe: it is Mr Cavafy.' He is on his way to the office, however, and 'vanishes with a slight gesture of despair'.

In 1934 the building was converted into a hotel, Greek-owned, with lavish Art Deco salons on the first floor. It sounded the classic Alexandrian spot: lashings of faded grandeur and a literary ghost or two.

No more, however: disappointment again. As I checked in I could hear ominous sounds of drilling. The Metropole has changed hands, refurbishment is under way, and soon, the elderly lift man tells me, it will be *tout nouveau*. Much the same has already happened to the city's most famous hotel, the Cecil, now owned by the Sofitel chain.

We ascended slowly in the lift, a wood-panelled kiosk about the size of a wardrobe. I had a seaview room on the fourth floor. Refurbishment had not reached there yet. The room was huge and sombre, and resonated to the noise of the tram terminus and coach station of Saad Zaghlul Square below, but as I threw back the shutters and took in the view – the westward curve of the bay along the Corniche, the ageing Italian-built apartment houses, the clouds massing behind the minarets of the Abdulkadir el Shorbagy Mosque – my heart lifted.

*

The city was founded by Alexander the Great in 332 BC. His body may lie beneath the city, perhaps around the busy junction of El Horreya and Nabi Danial Streets, but no one is sure. In Classical times it was famed for its lighthouse, the Pharos (one of the Seven Wonders of the Ancient World); for its immense library containing some half a million manuscripts; and for its seductive Queen Cleopatra the Fifth. In the square below the

Metropole stood the Caesareum, an enormous temple begun by Cleopatra in about 40 BC. This crumbled away long ago, but one of the granite obelisks which adorned it is now 'Cleopatra's Needle' on the Thames Embankment. It was brought to London in 1878, nearly sinking in the Bay of Biscay en route; six seamen were drowned, and are commemorated in a brass plaque at its base.

But this is only the bottom layer of Alexandrian history. The city's position on the Mediterranean has made it a crossroads of Greek, Turkish, Arab and European influences, and has brought it the chequered history and louche, cosmopolitan air which Durrell captures so richly in *The Alexandria Quartet*.

It is literally a city of layers. The city's topography is restrictive: the central area – hemmed in between the sea, desert and lake – has been constantly rebuilt. As the pace of new building accelerates, the archaeologists struggle to keep up. One morning I accompanied the eminent Alexandrian scholar Professor Mustafa Abbadi to see the latest find. On the way he reminisced about his days as a student at Cambridge in the fifties. When they asked him where he had learnt to row so well, he told them: 'On the Nile!' We are visiting the site of one of the city's old picture-palaces, the Cinema Diana, recently demolished. Beneath it they have found a second-century Roman villa, with cisterns and wells, and on its dining-room floor an exquisite, sexy mosaic of the Medusa. A young archaeologist pulls off the polythene tarpaulin, sprinkles her lightly with water. She glowers dangerously like those *femmes fatales* who flickered across the cinema screen above her. Her eyes are looking sideways, so she didn't turn the guests to stone when they walked in to dinner.

Down along the Corniche, a more ambitious rescue is under way. Two years ago, a team of divers under the flamboyant French archaeologist Jean-Yves Empéreur started bringing up pieces of the Pharos itself. Built in the third century BC, this immense lighthouse stood more than 400 feet tall and looked a little like the Empire State Building. Its beam was a fire magnified by mirrors or lenses, and fed (it is thought) by a fleet of donkeys carrying firewood up a spiral staircase.

The Pharos was destroyed by a series of earthquakes, and lies scattered over five acres of seabed below the headland. The divers have recovered Ptolemaic statues, parts of a sphinx, and one 75-ton slab of granite and marble, which was probably part of the parapet on the first floor of the lighthouse. Many of the statues turn out to have been brought from Heliopolis, the Pharaonic city near Cairo.

'Things do not change,' says Empéreur with a shrug. 'In the third century BC it was very *à la mode* to bring Pharaonic statues here, just as it was in the nineteenth century to take them to Paris or London.'

*

Durrell called Alexandria 'the capital of memory', a place where the past is always in the air, 'clinging to the minds of old men like traces of perfume upon a sleeve'.

Only fragments remain of Classical Alexandria, but its more recent past can be savoured just by wandering aimlessly through the streets, past shabby villas and Rococo façades and dusty bric-a-brac shops. The city seems like an ageing dandy fallen on hard times. Lingering over a café creme under the improbable chandeliers of the Trianon, or taking a lunchtime aperitif at the marble-topped bar of the Cap d'Or, it is easy to imagine yourself back in the Alexandria of Forster and Cavafy: a strange backwater of Classicism and poetry and sexual adventure.

Forster came here during the Great War as a Red Cross worker. He was in his mid thirties, a small, bespectacled man, already famous for novels like *Howards End* and *A Room with a View*. Here he had an affair – apparently his first – with a local tram conductor, Mohammed el Adl, and haunted the terminus below the Metropole. They quarrelled over a box of cakes. Mohammed's death, in 1922, devastated Forster. Cavafy was also homosexual, and many of his finest poems are about the boys he picked up in the billiard halls and brothels of Tatwig Street. Forster wrote a superb guidebook to Alexandria. Printed here privately in 1922, it is still the best guide to the Classical vestiges of the city. The first edition is rare because almost all the copies were destroyed in a fire.

The English have a long association with 'Alex'. For families working here during the British occupation of Egypt it was the summer bolt-hole from Cairo, an expat scene which Durrell summed up acidly as 'boredom laced with drink and Packards and beach cabins'.

Durrell, brother of naturalist Gerald, came here in the forties. His house can still be seen – just. You walk across the rail-tracks, down Suez Canal Street and into the narrow streets of a residential quarter called Moharran Bey. You see the tower first, dark sandstone, suggestive of a minor English manor house. The gates were bolted and guarded. The watchmen are under instructions to let no one in, and I wouldn't for a moment suggest they were open to backsheesh. The villa stands amid its rampant shrubbery like a forgotten folly. There is a walled garden with ancient fruit trees, and the remains of a stable, and washing strung across the porch. It is just an old address in the 'capital of memory'.

Actual memories of the old cosmopolitan Alexandria are fading fast, but not quite gone. At the Elite Restaurant Madame Kristina holds court behind the cash register. She is Greek, an ageless, matriarchal figure in the large Greek community. 'But one of my grandmothers was Austrian,' she adds coquettishly, 'which is why I am so blonde.' Her father was an immigrant shopkeeper; as a child she met Cavafy; she remembers the day Edith Piaf dined at the Elite. Even today it has a faded *fin de siècle* air, with its old French theatre posters and dusty check table-cloths. Does she think Alexandria was better in the old days? '*Mais oui!*' (Like many in this mongrel city she speaks several languages, sometimes in the same sentence.) 'But I have lived here so long, there is nowhere else to go.'

★

The current fate of Durrell's house is typical of the battle now being waged for the architectural heart and soul of the city. On one side, the well-known Roman family of Ambron, who built and own the house and are intent on redevelopment; on the other side, a local architect, Mohammed Awad, the president of the Alexandrian Preservation Trust. 'We have to battle,' he tells me. 'The old houses are just seen as cumbersome old structures that should be cleared away.'

It is often a losing battle. The billiard halls where Cavafy cruised have gone. The villas and picture-palaces are coming down, and the Cecil Hotel is a glum parody of itself. This was once *the* hotel in Alex, and during the Desert War the upstairs bar served as an impromptu HQ for General Montgomery. You can still take a sundowner in Monty's Bar but don't expect any kind of atmosphere – even the *Mona Lisa*, in lurid repro in the corner, seems to be waiting for you to leave.

But in the end it isn't just the architecture that gives the place its peculiar evocative charm. More, it is the people; and most it is an atmosphere, a mood as elusive as the aromatic, peachy smoke that wafts out of the hubble-bubble cafés. As the old man at the Metropole said: 'Soon it will be *tout nouveau.*' He sounds neither pleased nor regretful about it. Things change, but in the capital of memory, the past is always there to catch you unawares.

24

Mystery at Moonlight Cottage

The Disappearance of Jim Thompson
[1992]

The photograph has that eerie innocence: a casual event that is about to become a mystery. It is a faded snap showing three middle-aged people on a picnic, one Chinese and two Americans (see Plate 16). It is Easter 1967, in the lush surroundings of the Cameron Highlands, a former British hill-station in central Malaysia. Two of the people in the photograph, Dr T. G. Ling and his American wife, Helen, are now dead. The third, Jim Thompson, was declared legally dead in 1974, but no one can say for sure that he is. It becomes more probable – he would now be eighty-six years old – but how, when, or why he died is the mystery. This photograph is the last to be taken of him; he disappeared without a trace about three hours later.

Thompson was already something of a legend in South-East Asia. In the popular press he was known as the Thai Silk King. He settled in Bangkok after the Second World War and began his silk business hawking scarves in the lobby of the Oriental Hotel. At that time, Thai silk was virtually unknown, a local cottage craft. Within a few years – particularly after his designs were used in the musical *The King and I*, set in old Siam – Thompson had turned it into an international industry. When the rich and famous came to Bangkok, they bought silk at his shop on Suriwong Road, and they dined at his superb canalside house, built out of five original houses transported from the old Siamese capital of Ayutthaya. 'There was usually a Thai prince or two there, or an ambassador, or some no-account count,' recalls Barrie Cross, a former manager of the Oriental. 'There were only three menus at Jim's dinner parties. You could tell how important the guests were by what the cook served.'

Jim Thompson, one is often told, was a gentleman. He is sometimes called a snob, though others speak of his hospitality to the young and the broke who drifted into Bangkok: 'If you were interesting, Jim liked you.' Film footage shows an old-style American expat, tanned and a bit overweight, with a packet of Pall Mall in the pocket of his silk shirt, and a rapid, raspy, corner-of-the-mouth way of talking. He made a considerable fortune, most of it put back into the business or into his almost obsessive art collecting. He was, and remains, popular with the Thais, a man who fell in love with the country, and who genuinely benefited it. Nath Chaijaroen, for many years his translator, says: 'He was a good man, very diligent. He worked hard and always helped the weavers. They were poor people; now their children go to university, to medical college.' Thompson had a tinge of 'Quiet American' idealism: he once described his work as 'like a missionary, but with better visual results'.

These parts of the Thompson legend remain. His silk company (now owned by a consortium headed by his nephew Henry Thompson III) is doing better business than ever. An original block of shares, bought in 1950 for $2,500, was recently sold to a Japanese company for $25 million. Thompson silks, some featuring his own designs, command top prices in London, Paris and New York. His 'house by the *klong*' is visited by thousands of tourists every year. But there is also that other, chillier part of the legend, the question that hangs in the rooms of his house: what *did* happen to Jim Thompson that day in the Cameron Highlands?

★

In Bangkok no one has an answer to that question, but everyone has a theory. Many believe that the simplest explanation is the most plausible: that he went for a hike in the jungle, fell into difficulties, and died there. This is the view taken by his biographer, William Warren, and by some of his surviving friends. It is not quite the official story – there is no official story – but it is generally accounted the sensible story.

It is by no means the only one you will hear. Some say Thompson was kidnapped. As there was no ransom demand, it was either a kidnap that went wrong, or an abduction for a more complex reason. Others say it was a planned disappearance by a man tired of his own success. Alleged later sightings of him – in Tahiti, Macao, Hong Kong – are mentioned to support this. There is speculation that he was on a mission for the CIA, that he was involved in a planned coup, that he was being blackmailed because he was homosexual, and that he was the victim of machinations within the Bangkok silk industry.

And whichever theory you are listening to, you are sure to be dealt the wild card of the case, which is that a few months after his disappearance, Thompson's sister Katherine was murdered by an unknown intruder at her house in Pennsylvania.

Some of the theories sound alluring enough over a bottle of cold Singha beer. There is no hard evidence to back them up, yet the same is true of the supposedly simple theory that he got lost in the Malaysian jungle. The search was extensive. At its height there were 300 people combing the area: the Malay Police Field Force, aboriginal trackers, a detachment of Ghurkas, hotel guests armed with sticks and whistles. The US army sent helicopters and radar-tracking equipment. In nearly two weeks they found nothing – no shred of clothing, no spot of blood, no sign of a struggle and no body. The one constant in the puzzle, it seems, is a total absence of clues. As William Warren tells me, 'We really know nothing more about the case than we knew an hour after it happened.'

★

The climb to the Cameron Highlands is dramatic. At the cross-roads town of Tapah, you leave the heat and monotony of Highway One, which runs on down the peninsula to Kuala Lumpur, and switchback up through a lush, steep, misted landscape.

On Friday, 24 March 1967, Jim Thompson drove up this road in a taxi, intending – as it appeared – to spend a quiet Easter weekend with the Lings, who owned a cottage here. With him was an old friend, Connie Mangskau, an attractive Anglo-Thai widow in her mid fifties. They had flown down from Bangkok the previous day, spent the night at the Ambassador Hotel in Penang and then hired a taxi for the seven-hour journey to the Highlands. At Tapah they changed cars. There was a brief altercation with two Chinese who wanted to travel with them. Kidnap theorists have found this significant, but it probably was not. Shared taxis were, and are, the norm here. They arrived early in the evening. Ling, a Chinese-born, Harvard-educated chemist who worked for a pharmaceutical company in Singapore, was already there. Helen Ling arrived later that evening.

The Cameron Highlands, first mapped a hundred years ago by the Scottish surveyor William Cameron, became popular during the thirties as a cool-climate resort for British personnel working in Singapore and Kuala Lumpur. There are three villages, big tea estates, an eighteen-hole golf course and Ye Olde Smokehouse, a country hotel more English than any I have seen in England. Dotted through the greenery are bungalows and holiday houses in hill-station style: a cross-pollination of mock Tudor and Asian, with tall gables and verandahs. One of these is Moonlight Cottage, set in a twinkling garden of hollyhocks and scarlet salvia. This was the Lings' house. It is the last house up a winding track, twenty minutes' walk from the main road. There has been infilling since Thompson was here, but the cottage is still solitary. According to local lore, the house is haunted.

During the Emergency of the fifties, the place was used by the Communist guerrillas; it is said there were executions on the lawn. Malay shamans attributed Thompson's disappearance to 'bad spirits', as good a theory as some you will hear.

Today the house is owned by Wong Hoke Lim, a Chinese businessman from Kuala Lumpur. When I visited, the drive bristled with warnings – 'No Loitering', 'Please Respect Our Privacy' – and pictures of Alsatian watchdogs, but the place was deserted except for an elderly Chinese housekeeper and a sleepy chow who scarcely managed a bark. The housekeeper spoke no English. The name Jim Thompson, however I enunciated it, meant nothing to her. She watched as I strolled round the garden. She wondered what I was looking for, and so did I. Through the metal-framed windows, past mildew-spotted curtains, everything looked closed up.

On that Easter morning in 1967 Thompson and his friends attended a service at the Anglican church in nearby Tanah Ratah, then drove to the foothills of Brinchang Mountain for a picnic. This was the scene of that last photograph, taken by Connie Mangskau. But here comes the first possible tremor in the story. The picnic was not quite the easy-going affair it looks in the photo. According to Ling, Thompson had suddenly gone off the idea. In an interview with *Asia* magazine in 1974, Ling said, 'After everything had been prepared and we were about to go, Jim changed his mind. He said he didn't want to go, and he urged us to stay home. Well, the rest of us wanted to go, so he finally came along.' Thompson drank no beer with his lunch, and began packing up the hamper almost as soon as they had finished eating. 'He appeared nervous, which was very unusual for him, and he seemed anxious to get back early,' said Ling. 'Who knows why?'

They were back at Moonlight Cottage by about 2.30 p.m. Mangskau announced her intention to take a nap. The others, including Thompson, agreed. She retired to her bedroom, the Lings went to theirs, and the last they saw of Jim Thompson he was standing in the living room, preparing – they assumed – to do the same. He did not, however, go to his room. His bed had not even been lain on.

A little after three o'clock the Lings, resting but not sleeping in their room at the front of the house, heard the scrape of an aluminium deckchair on the verandah. A few moments later they heard footsteps going down the gravel path outside their window towards the drive. (This path is now grassed over, but you can clearly see the line of it.) These were, Helen Ling later insisted, the footsteps of a 'white man', not an Asian. She was sure she could tell the difference.

This is not quite the last record of him. At about four o'clock, a man matching his description was seen by the cook at the nearby Lutheran Mission bungalow. He came up the track to the bungalow, looked around a bit, and went away again. Shown a photo of Thompson, the cook said she was sure it was him, though she said he was wearing grey trousers, when in fact they were dark blue. Her statement is also problematic because of another witness, at the Overseas Mission Fellowship house, who said that she too saw Thompson at about four. He stood on a small plateau opposite the house for about half an hour, she said, and then went away

Given the Oriental vagueness about time, it is possible that both these sightings are genuine. It takes ten to fifteen minutes to walk from Moonlight to the Lutheran bungalow (which is a dead end), and a little more from there to the OMF house.

★

What happened to Thompson after that is the enduring puzzle. No one has an answer to that question in the Cameron Highlands any more than they do in Bangkok, but just about everyone

I spoke to seemed certain about what did *not* happen to him. He did not die in the jungle. Oh yes, you are told, people get lost in the jungle up here. But – dead or alive – they are always found again.

The terrain here is not, as you might think from reading the reports, the kind of luxuriant, hostile jungle in which disappearance is always possible. It is oak-laurel rainforest. In parts it is like an English woodland in high summer. It was denser then than it is now, says David Fitzstevens, an American aid worker who took part in the search for Thompson, 'but it wasn't that difficult to find your way. Those out there looking for him wondered how he could have got lost.'

Nor was Thompson a novice. He had stayed here before, and knew the area quite well. He had jungle training from his military days. He had hiked through Thailand on curio-collecting expeditions. Helen Ling remembered him talking on the subject: 'You know,' he said to her, 'if you keep your wits about you, you can never get lost here. All you have to do is find a stream and follow it out, and while you do, drinking its water will keep you alive.'

One theory is that Thompson was attacked and eaten by a tiger. There certainly were tigers in the vicinity, as Helen Robertson recalls. She is the Chinese-born widow of a Scottish rose-grower. She knew the Lings (her husband planted the garden at Moonlight Cottage) and she still lives at Rose Hill, a few miles away. 'At that time there were quite a few of them roaming about,' she says. 'I heard the roar of a tiger one evening at the back. I was cutting flowers. I ran down and told one of my men. We saw the paw marks all over the cabbage bed the next morning. At that time the tigers were all going for dogs.'

So does she think Thompson was taken by a tiger? She shakes her head. 'He cannot be dead here, because after that they had the army people, the soldiers, the *orang asli* [forest tribesmen], all trying to find him for days. They know the jungle very well. Even if he was eaten by a tiger there must be some trace, or clothing, or something left behind.'

In the Highlands the 'lost in the jungle' theory seems less sensible than it did in Bangkok. It is not even certain that he went into the jungle at all. He was a smoker, but when he walked down the drive at Moonlight he left his cigarettes and lighter. Nor did he take the pills which he carried in case of a gallstone attack. His silver pillbox, jokingly called his 'jungle box', was still in his room. About three hours of daylight remained when he set out. If either of the later sightings is genuine, he had still not gone into the jungle by 4 p.m., with only two hours of light left.

From the look of it, at least, Thompson had neither the intention to go very far into the jungle, nor the time to do so. If he did go into the jungle, and something happened to him – a tiger, a snake bite, 'killer bees', a heart attack, a fall into an illicit animal trap, a poisoned aboriginal dart, all of which have been mooted – he must still have been fairly close to Moonlight or to one of those other bungalows when it happened. In these areas, naturally, the search was most intense, but turned up nothing.

★

Back in Bangkok I heard about an Englishman known as 'Major David'. I was told that he was ex-SAS, ran a Mexican restaurant on Patpong Road, and had been involved in the search for Thompson. As it turned out, he was actually ex-Ghurkas, and when I finally met him, it was in a Pakistani restaurant in Manila, but the important part of the information was true.

David Shaw (Major, retd) is a laconic character with an eye that sizes you up. I was early for the appointment, but he was already there. He describes himself as a 'security consultant'. His clients include foreign companies setting up in Manila, and Filipino armed forces, both national and private. He is still in the business of jungle survival, he jokes, only now the jungle is Manila.

In March 1967 the men of the 2nd Battalion Second Ghurka Rifles were on cool-climate R & R in the Cameron Highlands after a ten-month stint 'killing Indonesian Communists in Borneo'. Among them was Shaw, then a lieutenant. When Thompson went missing, the Ghurkas formed a search party and Shaw, as the battalion intelligence officer – 'the shit at the end of the line' – was put in charge of it. They began their search on Tuesday morning, some thirty-six hours after the first alarm. It involved two companies, about 300 men, and Shaw insists it was very thorough.

'We swept the whole area,' he says. 'This wasn't a question of following tracks, because in military terminology you never walk along tracks in the jungle anyway. We were making straight-line sweeps along a ridge-side, then the other side, then checking back to the road. Using the bungalow as a centre, I would say we probably did a mile all round, maybe a mile and a half, which is a lot of ground in the jungle. And there was nothing. We followed a lot of tracks but there was nothing that looked anything to do with a white male. We turned up a baby, dead, and we turned up some tiger tracks, but the tiger was not dragging anything. Thompson was quite a big man. There would have been marks, there would have been blood.'

They searched for a week. Shaw is convinced that Thompson was not there, and pretty certain he never had been. 'This was a very high-calibre search party. The people we were using were excellent trackers. If we couldn't find anything in that area, there wasn't anything in that area.'

This is just one more opinion. It is based on first-hand experience, though there may also be an element of self-justification in it. But Shaw had something more to say, an 'impression' he had. He leant across the table, dropped his voice below the wail of

Islamic musak. 'I thought the whole thing was very shady,' he said.

In what way shady?

'Well, we were the only ones who took any real sort of interest. The effort put into the search by the Malays was pretty weak. The PFF [Police Field Force] came up, and they brought in some aboriginal trackers, but we thought they did a very half-hearted job.'

Was this, I asked, just a matter of laziness. 'I doubt it. The PFF were the best of the Malaysian groups. I've worked with them; I've trained some of them. These were professionals. They weren't like the military, they didn't have a colonel who was in charge purely because he was a younger sultan's younger brother. So I would doubt it was idleness. If it had been the Malaysian army, yes I would have said so, but not the PFF.'

So why weren't they looking?

'My personal feeling is that they *knew* he wasn't there, and they were just putting up a bit of front. I feel very strongly, from the attitude of people involved, that somebody up there knew what had happened. There was very little positive action taken by the Malays. The Americans made a bit of noise too, but it was all show. That can only lead to speculation, especially with the guy being what he was: a leading builder of a Third World industry, an international figure.

'It was weird. It was very weird.'

Another man with interesting memories of the search for Thompson is David Fitzstevens, a tall, red-bearded American who works for CAMA Services Inc., a Protestant aid organization running projects in Vietnam, Laos and Cambodia. In 1967 Fitzstevens was a sixteen-year-old student at the Dalat Missionary School, which had recently transferred to the Cameron Highlands from Vietnam. On the Monday morning, the day after Thompson's disappearance, the headmaster asked for volunteers to join the search party, and Fitzstevens was one of them.

At about midday, he and a friend were working through dense foliage in the woods below the back of Moonlight Cottage. He estimates it was about fifty yards from the house. 'We were coming up a slope, and there was this tree with big roots sticking out where the soil had eroded away, and something caught my eye. I shone my flashlight in there, and saw this small, bright, white object. It was some gauze, stuffed into the roots. It was very new, and it was very white. That's why I saw it. It couldn't have been there for long.'

He fished it out carefully. To a sixteen-year-old versed in Hollywood cop movies the implications were obvious. Thompson was a target for a kidnap gang; kidnappers used chloroform; here was a wad of gauze hastily hidden near the scene of the crime. At the least it showed that someone had recently been lurking in that area of jungle where there were no paths and no tracks, nothing at all except Moonlight Cottage fifty yards away, where Thompson was staying.

Excited by his discovery, Fitzstevens hurried back to Moonlight, where the local police had set up their headquarters. He found their reaction 'strange'. 'It was a kind of neutral response. They just said, "Well, thank you very much." I think they stuck it in a plastic bag. It was played down, a thing of no importance. And it's odd, but it seemed there was a relationship: after we'd turned this in, they moved us to another area entirely, a long way away.'

It is also odd, Fitzstevens thinks, that in all the sifting of the case that has gone on since, no one has made any reference to his discovery. There is nothing about it in the press reports, nor in the reminiscences of Connie Mangskau and the Lings, nor in Warren's biography. 'I've been waiting for twenty-five years for someone to mention it,' he says.

There may, of course, be some innocent explanation for the gauze – a hunter cleaning his gun, perhaps – but you wonder what else might have turned up, during the search or later, which the investigators decided not to mention.

★

Neither Shaw nor Fitzstevens has been interviewed before. They have no recollection of one another. Quite independently they raise these questions about the investigation of Thompson's disappearance. The search was only for 'show', according to Shaw, and at least one possible clue in this clueless puzzle was quietly ignored. And so suspicion steals back into one's mind, and one starts to shuffle once more through the deck of conspiracy theories.

The earliest, and perhaps most interesting, was the 'Pridi connection', which linked Thompson with a former Thai prime minister, General Pridi Phanomyong. It is interesting because it was advanced by a top-brass soldier – General Edwin Black, commander-in-chief of US forces in Thailand.

Black is now dead, but his views were outlined for me by his (and Thompson's) friend Maxine North in the office of her company, Starwagon Holdings, in Bangkok's business district. 'Ed's theory', she explained, 'was that Jim had been approached by Pridi's people, his "young Turks" as we called them. They were planning to stage a coup and install Pridi again. They wanted to know how the US government would react to this, and reckoned Jim should be able to gauge this.' In the Cameron Highlands, Thompson was spirited away to meet Pridi. Whether he went willingly to this rendezvous, or was abducted, is a variable in the theory.

There is certainly some foundation for this. Thompson had been a friend of Pridi, who led the 'Free Thai' resistance against the Japanese during the Second World War, and he was personally involved in the post-war power struggle between Pridi and his rival, Luang Pibulsonggram. In 1947 Pridi was ousted in a coup. Two years later he led an unsuccessful counter-coup. In the aftermath of this, three of Thompson's closest Thai friends – all former members of the Pridi government – were murdered in police custody, and his chief assistant in the silk business, a Laotian named Tao Oum, fled the country in fear of his life. This was, says Warren, a time of 'horror' for Thompson: his best Asian friends killed or imprisoned or driven into exile on charges which he believed to be untrue.

Pridi sought refuge in China. He disappeared from view behind the Bamboo Curtain in the mid sixties, believed to be based in Canton. According to the Thai government, he was behind the Communist insurgents then active in southern Thailand. In July 1968 a senior Thai official on a visit to Malaysia named Pridi as an 'architect of the Communist underground movement' in both Thailand and Malaysia. North and east of the Cameron Highlands the jungle stretches unbroken to the Thai border. This was the domain of the Communist guerrillas. If someone wanted to meet up with Pridi, a remote cottage in the Highlands might be a convenient rendezvous.

Apart from the customary lack of evidence, the Pridi theory has problems. Thompson's known links with the Pridi faction, says Warren, were 'strong in the late forties, maybe in the early fifties, but certainly not by the sixties. They were all long since gone by that time. People have a way, when they're talking about Jim, of sort of telescoping things that took place years apart.' Of General Black, Warren says, in his deadpan way, 'Ed was a nice man. He wasn't very bright, but he was a nice man.'

Nor does the theory explain why Thompson never came back. Maxine North's version – 'Jim knew too much [about Pridi's plans], so they had to keep him' – is rather crude. In his last years, which he spent in Paris, Pridi denied any knowledge of Thompson's fate, but then – to borrow a phrase from another cause célèbre of the sixties – he would, wouldn't he?

★

The bottom line of the Pridi theory, and of other political theories that have been advanced, is another question: was Thompson working for the CIA?

He certainly had the pedigree. During the war he was in the OSS (the Office of Strategic Services, the military intelligence wing which was a direct forebear of the CIA), and was briefly US consul in Bangkok. He was pre-eminently a man of contacts. On the one hand, he was in close social contact with military figures such as General Black and with CIA station chief Bob Jantsen. On the other hand, he personally knew and admired the North Vietnamese leader Ho Chi Minh, and had old friends from the silk business who belonged to Lao nationalist groups. This is a kind of fulcrum for covert political work. Maxine North, the doyenne of the conspiracy theorists, has no doubt: 'The CIA knew who he was going to meet down there.'

Warren argues, predictably but cogently, that Thompson did not have time to be a spy. 'I've known a lot of spies, because Bangkok is – used to be – quite full of them. But there was never much doubt who was. There rarely is, in a place like this.'

Perhaps the best ones are the ones you *don't* know about?

'I doubt if there were many you didn't know about, frankly. I really and truly do.'

I later spoke to Don Carmichael, who knew Thompson in Bangkok in the fifties. Carmichael was himself described to me as ex-CIA, though he denies this. He was, he says, 'a straight airline guy', though the airline in question was Civil Air Transport, the forerunner of Air America. This was put together by General Chennault in the early fifties as a supply-line to the

KMT (the anti-Communist Kuomintang) holed up in Burma. The operation, it is now well known, also involved shipping large quantities of opium out of the KMT's fiefdom.

Carmichael had, as he puts it, 'administrative status' in the outfit. He was later a 'consultant' in Washington for the US Department of Defense, and now runs a real estate business in Florida. I asked this 'straight airline guy', by telephone, whether Thompson had worked for the CIA. It depends, he said, what you mean by 'worked for'. 'I doubt if Jim was an agent, but 99 chances out of 100 he was a contact for the US intelligence people in Bangkok. He was a terribly knowledgeable man, with high-ranking contacts. He had contacts in Phnom Penh. He was certainly an intelligence asset. He didn't need the money, but he was a patriotic man.'

Much the same view is taken by Barrie Cross, an associate of Thompson in the Oriental Hotel and the son-in-law of Connie Mangskau. 'Jim was SEA Supply, which was the forerunner of the CIA, there's no doubt about that. I think it's true to say that once you're a member of a covert organization you can never really leave. I'm sure they consulted him. He was very aware politically. He knew what was going on.'

The veteran Indo-China reporter Alan Dawson introduces yet another twist. Like some other OSS veterans, he claims, Thompson had actually been rejected by the CIA. He was 'generally believed to be a secret agent', and both he and the CIA went along with this 'because it took the heat off the *real* agents in Bangkok'.

*

So one throws up the pieces and lets them land in another pattern of reminiscence and rumour. It could all fit into one superb, gold-plated conspiracy theory – the restlessness at the picnic as the meeting drew near; the sightings at the bungalows, which afford a clearer view of the road below than you get from Moon-light Cottage; the curious impressions of both Shaw and Fitzstevens that the exercise they took part in was more of a cover-up than a genuine search. This was 1967, the first flush of the Vietnam War. We now know something of what was going on behind the scenes: the missionary-spies working out of upcountry Thailand, the clandestine wooing of tribal armies, the Air America opium moves, the ground plans for the 'Secret War' in Laos and Cambodia. These contexts seem to legitimize a conspiracy theory: the maverick Pridi is only one possibility.

Thompson lives on in this limbo. You come to know the man a little, and to like him rather a lot: 'a curious, imaginative, engrossing, sometimes lonely man, who chose an unlikely course for his life'. People speak of him in a relaxed, anecdotal way; they enjoy telling the story, for the hundredth time – 'So I called Jim up . . .', 'Jim always used to say . . .', Jim with his creased silk trousers and his beer belly, Jim driving down a tree-lined street in his convertible, Jim clowning it up with his cockatoo, Cocky, Jim getting red in the face when he ate *thom yam kung* soup. I was surprised to learn from Nath Chaijaroen that he never mastered the Thai language: 'He used to say his tongue was not soft enough.'

In some of his friends there is a desire to let his bones rest in some sequestered niche of the Cameron Highlands. In others there is an opposite wish: to keep scratching away for a story they believe has not yet been told. After twenty-five years the case remains unresolved and somehow spooky, as if we were all still waiting for him to saunter back up the drive in time for a sundowner.

25

Crows

A Corvedale Story
[1990]

The snow came late and deep to the Corvedale. The operations of spring were suspended. It must have been 1981: we had been living in this Shropshire valley for three years, refugees from London, sequestered in a £12-a-week cottage with our two young children, in a rustic time-warp that would have seemed old-fashioned when I was a child. For the children these unexpected snows were paradise, as snow always is, but for the sheep-farmers of the area it was a disaster. They were out all day and half the night, struggling up to their stranded flocks, carrying up feed and carrying down dead day-old lambs.

We climbed Bouldon Ridge and looked back down over the valley. Patches of colour broke through the snow: the sepia line of the hedgerows, the apricot tinge of budding poplars. In the distance we could see the rookery near our house, straggling over the treetops above Tug Brook: oak and alder and misshapen pine, and the skeleton fingers of a few dead elm. It was late afternoon, the hour of commotion. We watched the birds rising and wheeling and settling back down, like specks of black paper in the updraughts of a bonfire.

We were too far to hear them but I could hear other rooks near by. They were up above us, the other side of the hazel coppice that ran below the ridge-top. They were making a racket of alarm. I thought we must have disturbed them, our voices carrying across the stillness.

We came up through the tweedy brown coppice, and out into

high pasture, and then we saw them. Twenty crows, maybe more – it was impossible to count them – caught in a trap.

The trap was simple: a large rectangular hutch of wood and stout wire-netting. The entrance was in the roof, an angled funnel of netting. It was big enough for a bird to get down it, but the angle made any return impossible. They were mostly rooks but there were a few carrion and hoodies in there with them. It was a strange medieval vision: a cage of angry black birds in an empty white field. The temperature was already near freezing. They were frantic with hunger; the bait, whatever it was, had long since been eaten up.

Part of me wanted to cut the netting and free them. I had my multiple-bladed pseudo-countryman pen-knife, and perhaps I could have done it. It was of course debatable whether I ought to. Crows are an enemy: they are not my enemy but they are certainly the sheep-farmer's enemy. They compete for the feed, they prey on weakened animals, and sometimes – one is told – they take out the eyes of lambs while they're still being born. These were the grim fortunes of war we were seeing here. But it wasn't that which stopped me. What stopped me was fear. I was quite certain that if we somehow opened up the trap the crows would come swarming out and attack us. They would try to kill us. They would take out the eyes of my children. I don't know if this was true, but there was an intensity inside that trap, a seething rage which scared the hell out of me.

The trap on Bouldon Ridge was another small chapter in an old story of persecution. Everything about the crow is old. They have been here for ever – continuously present in the landscape, ominously present in folklore. Our words for them are rudimentary, simple imitations of their call, not so much a name as an echo, so in a sense they have named themselves. The crow crows, the *corvus* caws, and the rook, in the Anglo-Saxon spelling of the word, says '*hrōc*'. To some we pretend familiarity, and address them with human names. The daw (*Corvus monedula*) is always Jack, and the pied crow, the apportioner of sorrow and joy, is Mag or in older days Meg.

Their features are unlovely, their manner shifty, their song 'poor and raucous', yet they have a brain-to-bodyweight ratio equalled only by the higher primates, and are documented as tool-makers and problem-solvers of remarkable skill. The family, *Corvidae*, has more than 120 species, and there are few corners of the world where this bullying omnivore has not found a niche (in fact I think the only region they are absent from is Antarctica). There are rookeries in the steppes of Central Asia, and white-necked ravens scavenging the African bush, and coast-dwelling crows who fish like ungainly black gulls, and deep in a forest somewhere there is the plush-crested jay.

When I was a child I was more than once taken to the Tower of London, and was in awe of the big, sinister ravens, and of their keeper, the Yeoman Ravenmaster, who sounded like he came from a fairy tale. I have an image of this man, with a weathered face under the squashy beefeater's top-hat, and of his brisk but respectful way with the birds. Was it he who told me, as someone certainly did, that in the old days people could get in free to the Tower Zoo if they brought along a dog or cat to be fed to the lions? This idea horrified me more than all the instruments of torture on show there – Skevington's Daughter and the rest. I thought of us doing that to our dog (at that point an Alsatian bitch called Velvet) – an unimaginable betrayal.

There is a complement of six ravens at the Tower, and by tradition one or two 'guests', but in the bombed-out city after the war there was for a short while only one raven left. His name was Grip. It is not improbable he was one of those I saw there in the 1950s. Ravens regularly live to twenty-five and sometimes much longer: a famous Tower bird, James Crow, was in residence for forty-four years.

Grip was named after Charles Dickens's pet raven, who lived in a stable and mimicked the language of grooms and coachmen. 'He would perch outside my window,' Dickens recalled, 'and drive imaginary horses, with great skill, all day.' In a letter to a friend he recounted the bird's death in 1841: 'On the clock striking twelve he appeared slightly agitated, but he soon recovered, walked twice or thrice along the coach house, stopped to bark, staggered, exclaimed "Halloa old girl!" (his favourite expression), and died.' Dickens immortalized Grip twice over – by making him a character in *Barnaby Rudge*, published in serial form that year; and by having him stuffed and mounted (see Plate 17). In this incarnation he was eventually purchased by an American collector, Colonel Richard Gimbel – a Poe enthusiast, who believed the fictional Grip had inspired Poe's poem 'The Raven'. He now stands in state in the Rare Books Department of the Philadelphia Free Library, which also has the original manuscript of Poe's 'The Murders in the Rue Morgue'. Grip, one might say, is not just a crow with a name, but a crow with a biography.

I pursue this little trail much later, at leisure, but the connection with the Tower ravens was one I made right there, standing in front of the crow-trap on Bouldon Ridge. I remembered watching them being shut up for the night in their straw-bedded cages near the Wakefield Tower. Across the years the two images met: a frisson of fear that seemed to pass, like a crackle of electricity, from my childhood to this moment with my own children beside me.

We watched the crows for a while, in the last low sun, but our curiosity seemed impertinent. The least we could do was leave them in peace. A few of the birds had settled down on the floor of the trap, exhausted and resigned. They would all die that night, taking their stories with them.

Notes

This is a brief dossier of background information on each essay. It gives some account of the sources I have used, some titles of useful or inspiring books on the subject, some updates or new material where necessary, some overdue acknowledgements and some occasional reminiscences. Unless otherwise stated, the books mentioned here were published in London.

1. *The Field of Bones*
(London Review of Books, *1999*)

I am grateful to the late Michael Strachan for generous advice on some aspects of this story. His biography *The Life and Adventures of Thomas Coryate* (Oxford, 1962) is indispensable to any student of Coryate. I have also drawn on his *Sir Thomas Roe, 1581–1644: A Life* (Salisbury, 1989). Two later travel books have followed Coryate's trails in Europe (Tim Moore, *Continental Drifter*, 2002) and in Asia (Dom Moraes and Sarayu Srivatsa, *The Long Strider*, New York, 2003). As for the legstretcher's own writings, the most recent appearance of the *Crudities* is the handsome old-spelling edition published by James MacLehose (2 vols., Glasgow, 1905), while the *Crambe* was last reprinted in 1776. The British Library has various first editions of the *Crudities*, including a copy presented to Henry, Prince of Wales; inserted in the back of this is a letter from Coryate to Sir Michael Hicks ('from my chamber in Bow Lane this 15th November 1610') – the only surviving example of his hand. The Indian newsletters are transcribed with minor omissions in Sir William Foster, *Early Travels in India, 1583–1619* (Oxford, 1921), pp. 241–76. A few of the notes Coryate left in Aleppo are published in Samuel Purchas, *Pilgrimes* (1625), Part II, Book 10, Chapter 12, and the last Indian fragments are in Part I, Book 4, Chapter 17.

The tantalizing information about the cache in Isfahan (see pp. 9–10) comes courtesy of Michael Rose (*London Review of Books*, Letters, 30 September 1999). My thanks also to Henry G. Coryat junior of Rhinebeck, New York, who wrote to me to say that his great-great-grandfather, Henry Coryat, who emigrated from England to Trinidad in 1805, considered himself a 'distant relative' of the author. Mr Coryat's researches have not confirmed a connection, but he did find that his ancestor had been born in Tétouan, in Morocco, thus invoking a faint possibility that Coryate left some progeny in the East (though there are, of course, many other explanations for Henry's birth in the Maghreb).

2. A 'Naughty House'
(London Review of Books, *2010*)

Further material on Christopher Mountjoy and his family can be found in my book *The Lodger* (revised edition, 2008), to which this piece is a kind of appendix. The records of the case examined here are in the London Metropolitan Archives: Middlesex Sessions Roll 526/179–80, 527/126; and Middlesex Sessions Register 2, fols. 26–7, 29–30. I am grateful to Christopher Whittick, senior archivist at East Sussex Records Office, Lewes, for some finer points of legal interpretation. The related references to Mountjoy's 'disordered' lifestyle are in the *Actes du consistoire de l'Église françoise de Londres*. This is in the library of the French Protestant Church, London (MS 4); entries relating to Mountjoy and Belott are transcribed in *The Lodger* (Appendix 3). On the accuser Adam Bowen, see William Moens, *Registers of the French Church, London, 1600–1636* (Publications of the Huguenot Society of London, 9, 1896), Vol. 1, pp. 19, 23; and Irene Scouloudi, *Returns of Strangers in the Metropolis* (PHSL, 57, 1985), p. 153. He may also be the Adam Bowyn listed in the Lay Subsidy Rolls of 1593 and 1594 as a foreigner resident in St Thomas's, Southwark: see R. E. G. and E. F. Kirk, *Returns of Aliens Dwelling in the City and Suburbs of London* (PHSL, 10, 1910), Vol. 2, pp. 449, 459. Possible but inconclusive references to the three French defendants can be found *sub voce* in the indexes of Moens and Kirk. On Jacobean Whitecross Street, see John J. Baddeley, *Cripplegate* (1921), pp. 186–9;

and on the Fortune Theatre see E. K. Chambers, *The Elizabethan Stage* (1923), Vol. 2, pp. 435–43. That one of those posting bail for the Frenchmen is described as a 'gardener' might suggest that Mountjoy's property was one of those 'garden houses' or 'summer houses for pleasure' associated with immorality in the suburbs by John Stow (*Survay of London*, 1598) and others.

3. Noticing Everything
(Weekend Telegraph, *1997*)

As is self-evident, this piece first appeared on the 300th anniversary of Aubrey's burial. The best general biographies of him are Anthony Powell, *John Aubrey and His Friends* (Oxford, 1948), and David Tylden-Wright, *John Aubrey: A Life* (1991). See also Oliver Lawson Dick's introduction to his edition of *Brief Lives* (1949) and Michael Hunter's to the Penguin Classics selection (2000). There is still no complete edition of the manuscript 'Lives'. Andrew Clark's (2 vols., Oxford, 1898) remains the most comprehensive, but suppresses some salacious material. I was first introduced to Aubrey by Roy Dotrice's wonderful one-man show, *Brief Lives*, directed by Patrick Garland, which I saw at the Criterion Theatre in *c.* 1968. My research in Oxford was assisted by the Revd Hugh Whybrew, then vicar of St Mary Magdalen, and Claire Harman.

4. Death of an Alchemist
(London Review of Books, *2001*)

Misconceptions about Kelley's last years are amended in the new (but still brief) article on him by Louise Schleiner in the *Oxford Dictionary of National Biography* (2004). There is still no full biography, though there is a very concise and factual one by Australian author Michael Wilding, 'Edward Kelly: A Life', published in the alchemical journal *Cauda Pavonis* (Vol. 19/1–2, 1999, pp. 1–26). My account of Kelley's post-1591 career is based on Bohemian documents collected by Josef Svátek in *Obrazy z kulturnich dějin Českých*

('Images of Czech Cultural History') (Prague, 1891), Vol. 1, pp. 135–89; on English dispatches from Prague in the British Library's Lansdowne manuscripts; and on material in Wilding's 'Life', pp. 17–20. On Kelley's stepdaughter see Susan Bassnet, 'Revising a Biography: A New Interpretation of the Life of Elizabeth Jane Weston' (*Cahiers Elizabethains*, 37, April 1990, pp. 1–8). Kelley's transcript of the Bohemian *Landtsordenung* is in the National Museum Library, Prague, MS VI D 17; I have compared its script with Kelley's last letter to Burghley, 18 February 1591 (BL MS Lansdowne 66/58, fols. 164–165v). Šimon Tadeáš Budek's account of Kelley's death is given in Czech by Svátek (pp. 156–7), but the original is in a Latin manuscript, '*Ars artium et scientia scientiarum*', now in Vienna (Österreichische Nationalbibliothek, MS 11133). Excerpts from Dr Dee's diaries (both quotidian and 'spirituall') are from Edward Fenton (ed.), *The Diaries of John Dee* (Charlbury, Oxon., 1998), though the long excerpt on pp. 48–9 is taken directly from Méric Casaubon (ed.), *A True & Faithful Relation of what passed for many yeers between Dr John Dee and some spirits* (1659), pp. 213–14. For assistance in the Czech Republic I am grateful to David Rehak, Michaela Kapanklova, Martin Orbach and Eva Holekova, whose whispered translations in the huge frescoed reading rooms of the Klementina Library lent an unusual glamour to historical research. My thanks also to Kevin Whelan and Liam Mac Cóil, who illuminated the Irish genealogy behind Kelley's Bohemian knighthood (see p. 45), and to Henry Schermer, who shared memories of the demolition of Most.

5. Mugshots and Miniatures
(The Independent, *1995*)

Karen Hearn's exhibition catalogue *Dynasties: Painting in Tudor and Jacobean England 1530–1630* (Tate Gallery, 1995) gives full information on the portraits discussed here. For further reading on English portraiture of the period, see Roy Strong, *Tudor and Jacobean Portraits* (National Portrait Gallery, 1969); and on portraits of Tudor and Jacobean authors see my *Shakespeare and His Contemporaries* (National Portrait Gallery, 2005).

6. *Canterbury Tale*

(London Review of Books, *1988*)

No account of Christopher Marlowe's boyhood is complete without the possible sighting of him as a nine-year-old 'boye' serving in a Canterbury 'victualling-house'. This was discovered by Andrew Butcher, the editor of Urry's book, and published by him in Daryll Grantley and Peter Roberts (eds.), *Christopher Marlowe and English Renaissance Culture* (Aldershot, 1996), pp. 1–18. In a court case of 1573 a serving-girl accused one John Roydon of sexually assaulting her, and in the course of her evidence mentioned that he employed 'a boye called Christopher Mowle' as a waiter or pot-boy. Butcher is correctly cautious, but I find it convincing. Mowle would almost certainly be bisyllabic, pronounced 'Moly' or 'Mowley', which is not too far from the 'Marley' favoured by Christopher in his signature of 1585. It is anyway the girl's pronunciation of his name, as recorded by the clerk; her estimate of the boy's age as twelve (while Marlowe was then only nine) is also subjective. A 'victualling-house' was a private dwelling licensed to serve food; Marlowe's father ran one in his later years. Marlowe's later dealings in the sphere of secret politics, referred to here *en passant*, are explored more fully in *The Reckoning* (1992, revised edition 2002).

7. *'An Explorer'*

(London Review of Books, *1991*)

David Riggs's biography of Jonson has held the field in the twenty years since its publication, but definitiveness is a perishable commodity, and a new (though identically titled) biography by Ian Donaldson (2011) looks set to succeed it. Donaldson is a leading Jonson specialist, one of the editors of the new Cambridge edition of the *Works* (7 vols., 2011). In the interim there have been some great documentary finds. One, discovered among miscellaneous manuscripts at Berkeley Castle, is Jonson's previously unknown elegy on the death of Thomas Nashe in *c.* 1601 (see Katherine Duncan-Jones, *The Times Literary*

Supplement, 7 July 1995, and *Ben Jonson Journal*, 3, 1996, pp. 1–19). Jonson speaks
warmly of Nashe as his 'deare freind', and a 'greate spirite', and fears his passing will cause a 'generall dearthe of witt throughout this land'. Jonson did not
praise lightly, and the poem adds a personal dimension of friendship to Jonson's obvious debt to Nashe as a comic stylist. Another discovery, as yet
unpublished, is an eighteen-page diary entitled 'My Gossip Johnson his foot
voyage and mine into Scotland'. This is nothing less than a first-hand account
of Jonson's trek of 1618, written by his travelling companion, who was also
apparently his godson – the primary meaning of 'gossip' at this time (from
Middle English *godsib*, 'related in god') was 'godfather'. The document was
found by James Loxley in the Cheshire county archives in Chester: see his article 'My Gossip's Foot Voyage' (*The Times Literary Supplement*, 11 September
2009, pp. 13–15). The diarist's identity is at present uncertain: he may be a
young man called Thomas Aldersey. This travelogue (which Loxley is editing
for publication) promises a wealth of new detail on the journey, about which
Jonson himself is oddly uninformative (see p. 79). The journey took about ten
weeks, we learn (from 8 July to 17 September 1618). One interesting detail is
that Jonson crossed the Tees by the footbridge at Croft-on-Tees, rather than
taking the more convenient ferry at Neasham – a detour, Loxley thinks, suggesting his determination to remain on foot throughout the journey, possibly
to fulfil the terms of a wager. This 'foot voyage' calls to mind Thomas Coryate's feats of walking, and Jonson's commendation of them – indeed the walk
may in part be a tribute to the late 'legstretcher', who had died in India the
previous December.

8. Cardenio's Ghost

(London Review of Books, *2010*)

Brean Hammond's edition of *Double Falsehood* (Arden Shakespeare, Third
Series, 2009) and Greg Doran's sparkling production of *Cardenio* (Royal
Shakespeare Company, 2011) have brought this lost play to new prominence.
The transmission of the text via an intermediary version by Davenant was

first proposed by John Freehafer in 'Cardenio by Shakespeare and Fletcher' (*Publications of the Modern Language Association of America*, 84/3, May 1969). Michael Wood's linking of the Robert Johnson song to *Cardenio* (see pp. 92–3) was briefly aired in his television series *In Search of Shakespeare* (BBC2, 2003); I am grateful to him for showing me his unpublished essay ' "A Sound from Heaven": New Light on Shakespeare's *Cardenio*', which gives a fuller treatment of the subject. Some years ago, noting that the earliest reference to the play spelt it 'Cardenno', I hatched a theory that the whole Quixote connection was a fallacious assumption of Lewis Theobald's, and the play was actually about the celebrated Lombard mathematician, magus and gambler Girolamo Cardano, whose rather picaresque autobiography, *De vita propria*, had been published posthumously in 1576. Fortunately I failed to convince myself.

9. 'The Life etc'
(2009)

This piece was written as an introduction to the tercentenary edition of Rowe's *Account*, published by Pallas Athene; I have incorporated some material which I added for a talk on Rowe at the Globe Theatre, December 2009. On the early biographers of Shakespeare see Samuel Schoenbaum, *Shakespeare's Lives* (1970). The case for taking them more seriously – or at least for listening more carefully to what they say – is argued with characteristic lucidity by the late Eric Sams in *The Real Shakespeare: Retrieving the Early Years, 1564–1594* (1995).

10. Cipher Wheels
(The Times Literary Supplement, 2010)

I am reluctant to add further to the tonnage of hot air which the so-called 'authorship controversy' has produced. A good, broadly impartial overview

of the candidates proposed is John Michell, *Who Wrote Shakespeare?* (1996). A
recent exposition of the Oxfordian case is Jonathan Bond, *The De Vere Code*
(2009). A sprightly defence of the pro-Shakespeare (or 'Stratfordian') position can be heard at www.shakespeare60.com. A heavily hyped feature film
on the subject, *Anonymous*, with anti-Stratfordians Jacobi and Rylance in the
cast, will have been released by the time this book is out: at the risk of sound-
ing like Nostradamus (who is oddly neglected as a possible author of the
plays) I predict that it will generate much heat but little light.

11. *Conversing with Giants*
(Granta, *1998*)

In its earliest form this was a lecture delivered to the Globetrotters Club at
Imperial College, London, in 1995. There are two good English translations
of Pigafetta's narrative: by Lord Stanley of Alderney (Hakluyt Society, First
Series, Vol. 52, 1874); and by R. A. Skelton (*Magellan's Voyage: A Narrative
Account of the First Circumnavigation*, 2 vols., New Haven, Conn., 1969). Both
are based on French manuscripts, the fullest and finest of which, reproduced
in facsimile by Skelton, is in the Beinecke Rare Book and Manuscript Library
at Yale University. It consists of 103 leaves of vellum, a text with illuminated
initials and paragraph marks, and twenty-three maps. The encounter with
the giant begins: '*Ung iour sans que personne y pensait nous veismes ung geant qui
estoit a la rive de la mer tout nud.*' The only contemporary Italian manuscript
(Biblioteca Ambrosiana, Milan) is less complete, and is peppered with Venetian slang and Spanish words; it was first published by Carlo Amoretti in
1800. Richard Eden's English abbreviation, 'A briefe declaration of the viage
or navigation made about the worlde, gathered out of a large booke written
hereof by Master Anthoni Pigafetta Vincentino', first appeared in his *Decades
of the Newe Worlde* (1555). It loses some of the impact of the original by changing the narrative pronoun from 'we' to 'they' ('One day by chaunce they
espyed a man of the stature of a giant'). In the 1577 edition read by Shakespeare (edited after Eden's death by Richard Willes and retitled *The History of*

Travayle), the reference to Setebos occurs on fol. 434v. On the New World 'prodigies', of which Pigafetta's giants are an example, see A. Wettan Kleinbaum, *The War against the Amazons* (New York, 1983); Stephen Greenblatt, *Marvellous Possessions* (Oxford, 1991) and *New World Encounters* (Berkeley, Calif., 1993); Marina Warner, *Managing Monsters* (Reith Lectures, 1994); Frank Lestringant, *Cannibals* (1997). My thanks to Matthew Kirkbride for additional research on Pigafetta's house in Vicenza.

12. *'Sneezing . . . Yawning . . . Falling'*
(London Review of Books, *2005*)

Leonardo's manuscripts and notebooks can be read in the magnificent series of facsmile editions published by Giunti, an old Florentine printing-house already in business when Leonardo began work on the *Mona Lisa*. These include *Il codice Atlantico* (24 vols., 1973–80), *I manuscritti dell' Institut de France* (12 vols., 1986–90), *I codici Forster* (3 vols., 1992) and *Il codice sul volo degli uccelli* (1976), all edited by the doyen of Leonardo literary scholarship, Augusto Marinoni; *Il codice nella Biblioteca Trivulziana*, A. Brizio (ed.) (1980); *The Codex Hammer* (aka Codex Leicester), Carlo Pedretti (ed.) (1987); and *Il codice Arundel 263*, Carlo Pedretti and Carlo Vecce (eds.) (1998), with chronological reordering of folios. The Windsor manuscripts are catalogued in *The Drawings of Leonardo da Vinci in the Collection of Her Majesty the Queen*, Kenneth Clark and Carlo Pedretti (eds.) (3 vols., 1968), and the Madrid codices are edited by Ladislaus Reti (New York, 1974). There is no complete English translation of Leonardo's manuscripts: the next best thing is the parallel-text selection of extracts (grouped by subject) by Jean-Paul Richter, *The Literary Works of Leonardo da Vinci* (2 vols., 1889, revised edition 1939), together with Carlo Pedretti's *Commentary* on it (2 vols., Berkeley, Calif., 1977). Sources for the extracts quoted in this essay, and further information on Leonardo's associates, can be found in my biography *Leonardo da Vinci: The Flights of the Mind* (2004).

13. *The Secrets of St Proculus*
(The Times Literary Supplement, *1999*)

According to latest reports, Mario Pincherle is still going strong, now aged
ninety-two. Some of the projects he spoke of in 1999 were duly published –
e.g. *La nuova Etruscologia* (1999), *La vera storia di Sargon di Accadia* (2001) and
Guglielmo Marconi (2002). One of his latest books, *Il libro di Abramo* (2009),
bears the characteristic subtitle '*I trentadue occulti sentieri della saggezza*' ('The
Thirty-two Secret Paths of Wisdom').

14. *A Renaissance Life of Riley*
(Sunday Times, *2004* and *2005*)

I have grafted together two reviews on related themes. Another excellent
study of the economic nuts and bolts of the Renaissance is Lisa Jardine,
Worldly Goods: A New History of the Renaissance (1996).

15. *Screaming in the Castle*
(London Review of Books, *1998*)

The classic study of the case is Corrado Ricci, *Beatrice Cenci* (Milan, 1923),
translated by Morris Bishop and Henry Longan (2 vols., New York, 1925).
Shelley's *The Cenci* is in *The Complete Poetical Works of Percy Bysshe Shelley*
(Oxford, 1921), as are Mary Shelley's comments on it. The manuscript Shelley
used may be the old '*dossier*' from the Palazzo Cenci later translated by Stendhal (*Revue des deux mondes*, 1 July 1837). Artaud's *Les Cenci* is in Vol. 4 of his
Œuvres complètes (Paris, 1964); an English translation by Simon Watson-Taylor
(*The Cenci*, 1969) includes a pair of brief essays by Artaud written before the
play's opening in May 1935. A later study by Belinda Jack, *Beatrice's Spell*
(2004), looks at various manifestations of her 'enduring legend' (there is an

interesting back-story to Nathaniel Hawthorne's obsession with her), and at some further visual refractions, such as the sculpture by Harriet Hosmer (1856) and photographic studies by Julia Margaret Cameron (1868). The appeal of the apocryphal Reni portrait continues – a reproduction of it is seen in a Hollywood apartment, undoubtedly with an intentional reference to Beatrice, in David Lynch's metaphysical noir *Mulholland Drive* (2001). What appear to be some echoes of the case are found in a Jacobean drama by Philip Massinger, *The Unnatural Combat*, first performed in about 1624, and thus antedating by two centuries the Romantic revival of Beatrice.

16. *Man in a Fur Hat*
(London Magazine, *1999*)

Kish's painting, catalogued as a 'portrait of Lord Byron as Manfred' by Hurlstone, was auctioned in London on 17 June 2008 (Bonhams Sale 15800: British, Continental and Old Master Paintings, Lot No. 310). The lot, which also included two 'framed documents' relating to Byron, was sold for £2,160. Less than three months later, on 9 September, the painting alone was resold for £1,800 (Bonhams Sale 15818: British and Continental Pictures, Lot No. 167). Though describing it as a portrait of Byron, the catalogue offers no date of composition, and therefore no support for Kish's contention that it was painted from the life. Nor does the sale price, which is about right for a generic, non-contemporary portrait of him. A larger but otherwise broadly comparable painting by Hurlstone, *A Boy of Venice* (1853), fetched £4,663 ($7,500) at a North Carolina auction in March 2011.

17. *'My Infelice'*
(London Review of Books, *2001*)

On the Walker family records see Stanley Jones, *William Hazlitt: A Life* (Oxford, 1981), p. 308; they were communicated to him by Micaiah Walker's great-grandson, John Field Walker. The eleven-page 'Journal Book' of March 1823 is in the Lockwood Memorial Library, New York State University, Buffalo. It was first published in full by Willard Hallam Bonner (*University of Buffalo Studies*, 24/3, February 1959); some of his transcriptions are corrected by Stanley Jones (*The Library*, Fifth Series, 26, 1979, pp. 325–6). The unexpurgated original letters to Patmore (also in the Lockwood collection) can be read in *The Letters of William Hazlitt*, Herschel Morland Sykes, Willard Hallam Bonner and Gerald Lahey (eds.) (New York, 1978), though this edition is also criticized for inaccuracy by Jones and others. The facsimile of Sarah's letter of January 1822 is in Richard Le Gallienne's privately printed edition of *Liber Amoris* (1894), p. 209; the text of it had previously been published in W. C. Hazlitt, *Memoirs of William Hazlitt* (1867), Vol. 2, p. 27. The document containing her letter of February 1822 is at Princeton (see my List of Illustrations, Plate 11, for details). It was first transcribed in Charles Robinson (ed.), *William Hazlitt to his Publishers, Friends and Creditors: Twenty-seven New Holograph Letters* (University of York, 1987), No. 7, but Robinson's contention that her letter is autograph is wrong. Though the script is slightly smaller than that of the accompanying comments, it is clearly in the same hand, i.e. Hazlitt's. The most recent edition of the *Liber* is in *The Selected Writings of William Hazlitt*, Duncan Wu (ed.), Vol. 7 (1998). I compute the approximate birth-date of Sarah's son, Frederick, from the fact that he was twenty-six years old on 30 March 1851 (census return) and twenty-eight on 6 October 1852 (death certificate).

18. Bet Rimbo

(London Review of Books, *2000*)

The photograph of Rimbaud first published by Claude Jeancolas in his *L'Afrique de Rimbaud* (Paris, 1999) – though its actual 'discoverer', according to other accounts, was a Paris gallery-owner, Arnaud Delas – shows him in a group of six Europeans at Scheick-Otman, a few miles north of Aden, in the early 1880s; he is simply dressed, bare-headed and (like the others in the group) carries a hunting-rifle. Another recently discovered photograph (see *Libération*,

9 September 2010) shows a group on the terrace of the Grand Hotel in Aden. It is the right place – Rimbaud often stayed at the Grand – but I am not entirely convinced, on visual grounds, that the rather elegant young man seated second from the right is actually the poet. One of the group has been identified as the explorer Henri Lucereau, who died on an expedition in October 1880; there is some debate as to whether he was still in Aden when Rimbaud arrived there in August. A full analysis is in Alban Caussé and Jacques Desse, 'Rimbaud, Aden 1880: Histoire d'une photographie' (*Revue des deux mondes*, September 2010). For more material on the Bet Rimbo see my *Somebody Else: Arthur Rimbaud in Africa* (1997), pp. 126–35. Here too can be found the three self-portraits taken in Harar; one shows him on the balcony of a house, but is too damaged to give any detail of the building. In a photograph by Rimbaud's Italian associate Ottorino Rosa (*L'impero del Leone di Giuda*, Brescia, 1913, p. 145) there is a low-built, street-side dwelling which he identifies as Rimbaud's house in Harar, though this does not invalidate the Bet Rimbo, as he certainly had more than one house during his years in the city. I am grateful to Gordon Wetherell, who has since been ambassador in Ghana and Luxembourg (a country scarcely bigger than an Abyssinian *gasha*) and is now governor of the Turks and Caicos Islands; and to Ron Orders, with whom I first visited Harar in 1994, and whose beautiful photograph of Bet Rimbo is reproduced here (Plate 12).

19. Joe the Ripper
(London Review of Books, *2008*)

All sources for the career of Joseph Lis-Silver, mostly police records of one sort or another, can be found in van Onselen's book. On the Whitechapel murders there are useful reference books such Stewart Evans and Keith Skinner, *The Ultimate Jack the Ripper Source Book* (2001), John Eddlestone, *Jack the Ripper: An Encyclopaedia* (2002), Donald Rumbelow, *The Complete Jack the Ripper* (revised edition, 2004), etc. Silver is one of over 130 suspects proposed over the years: a concise overview of them is given by Richard Davenport Hines (*Oxford Dictionary of National Biography*, 2004). The killer's nickname derives from the signature of a 'red-inked, defiant, semi-literate letter' posted in late September 1888, which was 'probably a hoax concocted by news agency staff' (Hines). The original police photograph of Mary Jane Kelly's body, in the City of London Police Archives, was not published in England until 1969 (in the *Police Journal*), though a more shadowy, and therefore less gruesome, reproduction of it had appeared in France a decade after the murders, in Alexandre Lacassagne, *Vacher l'éventreur et les crimes sadiques* (Paris, 1899, p. 257). There is an excellent article on the murders on Wikipedia, though those venturing into the labyrinths of online Ripperology do so at their own risk.

20. 'The wind comes up out of nowhere'
(London Review of Books, *2006*)

The best edition of Cravan's writings is the *Œuvres*, edited by Jean-Pierre Begot (Paris, 1992), which also has a trustworthy chronology of his life (pp. 265–78). Roger L. Conover's biography is now even longer-awaited than it was five years ago; his essay '*Arthur Cravan* by Roger Lloyd Conover' (*Four Dada Suicides*, 2005, pp. 12–27) expresses some Cravanesque doubts about the 'caging' of this free spirit in the confines of a Life. I am grateful to him for information on Cravan's Mexican sojourn; my thanks also to Alastair Brotchie of Atlas Press, John Pouttu and Kevin Jackson. Aside from the Spanish biography by Borràs and the comic-strip biography by Richardson and Geary, both mentioned in the text, there is a good account by Emmanuel Pollaud-Dulian (1998) at www.multimania.com. On Loy see Carolyn Burke, *Becoming Modern: The Life of Mina Loy* (Berkeley, Calif., 1996); Thom Gunn, 'Leper of the Moon' (*The Times Literary Supplement*, 30 August 1996); and Tanya Dalziell, 'Mourning and Jazz in the Poetry of Mina Loy', in *Modernism and Mourning*, Patricia Rae (ed.) (Lewisburg, PA, 2007). A good selection of her poems is *The Lost Lunar Baedeker*, Roger L. Conover (ed.) (New York, 1996). As well as her poetic memoir 'Colossus', which I quote from, there is a fine poem, 'Mexican Desert' (first published in the *Dial*, June 1921), which Conover calls 'a collaged recollection' of her journey with Cravan en route to Salina Cruz in 1918 (*Lost Lunar Baedeker*, p. 195). A novel by Antonia Logue, *Shadow Box* (1999), is an imagined account by Loy of her relationship with Cravan.

21. *Lingering Fever*
(The Independent, *1993*)

Alexander (or correctly Aleksandrs) Laime died of a heart attack on 20 March 1994, aged eighty-three. A biography of him by the Latvian author Andris Stavro, as yet untranslated, was published in Riga in 1999. See also Ruth Robertson's account of the expedition to survey Angel Falls, which Laime guided, in *National Geographic* (November 1949); and Tim Cahill, 'The Lost World', in *Jaguars Ripped My Flesh* (New York, 1987), pp. 39–59. The interviews on which this article is based were done in 1992; parts of them appear in *The City of Gold* (Channel 4, 1993), directed by Ron Orders. Another aged adventurer we met on this trip, the Dutchman Rudy Truffino, also died in 1994; there is an account of his life by the Dutch journalist Jan Brokken, *Jungle Rudy* (2004). Further material on El Dorado, and on Sir Walter Ralegh's 1595 expedition in search of it, can be found in my book *The Creature in the Map* (1995). Ralegh's own account, *The Discoverie of the large, rich and bewtiful Empire of Guiana* (1596), one of the best Elizabethan travel narratives, is edited with many supporting documents by V. T. Harlow (1928).

22. *Heading for Z*
(London Review of Books, *2009*)

Fawcett's own writings, listed by Grann, include eight scientific or expeditionary reports for the *Geographical Journal*, mingled with articles such as 'The Planetary Control' for the monthly *Occult Review*, where he appeared alongside Order of the Golden Dawn hierophants like Aleister Crowley and A. E. Waite. His last piece, 'At the Hot Wells of Konniar' (*Occult Review*, July 1925), probably appeared posthumously.

23. *The Capital of Memory*
(Mail on Sunday, *1996*)

Forster's affair with Adl was first chronicled in Vol. 2 of P. N. Furbank's *E. M. Forster: A Life* (1978). He was also thinking of his Alexandrian experiences when he wrote in 'Salute to the Orient!' (1923): 'nearer Port Said lie trouble and interest enough, skies that are not quite tropic, religions that are just comprehensible, people who grade into the unknown steeply, yet who sometimes recall European friends.' Some letters Adl wrote to him are in the Forster collection at King's College, Cambridge (where Forster lived for the last twenty years of his life, a sort of Legend in Residence, and where I remember him in the late 1960s, a small, venerable figure passing slowly through the college bar en route to dinner). The four assortedly coloured covers of the Faber paperback edition of *The Alexandria Quartet* belong to that time too. In 2007, on the fiftieth anniversary of the publication of *Justine*, the first of the quartet, Dr Mohammed Awad launched a new campaign to save Durrell's house, the Villa Ambron, and as far as I know it is still standing. On Constantine P. Cavafy (or Konstantinos Petrou Kavafis) see the standard biography by Robert Liddell (1974). There are many English editions of his elegant and elusive poems, but the translation by Rae Dalven (*The Complete Poems of Cavafy*, New York, 1961) has the added benefit of an introduction by W. H. Auden. Michael Haag's *Vintage Alexandria: Photographs of the City 1860–1960* (New York and Cairo, 2008) has portraits of these authors and evokes the city they knew. I am grateful to Valerie Teague of the British Council for introductions to the invariably charming Alexandrians mentioned in the article.

24. *Mystery at Moonlight Cottage*
(Weekend Telegraph, *1992*)

There is little further to report on the Thompson mystery, though a recent flurry in the Malaysian media may be worth mentioning. According to a

Cameron Highlands hotel manager, Mr Lim Wai Ming, a local farmer on his deathbed confessed to his family that 'he had once knocked down and killed a European man and buried him in an unmarked grave.' This claim is unsupported – no name for the farmer, no location for the grave – but a former Malaysian police officer, Captain Philip Rivers, backed up the possible connection with the Thompson case. 'In 1967, it was rumoured that a lorry had struck Thompson on the road, but this was not reported to the police. It was said that the driver in his panic placed the body on to the back of his vehicle, drove off and buried the body in the outskirts of a vegetable patch. An alternative story says the culprit was driving a timber lorry and the body was disposed of at a sawmill' (*The Star*, Kuala Lumpur, 23 March 2010). A few days later Rivers added a further twist. In about 2000, he claimed, when the old hospital at Tanah Rata was transferred to new premises, a box was found containing human bones which had been 'brought by *orang asli* [forest tribesmen] from the jungle' (*Ipoh Echo*, 1 April 2010). He speculated that these bones might be Thompson's and urged local authorities to have them tested, but as far as I know, this has not been done. The best account of the mystery is still William Warren's *The Legendary American: The Remarkable Career and Strange Disappearance of Jim Thompson* (Boston, 1969), with frequent paperback reprints in Bangkok to feed the continued interest in the case there.

25. Crows

(1990)

This piece first appeared (along with a few others here) in a small collection published in the United States by Akadine Press, *Screaming in the Castle* (Pleasantville, NY, 2000). I have here pursued the story of Grip a little further than before.

Index